Reading
in the 1980s

Reading
in the 1980s

Edited by Stephen Graubard

R.R. BOWKER COMPANY   New York & London, 1983

With the exception of "Reading, Writing, and Publishing in Academia," by
Herbert S. Bailey, Jr., which is published here for the first time, the essays in
this book appeared in the Winter, 1983, issue of *Daedalus,* the Journal of the
American Academy of Arts and Sciences.

Published by R.R. Bowker Company
205 East Forty-second Street, New York, NY 10017

Copyright © 1983 by American Academy of Arts and Sciences

Printed and bound in the United States of America

Library of Congress Cataloging in Publication Data
Main entry under title:

Reading in the 1980s.

    1. Books and reading—United States—Addresses, essays, lectures.
2. Book industries and trade—United States—Addresses, essays, lectures.
I. Graubard, Stephen Richards.
Z1003.2.R43 1983   028'.9'0973   83-11753
ISBN 0-8352-1758-2

Contents

vi   *Contents*

Preface to the Issue:
"Reading: Old and New"

A S THOSE WHO HAVE KNOWN *Daedalus* in the past will recognize at once, the Journal's format has been changed substantially. A larger, bolder typeface, together with other changes, produces copy intended to have greater aesthetic appeal. While design improvement would have been reason enough for the changes made, practical considerations also intervened. We believe that the new format will prove inviting and make more readable a publication that aspires to reach a wide and disparate audience.

The decision to modify the appearance of the Journal at this time, while not originally linked to the subject of the issue—reading—is a happy conjunction that we think fortuitous. The Editors, wishing to celebrate the founding of the Journal as a quarterly twenty-five years ago, decided on visual changes that would help realize the editorial purposes voiced by Gerald Holton, the Editor in 1958, when he said that *Daedalus* had come into being to "give the intellectual community a voice of its own." This has been our major aim in all the intervening years. We have consistently sought to publish contributions from men and women of diverse opinion. Striving always for a certain catholicity in theme, we have ranged widely, believing that no area of knowledge, field of scholarship, or question of public policy could be declared "off limits."

During the summer of 1982, when draft essays for the present issue began to trickle in, I prepared a report for the Records of the American Academy of Arts and Sciences that told something of what the issue might eventually contain. I wrote at the time:

In 1963, *Daedalus* published an issue entitled "The American Reading Public." Twenty years later, in the winter of 1983, we propose to publish a collection of new reflections on books and reading in the twentieth century. At a recent meeting at the Academy to discuss the issue, those present agreed that it has become impossible to think in terms of "the" American reading public—it is time to acknowledge that there are many reading publics in this country, and that we do not know nearly enough about any of them. Who reads? Why do they read? Is the habit growing, declining, or simply changing? In asking these questions, do we start with a cultural bias in assuming that it is good for people to read, that they ought to occupy themselves reading serious books, and that this ought to be a lifetime pursuit? What possible reason do we have for believing any of this? Who is Dr. Johnson's "common reader," and what is he reading today? If there exists now, as never before, a mass of people capable of reading, does it necessarily follow from this that they will want to read or that they should want to?

That we have gone a certain distance in treating these matters, the readers of this issue will readily acknowledge. Still, what may seem most striking are the number of puzzles raised by these seemingly simple questions. It appears, for example, that we know considerably less about the "American reading public" today, about its tastes, needs, and habits, than we would like to imagine. Also, we are remarkably loathe to consider how changes in reading habits may relate to other larger societal changes. We hold television responsible for the abandonment of reading by children and adults alike, yet the reasons for this withdrawal—if indeed it is taking place at all—are in fact remarkably complex. We have not inquired closely enough into how those who enjoy both leisure and substantial amounts of discretionary income in this country today choose to use them, how habits are changing, or why. Nor have we asked what happens to books— serious books—when they come to be appropriated principally by adolescents and young adults, who read them to meet course requirements set by a small army of teachers and professors of literature. As for the popular books of the day, which sell in the hundreds of thousands or millions one year and are unavailable the next, we know almost nothing about why individuals buy them, what they find in them, or how taste for such books relates to taste for other equally attractive consumer goods. Indeed, these books are rarely reviewed seriously, and their examination by literary critics is virtually nonexistent.

Literary criticism today, in the United States as in many parts of Western Europe, appears frequently to be an intellectual exercise pursued by "dons" writing for colleagues and students. The nineteenth century's "man of letters," who continued to enjoy a certain influence well into the twentieth, has disappeared, leaving a large cultural void that no other figure or institution seems able to fill. Our knowledge of what individuals read in various parts of the world today and the role criticism has in forming public taste and creating reputations, in inculcating the habit of reading and creating an appetite for books, is remarkably limited. Statistics across national frontiers reveal little of substance; they tell us less than we need to know about the books that are read or the reasons they are selected. As for insights into the more subtle social and cultural differences revealed by contemporary reading habits, one must acknowledge that the subject awaits investigation.

We hear a great deal today about growing illiteracy, not least in the United States. Statistics that tell of the tens of millions who cannot read—not to speak of the aliterate millions who choose *not* to read—add fuel to the arguments of those who deplore the state of American education, often linking it to the depressed state of the nation's economy. Still, how illiteracy incapacitates the individual in today's world, what its real human costs are—and not only its social costs—proves surprisingly difficult to determine. Indeed, it is no less difficult to enumerate the benefits that are commonly thought to attach to reading. Cultural deprivation is a subject that is only slightly more ambiguous than that of cultural privilege.

In our all-too-easy satisfaction with at least certain of the books that appear on the school and college reading lists of our young people, we ask too few questions about how such books are read, whether they succeed in taking individuals out of themselves, out of their own limited society, to show them the possibilities of some other, or whether they serve mainly to reinforce local and particular prejudices. Reading is done for such various purposes today that it is not enough simply to praise it as desirable; a more searching inquiry into its character is called for. To see reading principally as a useful activity is almost certainly to see it too narrowly. It may be most liberating for those who simply accept it as one of life's great pleasures. Yet, to argue in this way is to risk being charged with nostalgia, of showing insufficient understanding of all the "uses" of reading. For many, reading remains the preferred route to securing information, to finding answers for specific questions.

If information-seeking is the prime purpose of reading, then the questions asked, the answers sought, and the role technology plays in facilitating this search become all-important. Whether the computer, for example, will in the foreseeable future substantially reduce the need for conventional books in many fields, and whether efficient storage and retrieval of data will soon become an even greater challenge to our engineering ingenuity, has implications for all learning and scholarship.

Those who "fear" the computer are not so much worried that telephone directories and other reference "publications" will soon go out of fashion. Their worry, rather, is that we will increasingly think of knowledge as "information," exulting in our new databanks when we ought to be examining critically the hypotheses we fashion. The existence of vastly improved technology for the rapid transmission of information raises fundamental questions about what kinds of information are worth securing and whether information is indeed our chief lack. Basic questions are being raised about "styles" of scholarship and about how the new technologies influence them. For those who rejoice in the promise of this technology, seeing in it only limitless benefits, there are no problems. Others are considerably less sanguine. More cautious, they rarely argue as Luddites, but their misgivings are all too patent.

Between a "high modern culture," inaccessible to many, that leads some to yearn for the "classics" of another day, and a "modern technology" that seems to threaten certain traditional humanistic values, there are substantial numbers who crave a different kind of reading and learning experience. Their search is for a "good read," and they still look to others to introduce them to such books. But the culture seems no longer able to produce these once-traditional middlemen, and the new "keepers" of literature have little to recommend to a reading public seeking guidance. Indeed, most scholars today do not imagine one of their principal obligations to be the enlightenment of an uninstructed anonymous public. Inevitably, others move in to do what scholars either refuse to do or believe cannot be done.

Among these, book clubs and bookstores are, each in their own way, influential. Since their commercial interest is to satisfy readers, to create a market for books, understanding today's reading public has become a business necessity for them. If they cater to prevailing opinion and taste, they also do much to create both. They may sometimes know what will sell; this, however, does not guarantee that they will have available the books they believe the public wants. Most authors do not simply write for a market that booksellers are able to describe, although a number of them—sensing market trends quite as accurately as knowledgeable businessmen and knowing how their own economic interests are likely to be served—do. Readers' interests, however, can be quite complex: many know what they are looking for, insist on being allowed to choose, and will not be satisfied with the book that the club or the bookstore simply wishes to dispose of. Mass merchandising has its own conventions and rules, and while such enterprises have been highly successful, they have not destroyed the profitability of specialized bookstores that cater to more specific tastes.

If the book club has an interest in making available certain kinds of books but is not always able to secure them, this is of course the perennial problem of the publisher. Whether he is looking for a commercial success, knowing that a good book will sometimes do as well as one specifically crafted for a mass market, or whether profits figure less in his calculations, there are limits to what the publisher can do to create a market for his product. This is true particularly for works written principally for that segment of the reading public whose interest is in books of "high" culture. For such works, "word of mouth" publicity seems to be all-important.

Whether we live today with largely outmoded notions about reading—knowing less about the reader, author, publisher, and bookseller than we pretend—whether the book in our time remains a largely unstudied artifact whose creation and distribution seem surprisingly mysterious, no one will contest the proposition that we lack anything like a "general theory of the book." Indeed, we probably know more about the book historically, in its seventeenth and eighteenth century forms, than we know about its condition in the contemporary world. Scholars have made substantial contributions to our knowledge of the early book; there is no comparable literature on the book today.

If this is so—and there is much in this issue of *Daedalus* to suggest that it is—the effect on reading of technological inventions already in place, or likely to be introduced soon, becomes a matter of great importance. We know, from the Fall 1982 issue of *Daedalus,* "Print Culture and Video Culture," that television did not in any significant way destroy print. It may in fact have made certain unacknowledged contributions to print—in demarcating certain areas where print was clearly a superior system for communicating certain kinds of information and for giving pleasure in a way that a purely visual medium cannot. But such discovery in no way negates the substantial impact that television has had, not least on print. There is every reason to believe that equally large impacts will be registered in the future. If reading has lost its monopoly status in extending the personal experience of the individual—if indeed it ever enjoyed such a status—we are obliged to ask what the new audiovisual media promise to give in the way of new instruction and what the cultural consequences of that instruction may be. Similar questions, obviously, can be asked about computers and about the coming electronic era they are said to herald.

If there is indeed a "new literacy," those who lack such literacy must in time be seen as disadvantaged. Just as book reading proved a boon to those capable of it, computer reading will also give an advantage, especially to those who know how to exploit the computer's multiple uses. While computer skills may initially simply supplement existing skills—particularly reading and writing—they are expected, in time, to contribute to the growing twentieth century emphasis on the visual, with all of the liberating influence that such an extended "vision" is likely to give.

In the new world of the "electronic reader," publishing will change radically. The notion that the computer's principal function is to store facts shows a lack of appreciation of the computer's role in graphic representation, in creating an aesthetic awareness now lacking. The prospect we are offered is not only of a more efficient production of texts, but also—and very significantly—of a new relation between author and publisher, and between both and the ultimate consumer, the reader. Author and reader will, it is said, enjoy wholly new kinds of independence in the electronic era. While dangers inhere in the processes imagined, and while these are acknowledged, those who have the greatest faith in the new technological possibilities see little cause for fear. They argue that the new technologies give promise of inaugurating a new age of reading, with wholly new excitements in prospect.

What, then, will happen to more traditional forms of scholarship, to the kinds of interests that have dominated, in recent decades, in particular academic disciplines? How much has scholarship in fact been wedded to particular communication technologies? Will new technologies make possible new kinds of inquiry? Will they, for example, substantially encourage certain kinds of large-scale study, making many contemporary scholarly monographs seem timid and modest, expressing nothing so much as the limitations of a single mind working on its own in a library of bound books?

The question is not asked rhetorically. For those who have never believed that technology alone explained the character of scholarly inquiry, other forces—social, cultural, political, and institutional—are no less vital. If an essay like "The Englishness of English Literature," published in this volume, has not been frequently attempted, it is not because existing technology militated against such inquiry, but because other forces made study of so broad a theme seem hazardous. Specific conventions of British literary scholarship in the twentieth century may have discouraged scholars from attempting such broad-brushed literary inquiry with such unconventional ideological implications. Fashion in scholarship, as in reading, needs always to be considered.

The issue, in a slightly different form, has importance for the kinds of literary scholarship and literary criticism practiced in our day. How are we to explain, for example, the rapid changes in styles of literary study. Why, for instance, have certain traditional philological interests—so paramount in our universities even in the early part of this century—disappeared so totally? Why has the purely biographical interest in literature apparently receded? Or, do we exaggerate that particular "recession," forgetting how many universities remain faithful to it? The "new criticism," the innovative textual criticism of yesterday, still has its advocates, but it is increasingly obliged to share whatever place it enjoys with other "critical" schools, more contemporary, concerned with texts in new ways, as preoccupied with "readers" as earlier schools were with "authors."

How are we to explain these new intellectual interests in scholarly circles? Ought we to agree with Frank Kermode that much of this new academic criticism is largely incomprehensible to laymen, that it can have little interest for those outside the literary guilds? Or, ought we to insist that when learned men and women in so many places choose to debate such issues, believing them to be important, that it behooves us, whatever our profession, to know something about the controversies now dividing scholars in the humanities, specifically those who are concerned with literature?

The last essays in this issue are integral to our larger purpose, which is to discuss how reading is perceived in this country today. For better or worse, literary scholars divide on how a text is to be read, on what able students need to learn if they choose to study literature. Indeed, the larger question of how students ought to be introduced to literature is opened. This links up with a growing public debate on what kinds and levels of literacy need to be achieved, by whom, and for what purposes.

Many are unhappy with what the young read; many more are concerned that so little is read. Adults, who once appropriated certain books for themselves, believing they were intended for them and not for their adolescent children, are now quite prepared to share the wealth, if not to abandon it altogether. Many choose other pursuits for their leisure hours. Ought this to be a cause for concern? Why?

Are such changes adversely affecting society and culture? Or, is there too much nostalgia in all such concern and fear? Ought we not to recognize that reading has always had a purpose—moral if not utilitarian—and that a good deal of what is published today continues to serve one or both of these purposes? May it not be true that new ways of reading may serve in ways that are still scarcely acknowledged?

So, also, with the ways in which literature is taught in many colleges and universities in the country today. A great deal of contemporary literature is admittedly difficult, opaque, and unconventional; yet, can we really offer this as an excuse for its neglect? Or, is it not imperative that we examine the intellectual and critical expressions of our day, realizing that some will not bear close or constant scrutiny, but that others will? In literature, as in criticism, as in all the arts, the contemporary clearly deserves some place. The disputes that go on about its quality and utility may be as revealing as anything that can be said to express our consensus about its value.

The Rockefeller Foundation is to be thanked for making this issue of *Daedalus* possible. A more difficult or more controversial subject could not have been chosen.

S.R.G.

Frank Kermode

The Common Reader

O VER THE PAST FEW YEARS, we have heard a good deal
about a possible and desirable "science of literature" that
would have linguistics as its principal model; and it would
be reasonable to maintain that we have seen marked advances in
descriptive and taxonomic techniques, especially in the analysis of
narrative. Unprecedentedly large numbers of people now seek, or are
compelled to undergo, formal instruction in literature, and part of
the motivation of this new science is undoubtedly a desire to develop
a systematic body of information that can be taught and learned.
Another part is the wish to establish a decent claim to exactness; for
in the modern university, whatever is spent on the "humanities"
must be got at the expense of the natural sciences, with their insatiable appetite for money.

There is nothing very new about such desires and claims; in some
form or other, they have existed ever since the vernacular literatures
were admitted as subjects for study in the universities. In former
times, the model for imitation might be classical philology or com-
parative philology; more recently, it has been post-Saussurean linguistics. Yet there has always existed, along with these scientific aspirations, a strong current of "antipositivism," a conviction that the
study of literature could only be frustrated by attempts to ape either
the exactness or the utility of the hard sciences. And this opinion has
survived along with all the latest things in "theory." Over the past
few years, we have seen the successful publication of new kinds of
literary criticism that are frankly incomprehensible—and of course
totally without interest—to nonprofessional readers, and it ought not
to seem surprising that they have produced a backlash. The protest-
ers argue that the business of literary criticism, however they may

define it (as the common pursuit of true judgment, the elucidation of works of literature, etc.), is certainly not the arcane and pretentious affair it is represented as being by the latest "theorists." And as often as not, they will at this point refer to Samuel Johnson as a great critic seraphically free from taint of theory, and remind us that Johnson said that he rejoiced to concur with the Common Reader, implying that all good critics must do likewise.

Johnson concurred, specifically, with the opinion of the Common Reader on Gray's "Elegy in a Country Churchyard," and added this: "By the common sense of readers uncorrupted with literary prejudices, after all the refinements of subtilty and the dogmatism of learning, must be finally decided all claim to poetical honours." And it is to this Common Reader, endowed with common sense but innocent of subtlety and learning, that many refined, subtle, dogmatic, and learned literary critics now profess to cede all judgment.

It is as well to be clear what Johnson meant. In rejoicing to concur with the Common Reader, he was of course making it evident that he himself was a different animal altogether, though capable of understanding judgments that were unprejudiced and incorrupt. That he could speak so of the consensus of unspecialized opinion is an indication that he was talking about a state of affairs historically very different from our own. Johnson was not a teacher of literature in the modern manner, and critics who nowadays say that they yield to the authority of the uninstructed are in a very different position from his. Why, what, and whom are they teaching? Helen Gardner, a devout supporter of the Common Reader view, has spent her life teaching literature to the expensively educated. In her recent book,[1] she compares her students to camels, who pause at the Oxford oasis to fill their humps with reading before striking out across the desert of modern life. But she also believes that some people are better readers than others, and I suppose she would number her Oxford students among them; they are already *un*common readers, and unless the teacher secretly believes that reading cannot be taught, will presumably be even more uncommon by the time they leave the university. To believe otherwise would surely destroy the spirit of all but the most cynical and self-serving of teachers. Yet Dame Helen warmly applauds Dr. Johnson and Virginia Woolf, who took *The Common Reader* as a title for her collected literary essays, for appealing from the judgment of professionals to the common sense of "those who read widely for enjoyment."

The Common Reader is of course not a person but a constituency, and everybody not seeking to grind an ax must know that by now it is a pretty rotten borough. Whether or no there is a causal connection, the dissolution of the Common Reader has proceeded *pari passu* with the establishment and growth of the profession of which Dame Helen is such an ornament. A large-scale history of the Common Reader is certainly a professional desideratum (though it might find but few common readers). Erich Auerbach sketched a part of that history when he investigated the expression *la cour et la ville:* "The absence of function, common to the aristocracy that had been stripped of its feudal character and to the wealthy bourgeoisie which had begun to turn away from gainful occupations toward *otium cum dignitate*, fused these two groups into a single class, namely *la cour et la ville."* But as this class expanded, it recruited on a large scale from *la ville*, and in the course of the eighteenth century, "the 'public' came . . . to be dominated by *la ville, the bourgeoisie."* This public came into existence as a direct consequence of the development of the vernaculars and of printing. Auerbach says that it "determined the character of literature and the literary language throughout Europe."[2] It was an "elite minority," clearly differentiated from the uneducated on the one hand and the specialists on the other. In fact, it was Johnson's Common Reader.

Johnson took an interest in this phenomenon, and of course understood that it had undergone a historical development. He remarked, for instance, that in Milton's time, reading was not a general amusement: "Neither traders nor often gentlemen thought themselves disgraced by ignorance. The women had not then aspired to literature, nor was every house supplied with a closet of knowledge." Of his own time, however, he says that "general literature . . . pervades the nation through all its ranks." There is here a touch of hyperbole, but it is clear enough that Johnson characterizes the Common Reader sociologically; he speaks of him (or it) as a class. Reading was one of the things that was done, in his time, by people of some income and some leisure. Occasionally he even suggested that they read because they could think of nothing else to do: "People in general do not willingly read, if they can have anything else to amuse them."[3]

That last sentence might adorn the wall of any modern publisher's office, but the point is that leisure and income are now for the most part otherwise employed than in reading. We still speak of "the general reader," but not very hopefully, and it is acknowledged that the kinds of people who constituted the class of the Common Reader have now thought of other things to do; the class is as nearly obsolete as "polite literature," which is what it once chose to read. Its rapid decline dates from the last quarter of the nineteenth century; one symptom of it was the sudden demise of the three-decker novel that had helped to fill the leisure time of large numbers of bourgeois families. The effect on literary production is very noticeable at the same period. Crudely speaking, there was a new public to satisfy, but its requirements were not always consistent with the aspirations of authors who thought of themselves as artists. Hence the new importance of such editors as Edward Garnett, middlemen between artist and public. Garnett wielded extraordinary power over a host of writers, including Conrad, Galsworthy, and Lawrence, and they submitted to it because the gap between art and the public had to be closed if they were to survive.[4] The literary agent was another new trade, another sign that the concurrence of specialist and Common Reader now called for professional intervention. The ample provision of ephemeral writing for the masses made it more and more obvious that serious writing must be content with its own small audience; the avant-garde took pride in the fact, but eventually its products were to be saved by the creation of an artificial class of readers who taught, or were taught, in colleges. The division widened as cinema, radio, and television took over the task of filling people's leisure time; and all the duties of the old Common Reader have now virtually devolved upon professional students of literature. The competition for mass markets (for common readers in a looser sense) is something that does not concern these professionals, who generally have nothing whatever to do with the promotion or censure of the most widely read books. Pale descendants of the Common Reader, they have none but the most transient contacts with common readers.

The nature and extent of such contacts are worth more study than they get. We must expect a good deal of variation from one country to another; the only study I know of confines itself almost exclusively to West Germany, where the position is different from those in the United States or in the United Kingdom. Yet there are resemblances also, and we have something to learn from the work of Peter Uwe Hohendahl,[5] who assumes a split between "elite" and "mass" culture, and sees that it must affect criticism. Broadly speaking, the elite is still under the influence of notions of aesthetic autonomy that had their origins in the thought of the late eighteenth century; the masses assume that naive realism is the proper aim of writing. This division indicates the end of what Hohendahl refers to as "the public sphere," a Frankfort term that in this connection means something very close to Johnson's Common Reader. Hohendahl happens to believe that the remedy for this split is the socialization of private property; but we need not follow him in that direction to benefit from his empirical observations.

In Germany, there is still a clear difference between the reviewing of books, *Tageskritik*, and the study of literature in the universities, *Literaturwissenschaft*, such that it is unusual to find the same persons doing both. The effect of *Tageskritik* on readers seems to be very limited; at a date in the late sixties, it appeared that of the one hundred seventy thousand people who read reviews in the journals or class newspapers (a number estimated to be about a quarter of the total professing some interest in literature), very few took any serious notice of book reviews. The aesthetic assumptions of the reviewers do not coincide with those of the readers; indeed, "the literature that is actually read is not the literature that is discussed" by reviewers.[6] Best sellers are rarely reviewed at all, except in provincial newspapers. Rather, the publishers work directly on the public, arranging "media events" and general support from newspapers whose owners find the promoted book ideologically congenial. Such books are, in their way, instruments for the capitalist oppression of consumers; and by paying no attention to them and concentrating on work that meets their own irrelevant standards of merit, the reviewers are abetting the exploitation. All they do is serve as cultural extras to the papers they write in; and they use a narcissistic jargon mostly incomprehensible to their readers.

It was for these reasons that the New Left eventually turned its fire on the practitioners of *Tageskritik*. They served the ruling system; aesthetic autonomy has no real meaning in an age of mechanical reproduction. What the critics ought to concern themselves with was political praxis; to stop reviewing randomly chosen books and concentrate upon the mechanisms by which books are produced and sold. As it turned out, both *Tageskritik* and *Literaturwissenschaft* survived these assaults. There is, to be sure, more consideration of "trivial literature"; the authority of professors is somewhat reduced; but the end of bourgeois criticism still seems a long way off. In his famous essay,[7] Walter Benjamin spoke of an art appropriate to an era of mass production, an art lacking *aura*—that uniqueness, authenticity, historicity, which mass reproduction necessarily destroys. But *aura* is what most of us literary critics are interested in. To the New

Left, and indeed to Benjamin (who had marvelous antennae for *aura*), our interest makes us more or less unconscious kin to Fascism.

As I remarked, Hohendahl's material is not quite the same as ours, and any critique we ventured would also differ from his. We rarely think of criticism as an "institution"—rarely consider it as part of the entire social nexus. But it is hardly to our credit that we fail to do this, and the absence of any effective critique of criticism goes some way to explaining why our criticism is in such a peculiar state. One significant difference from the German situation might be mentioned at once. In the United States and perhaps even more in the United Kingdom, *Tageskritik* is very often, perhaps one could say normally, the work of the same hands that produce *Literaturwissenschaft*. The writers use a different tone, but are essentially academics; either they are talking to an audience that consists, approximately, of their former students (the new Common Reader), or they indulge themselves as wits or punsters. The dyer's hand is visible, though there may be attempts to conceal it; and it can hardly be denied that their aesthetic expectations, the general set of their interests, are very different from those of their audience, even in the posh Sunday papers, which have a circulation of a million or more. That circulation is maintained by means quite other than those employed by the academic reviewers, and it is easy enough to see that, to the New Left, the reviewers must seem to be passive instruments of a vicious system, contributors to "systematically distorted communication."

The historian of the Common Reader would need also to be the historian of reviewing. He would find in the great nineteenth century quarterlies, and in *The Atlantic Monthly* of Brownell's day, long and lucid reviews of important books. The Common Reader still existed; such reviews were bourgeois family reading. To find anything comparable now he would have to look to such journals as *The New York Review of Books* and *The London Review of Books*, but even there he will find dons writing for dons and their pupils—a very different audience, very differently recruited. The reason for the change, I've already adumbrated: first, the relatively uneducated have found amusements they prefer to reading; second, the universities have taken over both the production and the criticism of literature, except—and it's of course a large exception—for the books that are read by millions.

A few freaks aside (the latest being *The White Hotel*), how do English-speaking critics respond to best sellers? On the whole, when they look at them at all, they do so with a holiday air, as if they were doing something that wasn't really their business. Edmund Wilson was, among many other things, the greatest *Tageskritik* of his time. In a piece called " 'You Can't Do This To Me!' Shrilled Celia," he took a look at Lloyd C. Douglas's wartime best seller, *The Robe*. ("I lately decided that it was time for me to take cognizance of it," he says, meaning by "lately" not, I think, "recently" so much as "belatedly," for he explains that the book has sold about a million and a half copies in hard cover in rather less than two years.) Having provided samples of the prose, he goes on to say how very old-fashioned the book is, just like *Ben Hur* and *Quo Vadis*. The puzzle for Wilson is that this "almost unrivalled fabric of old clichés" should hold the attention of 7 million Americans, when it is "difficult to imagine that any literate person could ever get through more than two pages of it for pleasure." Yet the work has "a certain purity"; and the fact that all those readers should prefer this long and tedious novel to "livelier and easier productions which have been specially flavored to please them" testifies to the longing of the ordinary reader for "moral light." Wilson concludes that "the ordinary reader, even in our ghastly time," is in decent moral shape; but that anybody who supposes Mencken had improved American taste had better think again.[8]

I doubt if the attitude of reviewers to popular books has altered much since that article was written, almost forty years ago; Wilson cannot conceive of himself concurring with ordinary readers. When they read, they do different things, and for different reasons. Like shepherds in a pastoral, the Common Reader is granted a certain moral purity, but no refinement. Or, like the shepherds' flocks, they look up, and Douglas feeds them. Nowadays we might rather say that his successors exploit them. The latest notice I have seen of a current best seller in a highbrow journal—*The London Review of Books*[9]—is by John Sutherland (author of a good book on the publishing of best sellers). His subject is Jeffrey Archer's *The Prodigal Daughter*, topping the list as I write. Sutherland tells the story, which is about Florentyna, a prodigious child who grew up to be vice-president and then president of the United States. He then criticizes the style, just as Wilson did: "The result is the kind of novel one imagines a *Time* Magazine team turning out." Why, then, do people like it so much? Well, there is "an insatiable appetite for fables of success"; and such fables do best in America, which is why Archer, an Englishman "with a shrewd eye to the market," made his book a "tatty rewrite of the American dream." Like Wilson, Sutherland censures the derivative nature of the best seller's prose, and associates the success of the book with what he takes to be well-understood characteristics of the American way of life. The space between the reviewer and the novel, and the people who like the novel, is accepted as unbridgeable; and there is no attempt to explain why this should be so, or what the consequences are of its being so. Sutherland has, exceptionally, made a point of studying the best seller; that is, when he is wearing his *Literaturwissenschaft* (subsection, sociology of literature) hat. As a reviewer, in the *London Review,* he assumes that he is talking to the new Common Reader, who shares his assumptions and wouldn't be seen dead with a copy of *The Prodigal Daughter,* but might be amused to read a bit about it, simply as a curiosity having nothing to do with literature but only (as Leavis said unfairly but brilliantly of the Sitwells) with the history of publicity.

Meanwhile the academics go on producing their editions of the classics, or, more usually nowadays, developing theories of everything; of both classes of work, it may safely be said that the ordinary reader cannot afford to buy them, and could not read them if he did. Even in Germany, the most successful new critical school—that which deals in "reader response"—has very little to say about that reader as a social being, a person who opens a book and reads it. In England and America, a few Marxists—and they pretty rarefied— apart, the matter of the relation between professional critic and audience is hardly ever mentioned, except in the sort of vacuous observation about the Common Reader I have mentioned. As to why ordinary readers should be so different from us—why they used to be moral and dull, and are now possessed of an insatiable appetite for success and are still dull—nobody ventures an opinion.

Yet such power as there may be to influence our literary culture must be in the hands of these critics, who teach in the colleges and moonlight in the reviews. How do they, and how ought they, use that power? I have assumed that the modern Common Reader passes through a university. The number of people now teaching literature is probably greater than the total of critics who formerly existed throughout history, and they must have some effect on the millions of readers who frequent their classes. Does good come of this? Richard Poirier says he sees "no reason in the world" why common readers should care to read the classics or serious contemporary fiction and poetry; "I don't think it makes them better people, better citizens, better anything." By some criteria, he must be right. Indeed, it is immodest to propose that by making people read these things we are improving them, ethically or civically. All we dare claim is that we are making them better readers. We might or might not go on to claim that bad reading (of the Bible, for example) has often had disastrous consequences; or that a society containing subtle readers is at least a more interesting, perhaps a richer, society than one that doesn't; or that good readers are likely to be more resistant to the exploitative forces of "the ruling system." But we should not say we are improving them, except as readers.

And that is surely enough for anybody to attempt: the reconstruction of the Common Reader on a new, historically appropriate plan. We need to remember Johnson's remark, that reading is not willingly undertaken if there is something else to do; that the acquisition of the knowledge and technique to do it well is arduous. People will sweat for them only if assured of the authenticity of the authority that asks them to do so. Such authenticity is largely institutional, but we have to manage without any central authority ourselves. If there were one, with power to bind and loose, to make and uphold canons, even to issue an *index librorum prohibitorum,* the job would be easier. It would be easier, too, if we did not devote quite so much of our energy to showing how clever we are, either in the manipulation of texts or in the rarefied exercise of theory and methodology. If, in short, we had a full and daunting sense of our responsibilities toward the Common Reader, conceived not as some fictive outsider whose word, it pleases us to say, is our law, but as the students in our class, who, as we are now continually lamenting, know nothing and have never acquired our own need to be on speaking terms with the past. As Philip Rieff likes to point out, the world of rock and pop pretends to have no past, and they live partly in that world. Some make the mistake—understandably, but it *is* a mistake—of treating the past as synonymous with authoritarian oppression. I am sure Rieff is right in speaking of them as "disinherited."[10] He believes that the only remedy is the restitution of authority, the promulgation of "interdicts" and the inculcation of "the knowledge that is in repetition." It is true that "unified cultures" tend to be authoritarian, so the culture of the new Common Reader, however subtle and various, would need authority. There is something to be learned, perhaps, from the success of F. R. Leavis as a teacher: these books prescribed, those proscribed; a bold doctrine of minority culture, and the creation of an image of it that made the young want to join it. As Donald Davie, who underwent that influence, has recently remarked,[11] it was at least as encouraging to be told what you should not read as what you should. There was a canon; and where there is a canon there is authority.

Philip Rieff believes that by authoritarian prescription we can make our students "sovereign selves."[12] I imagine he would allow in that remark a certain ethical component. There, I hesitantly disagree; hesitantly, because I don't know what Professor Rieff could bring off, but know the sensible limit of my own ambitions. I agree with Poirier; I daresay he would accept my view that reading, as we ought to teach it, can make not a good person, but a subtle, questioning one, always with the possibility of corruption yet richer and more enriching. How did we ever come to suppose that we were equipped to make people good? To be realistic, we cannot do that, any more than we can fill the humps of the young with supplies of reading for later use. There are soft drinks available everywhere; nobody needs that warm stale water. To be realistic again, we have little to do with the oppressed, with the hapless victims of television and advertising, insofar as they constitute an inaccessible mass. We have to do with the new Common Reader, who has to be our creation, who will want to join us, as people who speak with the past and know something of reading as an art to be mastered. We are carrying something on, but have the responsibility of making the generation that will agree that carrying it on in its turn is worth the effort. In the end, that is the only feasible task of reviewers as well as academics. And every narcissistic, venal, or impudent review, every clever academic stunt, is a dereliction of this duty of continuance and creation. That, I think, is where we may speak of the morality of the business: in terms of our duty to the only real Common Reader, and the strong temptations to neglect it.

ENDNOTES

[1]*In Defence of the Imagination* (New York: Oxford University Press, 1982), pp. 41-2, 47.
[2]*Literary Language and Its Public in Late Latin Antiquity and the Middle Ages* (London: Routledge & Kegan Paul, 1965), p. 333.
[3]*Boswell's Life of Johnson,* edited by G.B. Hill and L.F. Powell (Oxford: The Clarendon Press, 1964), pp. iv, 218 (May 1, 1783).
[4]Garnett's role is documented in George Jefferson's *Edward Garnett: A Life in Literature* (London: Jonathan Cape, 1982).
[5]*The Institution of Criticism* (Ithaca: Cornell University Press, 1982).
[6]Ibid., p. 133.
[7]"The Work of Art in the Age of Mechanical Reproduction," in Walter Benja-

min, *Illuminations,* edited by Hannah Arendt (New York: Harcourt, Brace and World, 1968), pp. 219-53.

[8]*Classics and Commercials* (London: W.H. Allen, 1950), pp. 204-8.

[9]4(15) (August 19-September 1, 1982): 18.

[10]*Fellow Teachers* (London: Faber & Faber, 1975), p. 97.

[11]*These the Companions* (Cambridge: Cambridge University Press, 1982), p. 78.

[12]Rieff, *Fellow Teachers,* p. 175.

Elizabeth Hardwick

Reading

R EADING—what sort of subject is this? There are "reading scores," and "my early reading," and "reading the future." There are neurology and pedagogy and linguistics and dyslexia and lipreading. And then there is plain reading for information and pleasure—neither very plain indeed.

In writing about reading, one is imposing more reading, a grave decision if the "worry" about reading, the decline of it, is more than a rumor. Virtue and pleasure attach to our subject. Virtue is conferred upon it from the outside, and the pleasure is to be subjective. It does not seem suitable to take a legislative tone, to invade by way of advice or censure, this solitary, private act.

I like the phrase "functional literacy." It is, apparently, a diminished, but not entirely neglected, condition. Fifth grade, we hear, and what does that mean? Fifth grade is a state with many word-blessings. Lilac and rose (lipsticks); sheer black (stockings); men and ladies (toilets); bus stop, exit, take one before meals, 80-proof, on sale, free. But if I understand the term "functional literacy," these words do not lead anywhere: fifth grade does not move to sixth, nor does *exit* to *perilous curve*. It is hard to understand a stasis, a cutoff, after the "functional literate" has arrived at "zip code," an arcane bit of interesting and useful reading. There is some perturbation in the condition, and perhaps statistics are not able to keep up with the leaps and bounds that mere function provides like a set of muscles.

Figures about illiteracy among us may stun the mind of one looking out on a street filled with automobiles, hearing the planes whining down to the airports, knowing of sonics and stereophonics and miraculous little chips. We are, in literacy, forty-ninth among the 158 members of the United Nations, and that means 60 millions among us, including 47 percent of black youth, do not, cannot read. This fact seems to call up an ancient rural folk living in brutal, repetitive isolation, centuries past, one day like the next, the hut, the unlettered darkness. But that is not true; the illiterate are of course utterly contemporary in look and experience of life, and their plight is like some crippling or myopia, personalized and yet hidden, at least in some part of its manifestation. The scandal of it, surrounded by words like priorities, tax base, overcrowding, unfortunate methods of instruction, and the easy absorption of the figures without alarm would seem to indicate one of those shiftings in our apprehension of national destiny. The sacred school, the devotional teacher, the alphabet on the wall, the cutout apple in the window—these are nostalgic, small-town images whose hold on the imagination is merely sentimental. It appears that we can "live with" our expanding illiteracy and that it is to be thought of as a handicap, individually unfortunate, but not a stain on the national psyche. Education, then, is a sort of option, a curious settling down of the American half-serious utopian claim.

To speak of a passion for reading is rather self-aggrandizing, as perhaps it would not have been in the past. This act, except for purposes of the classroom or for information, is self-propelled, unmortgaged, so to speak, not subject to obsolescence or engine trouble or the need for maintenance. It is not often that one is scolded for it, although biographies tell of the wishes of parents to interrupt on behalf of unchopped wood or expensive candles. Perhaps the love of, or the intense need for, reading is psychological, an eccentricity, even something like a neurosis, that is, a pattern of behavior that persists beyond its usefulness, which is controlled by inner forces and which in turn controls.

There seems to be a good deal of "practice" necessary to sustain the gift of genuine reading, practice being the adding of one book to another, the development of tone. Impediments to reading on the part of advanced students of literature are far from uncommon—not a reluctance before the act itself, but a sort of deafness in the matter of aesthetic tonality.

Too violent a contemporaneousness in the souls of some readers inhibits discussion and somehow infects the air, but with such subtle penetration it is hard to define. Things go on in a chatty manner, hardly to be understood as different from gossip about one's friends. This may be thought of as propitious, the current right to remove literature from too great a degree of pedagogy and to restore it to experience. And, since about works of art there is no right opinion, it is something beyond that which troubles.

Tonalities and nuances give pause. Relentless contemporaneity produces some of the same reading defects, spiritual as well as vocal, that one often notices in the American performances of classical modern drama. The actors cannot get out of their own skins, despite the period costumes, the parasols, the old serfs shuffling in with a tea tray. *Madame Bovary* is an example that comes to mind because the text does not require exegesis. The students who have chosen literature for their university study are pleased to read the novel, perhaps again and again, and nothing onerous attaches to it as a "requirement," such as might be felt in many cases about the burden of Spenser or Milton.

As the discussion goes on, we hear that Emma is "too romantic"; Ms. Homais is "just pretentious"; Charles is a "clod"; Rodolphe is "selfish"; and Leon is "weak." The adjectives are to the point, naturally arrived at as descriptive efforts. Yet something is askew in the tone of the discussion. It is too intimate, too cozy; the distance has been traversed with a disfiguring speed. A masterpiece of created "tiresomeness," becomes "tiresome," and that is not the same thing. There is a sort of present tense of judgment that establishes a feeling of equity between author and reader.

In the latitudinarian air of the classroom, and no doubt elsewhere, there is the tendency among readers to populate works with themselves, their friends. There is too much self-esteem and too little surrender. So the students say this novel, with its diversions, "drags," and Chekhov doesn't make a "real point," and Jane Austen is often silly, meaning that, in their view, the throb of afternoon calls, the bow at the ball, cannot bear the intentions attributed to them by the characters and, along the way of course, by Jane Austen herself. The personalization of fiction, the reduction of it to the boundaries of the reading self, often one who has lived for only a few decades in the twentieth century, is an intensive democratization not quite so felicitous for the spread of literature as one might have predicted. It bears some relation to the deformations of Socialist Realism—that is, the inclination, in this case, unconscious and without ideology, to impose current conditions upon the recalcitrant past. Some feminist critics wonder why Dorothea Brooke, after the "disaster" of her marriage to Casaubon, wants to marry the vaguely nitwitted Ladislaw? Dorothea has the money to "make a new life," and in any case, she could go to work, if there was work then for women. So, psychologically nothing is to be accepted as given, created, composed, in accordance to the truth and imagination of its own terms.

On the other hand, less knowledgeable readers do not, in my view, read for a validation of their own experience. The stack of romances at the supermarket is noticeably shorter at the end of the day, showing the movements of commerce. For certain women, these seem to be a sort of daytime gift to themselves, as the washing machine growls through its cycles. It is something of an insult to ordinary people to imagine that they, for the moment, believe it possible to be as fascinating and sexy or as romantically cruel as the impossible characters on the page. They, the readers, will not experience in life a charming, interesting, detailed betrayal, but, if any, a dull, extended, paralyzing impasse. These mass-produced entertainments are rather like a glass of beer—Miller Time. They offer little instruction about the reading public for works with the claims of literature, are not in competition with them, and cannot be discussed except as items of capitalist market seduction.

One of the results of genuine power in business, in politics, in law and medicine, is that there is no time to read. Time, that curious loss in a world of time-saving, is indeed running out, we might say. It takes with it the time-consuming reading. No doubt those who address their print to the powerful adjust their psyches and perhaps their styles to the inevitable reduction to memo and summary that lies ahead—summary, the passageway of information to those whose attention is solicited for the sake of the country, the legislative plans, the conduct of wars, the dilemmas of justice. Not reading has certain benign aspects for the powerful, who are thereby spared deprecations, advice, rumors, and plain insults.

For the chic and the rich, a certain ectoplasmic culture—thought to be taste—is considered of value. A crossword puzzle familiarity with names and tags is preventive, warding off embarrassment. Names have a glow, like a pear in autumn, and are a sweetening acquisition. The list is not punitive either. Renaissance, perhaps, but not necessarily the Risorgimento; Hamlet and Macbeth, but not Laertes and Macduff; Lazarus is metaphorical and Ezekiel isn't; Dante, yes, but no shame will attach itself to a smile of confusion about Brunetto Latini, who, except for his learning, is very like one's friends. In the television program about the Duke of Windsor, Mrs. Simpson had to explain to the Prince of Wales who Emily Brontë was—all done with a tolerant smile.

This is as it must be. Knowledge of literature is an idiosyncracy, professional sometimes, and a scarcity otherwise. The literature of history and philosophy are also little mandarin buttons worn on the caps of a few. Perhaps a certain discrete honor accompanies these accomplishments, but the large, educated, reasonably prosperous public will for the most part want to buy and read books that have elements of current interest, either in the immediacy of the subject matter or in the strength of striking ideas. Yet, a considerable number of difficult and supremely valuable books are published each year, and someone buys them for the purpose of reading, else they would not be made available. This seems all we can ask, and what education and self-education have failed to stimulate cannot be forever lamented. And of course there is always the humbling fact that even the greatly learned and devotionally pursuing will indeed care and pursue less than they might.

When one considers the nature of contemporary fiction and poetry, it would seem to deny the supposed lack of sophisticated culture and ready-reference comprehension on the part of the reader. The greatly admired authors are freely anarchic and demanding. It appears that those who read at all have read a lot. Much important contemporary writing is intensely "literary." These compositions are not addressed to a void, but rather assume a common culture out there somewhere. Skimming the pages of a book of poetry that just arrived in the mail, my eye comes upon Faustus, Uccello (followed by a single-word sentence: Bird.), Orpheus, Alcibiades, Degas, Crivelli, Bechstein, Poussin, Myshkin, Beauvais, for a beginning list in verses that might be called "open."

For a writer like Borges, the library is the landscape of human drama; it is experience, tragedy, social history. Among our own writers, satire and parody and mimicry are directed to a mind that must itself be richly aware of banalities, old movies, literary texts, conundrums, puns, a torrent of references. Ellipses, allusiveness, disconnection, are to be filled, identified, connected by the imagination and knowledge of the reader; otherwise the creative effort, so detailed, so mindful of tone, will have been in vain. "Description of physical appearance and mannerism is one of the several methods of characterization used by writers of fiction," John Barth says in an early story. "But to say that Ambrose and Peter's mother was pretty is to accomplish nothing." This asks of the reader a contemplation of

physical description in narrative; it also, perhaps, asks him to smile—
knowingly.

Proust left a short book titled *On Reading*. It says, of course, many beautiful things about himself, about decoration (William Morris), Carlyle, Ruskin, the Dutch painters, Racine, Saint-Simon—on and on. And then somewhere in the pages he notes the insufficiency of reading and says that it is an initiation, not to be made into a discipline. "Reading is at the threshold of spiritual life; it can introduce us to it; it does not constitute it."

So, perhaps we should not solicit, insist, badger, embarrass, on behalf of this almost free pleasure.

Lola L. Szladits

Answers and Questions

R ESEARCH IN THE HUMANITIES is the quest of a potentially
unexpected answer to a possibly ill-defined question. If one
question leads to another, the answers received might map a
different subject from the one that got it started. In any research
assignment, major *or* minor, the right question may become obvious
only in the end, and its truth apparent in the understanding, interpretation, and transmission of a series of answers. The intellectual process of any well or ill-defined plan is painstaking and lengthy. Perhaps the briefest definition of humanistic research could be: "An ar-
ticulate person in search of an unarticulated question."

During the fifties, The New York Public Library searched for a slogan to define its mission and came up with a comprehensive label:
"The House of Answers." It perhaps generated more questions than
answers, but unfortunately, no statistics were kept to sum up its fifth
decade as a public institution. In its statuary and inscriptions, the
building proclaimed Truth and Beauty—History, Drama, Poetry, Religion, Romance, and Philosophy. As one of the world's great research libraries, its bronze doors were open to everyone, with no
questions asked about individual need or purpose—and this, in stark
contrast to the British Library or the Bibliothèque Nationale, its older brethren. In its reading rooms, classified by subject, by language,
and by form—as in the case of periodicals, maps, and prints—seekers
of answers could narrow their questions. Open shelves in the Main
Reading Room made it easier for the uninitiated to grope for general
reference books. As a last resort, librarians were ready to help in
clarifying the ill-defined question. The beauty of research in action
lay in the material and intellectual freedom that the building and its
tools offered. In the sense of time and space, the researcher was able

to read, cogitate, and digest for as long as he or she wished. The quest seemed unlimited and timeless.

Like so many cultural institutions in New York, the Library was the only one of its kind, unique in form and substance. Its substance was shaped by individual collectors and institutional policies. Nothing was too small or too ephemeral to keep, because the trivialities of today could become part of history tomorrow. A modern diet manual would be treated with the same respect as a bygone Victorian menu. One specialized librarian, in fact, urged his staff to justify the purchases they *didn't* recommend, rather than those they did. Harry Miller Lydenberg, the Library's greatest collector-director, laid the foundations of the Slavonic Division personally in one fell swoop. He himself brought from Russia in 1924 some of the rarest pamphlets in the West, thereby expanding the nucleus of 1,000 volumes in 1899 to a collection of 24,000. His acquisitiveness justified itself, for during the Second World War, the Slavonic collections in the British Museum were destroyed. In this country, when some of the Library's treasures were sent to vaults for safekeeping during the war years, it was Lydenberg who, while assigning priorities to the treasures that had to be transported, urged his staff to evacuate pamphlets first, because those collections might contain unique copies. Of Gutenberg Bibles there were more. In building collections for the public, the question of how frequently an item might be called for never came up. It seemed immaterial whether or not one reader in fifty years might call for it; all that mattered was that it was available. The collections were built by scholars with extraordinary knowledge of their fields, and with boldness of action, dedication to the common good of scholarship, and a united purpose. The record speaks for itself in the Library's catalog; in books that are based on research conducted, often, in just one location; in the names inscribed on the Library's columns. Despite Samuel Johnson's judgment that "no place affords a more striking conviction of the vanity of human hopes than a public library," The New York Public Library became a monument to combined generations of human hopes as expressed by all Americans, those who were already here and wave upon wave of immigrants.

When the English public library system was established, its formal charter, the Public Libraries Act of 1850, stated that it was done for "the purpose of education, recreation and information." The history of libraries on both sides of the Atlantic runs parallel, and in both countries, information seems to be crowding out education and recreation. The advances made in computer applications during the seventies coincided with the proliferation and rising cost of publications, and with rising wages and expectations and decreasing space as well. At the same time, the introduction of databases, collaborative acquisitions between libraries, and commercially distributed microfiche publications did much to solve the problem of inadequate space. By the mid-seventies, it was no longer possible to maintain service on the level of the previous two decades, and the Library had reluctantly to cut back on the number of hours it would remain open. The special eagerness with which readers crowded into the Library's historic Main Reading Room seven days a week is now a memory. Transportation in the City has grown increasingly expensive and inefficient, and all but gone are those readers who in the past would spend a day of leisure, walking through and reading exhibitions, sampling books without taking note of the passing of time. Gone, too, are the crowds waiting in line to read, standing up if necessary, during the Christmas recess at university campuses. Photocopying has replaced personal trips and the reading of original manuscripts. In many cases, research from film has taken the place of studying the real thing.

The need of books and scholarship, of a quiet place for study and contemplation, was never felt more acutely in the Library's seventy-five-year history than during the depression. The staff, ill paid and overworked, made up of those who had come to New York from all parts of the country and of recent immigrants who supplied language skills; of maintenance staff and craftsmen of Scandinavian, German, and Italian descent who polished the long study tables, the bronze, and the marble—all found a home in the beautiful building. Some lived in rented rooms, some in cheap hotels. They did not mind if the hours of service were long. Many of the staff were young, aspiring college graduates attending library schools that had just begun teaching bibliography and librarianship on a college level, leading to a bachelor's degree in Library Science. (This undefined, book-centered discipline developed into a recognized profession, with classification and cataloging at its core.) Misery created a community of spirit within the book-lined walls. Both senior and junior staff served the public with courtly formality. With temperatures often in the 90s, male staff at the Information Desk nonetheless always wore jackets, and one much-loved curator of memory never set foot in the public corridor in shirtsleeves. Guards in uniform stood stiff at attention. At the same time, the well-known kidding of New Yorkers took place in manned elevators that bore a close resemblance to those of the now vanished Metropolitan Opera House. In the face of all sorts of historic woes, the Library reflected within its doors the spirit of New Yorkers. It lasted into the fifties.

During the fifties and sixties, as the demand for research materials in traditional and new fields grew, the pace quickened. Readership increased rapidly, and the need for a different sort of reading room became apparent. The Mid-Manhattan Library, which opened in the spring of 1982, is the realization both of increasing demands and the change in demography and age groups in the City. Decentralization also came in the mid-sixties, when a library for the performing arts was built at Lincoln Center. With its tools no longer contained in one building, scholarly research within the City became more cumbersome, but during these two decades, students' needs were also adequately met by expanding university campuses in the metropolitan area. Except for unique materials, the Library no longer held the same eminence it once did—even nationally. In the mid-fifties, for example, older institutions on the Eastern Seaboard faced a growing challenge—both intellectual and financial—from such extraordinary collections as the modern literature collection at the Humanities Research Center of the University of Texas (Austin).

Today, it is possibly true that the need for and interest in the humanities are on the wane. It cannot be quantified, but it is visible both in the quality and quantity of readers and their work. Fields tend to become narrower, restricted, as some studies are, to major authors or major trends. There is a marked tendency to turn out whatever work is required in the fastest possible time. An old-fashioned humanist has trouble understanding research today: instant answers to quick questions. Research—and it cannot be stressed sufficiently—is not identical with information, and in its long-term duration, includes contemplation and articulation. In print, some thoughts read like *non sequiturs,* almost as if words had gotten in the way. Quite often what seems to be lacking is concision or, perhaps, the essence of what Pascal wrote: "I have made this letter longer than usual, because I lack the time to make it short."

The Library met the challenge of the sixties: it continued to collect in depth, but at the same time, witnessed a deterioration of its much abused collections. By the end of this socially turbulent decade, the need for increased security in our vulnerable building became apparent. New planning to suit changed circumstances became imperative in the early seventies, as the Library's endowment decreased in value and the budget could not be balanced. Older tools no longer seemed to suffice. A card catalog of 10 million entries was deteriorating, and technology, with its electronic aids, promised a different departure. The use of the computer for indexing and cataloging came onto the horizon, and computer technicians who were also trained in the humanities, while small in number, were intellectually sound and hopeful. Neither the means nor the end would be economical. Today it would seem that ends and means, cause and effect, are what require a certain amount of sorting out. Like many cultural institutions, the Library, although it endures, is experiencing the ills of a society that has lost its way.

In the seventies, an increasing number of specialized articles dealt with the use and adaptability of electronic hardware to bibliographic purposes: indexing, data processing, information transmission, and the replacement of card catalogs. Within specialized library literature, certain guidelines were set, always with the warning that machines are only as good as the people who adapted and made use of them. Electronic photocomposition of books was being tested and perfected, and books could be distributed in unprecedented quantities. Anxiety surrounding the survival of the book in its original form, the codex, increased with the distribution of cassettes. In response to the dangers threatening the book, "International Book Year" was launched in 1972, and the International Federation of Library Associations published its proceedings in 1976, under the title *Reading in a Changing World.*[1] In his contribution to that volume, "Books as a Way of Life," Gordon N. Ray sounded the warning: "Those who believe in books should regard with extreme distrust . . . all proposals to turn libraries into 'information centers' and librarians into 'media specialists.' " Certain factors in the way electronics and books serve different purposes are never going to change: the book is portable; it is adaptable to human needs; it may serve to give permanent information; its pages are easily turned when certain passages of text are required; it can be used immediately, once supplied; and its pages can be annotated if required. We approach a book entirely differently from the way we approach a screen, whether it is a database, a microfilm, or a cassette.

In closing a decade during which certain distinctions became blurred, and that witnessed a rise in illiteracy and aliteracy (the abandonment of reading by those who can read but refuse to), UNESCO, in a "World Congress on Books" held in London this past summer, formulated its declaration and recommendations. In it, three hundred participants from eighty-six countries declared their "continued support of the principles and objectives established ten years ago during the International Book Year 1972."[2] The most important statements concern the future:

Books, we believe, retain their pre-eminence as the carriers of knowledge, education, and cultural values in human society. They serve both national development and the enrichment of individual human life. They foster better understanding between peoples and strengthen the desire for peace in the minds of men, to which UNESCO is dedicated. . . . Looking forward, we seek a world in which books are more readily available to more people, and in which the ability to read and the will and desire to enjoy the fruits of reading are more widely sought by all societies.

It is not as if mankind did not have its prophets. Great writers, who know that memory itself is being threatened, are warning us, with increasing urgency, that we are in danger of losing it. Jorge Luis Borges reminds us that libraries are mankind's memory and imagination,[3] and Czeslaw Milosz in his 1980 Nobel Lecture said:

Our planet that gets smaller every year, with its fantastic proliferation of mass media, is witnessing a process that escapes definition, characterized by a refusal to remember. Certainly, the illiterates of past centuries, then an enormous majority of mankind, knew little of the history of their respective countries and of their civilization. In the minds of modern illiterates, however, who know how to read and write and even teach in schools and universities, history is present but blurred, in a state of strange confusion.[4]

Will George Orwell's prophecy in *1984,* of bookless homes, become a reality? Joined to this question is another: How will written traces of man's creative spirit be preserved if artistic composition is conveyed on a magnetic tape? Is posterity going to be left with only the grin of the Cheshire Cat? If we are heading for a paperless society, will Milosz's warning become a reality, and how many of us will then feel the anxiety of the poet: "a foreboding of a not distant future when history will be reduced to what appears on television, while the truth, because it is too complicated, will be buried in the archives, if not totally annihilated." It may be too late by then to take any action, especially on a national and international scale.

In articles written by librarians, the layman might notice certain characteristics: the survival of libraries themselves is questioned, and such terms as "libraries of last resort" have crept into the language. (There are also "user-friendly" computers.) The directions in which libraries might go are described as "warehouses of knowledge" or "the information marketplace"—of which the library may become an extension. These articles ask whether librarians should try to transform their libraries into businesses, and whether businessmen should not try to get into the library business themselves. Many already have, and commercial enterprises are clearly visible in the explosion of computer software, most of it requiring printed catalogs and publications that call for the same handling as reference material. Since entire libraries are now transferred both in time and space, catalogs and announcements to accompany them must be provided for. What is missing from all discussions is a fact never questioned in the past few centuries—that we are masters of our future, not victims of machines nor of the circumstances they may have created. Librarians can—and ought—to control their own computer programs, lest they sell out to businesses that would impose theirs.

Finally, to pose the basic questions: What has gone wrong, and how, if at all, can a balance be struck in raising a generation of readers? To these, there are no simple answers. Reading as a way of life starts early and when it is, is rarely abandoned. The discipline requires a great deal of time, and is frequently exercised at the expense of life's other pleasures. Especially in a society that offers so much in material goods, it may be hard to impose reading and study on urban children. It is becoming quite clear, however, that television is a poor substitute. Perhaps whatever reading our society offers, it is not the kind either young or old want, and the rejection of reading by millions may be valid on that count alone. Young readers are conditioned by the mode and material they read, and mechanical means of transmitting information convey, however subtly, the fallacious notion that those means are identical with reading, and that information and education are one and the same. There is no doubt that in this country, anyone in need of a specific book, or of one he (or she) has not identified, can be satisfied. It is equally certain that a materially wealthy America cannot afford a spiritually poor citizenry.

I submit that to be well informed is not synonymous with being well educated. Experience does not equal education. Informed opinion is not the same as an educated view. Mysteries of the act of creation cannot be penetrated through the use of a machine. Understanding and interpreting history require more than data in statistical tables, and balanced minds are better than balanced budgets.

ENDNOTES

[1]G.N. Ray, "Books as a Way of Life," *Reading in a Changing World,* Papers presented at the 38th session of the IFLA Council, Budapest, 1972, edited by E. Mohrhardt (München: 1976), pp. 20-30.

[2]"UNESCO's London Declaration: Towards a Reading Society," *Library Association Record* 84(6) (June 1982): 213.

[3]J.L. Borges, "Burning Books," *Horizon* 24(6) (June 1981): 58-60.

[4]Czeslaw Milosz, *Nobel Lecture* (New York: Farrar, Straus & Giroux, 1981), pp. 14-15.

Daniel Aaron

An Informal Letter to the Editor

D<small>EAR</small> <small>STEPHEN,</small>

You'll recall that during the *Daedalus* symposium held last June on the general topic "The American Reading Public," some reference was made to the recently launched Library of America. Richard Poirier and I, speaking as members of the Library's Board of Directors, briefly discussed its origins and prospects. Since then, the success of the Library in a slack economic period has surprised its sponsors and ill-wishers alike. The reviews and comment have been overwhelmingly positive, the brickbats few. We shall know soon enough whether it is destined to become a national institution, sink into oblivion, or just plug along. For the moment, it happens to be alive and kicking. Hence I take this occasion to speculate a little on why the Library has received so much attention and to ask what, if anything, this tells us about at least a part of the American reading public today.

When Edmund Wilson proposed the publication of an American library in a series of hardcover volumes that would stay permanently in print, he didn't advance his idea as a promising financial venture. He thought the public deserved the opportunity to buy the works of American authors in good, affordable editions. I think he would have been pleased by the reception of the Library of America, but it would have made no difference to him if the volumes sold widely or not. All the same, one can't help being struck by the number of people who read about the project in, say, *Parade*, the Sunday supplement, or in other newspapers and magazines, and who took the time to write for more information.

Of what sort they are, or how representative of the public at large, can only be guessed. A breakdown of the more than 2,600 letters provoked so far by the *Parade* piece alone offers a few clues regarding the motivation of prospective subscribers, but nothing conclusive. The letters come from forty-seven states and two Canadian provinces. The majority of correspondents live in small towns and villages, where, presumably, bookstores are a rarity. One Missourian writes that he can't find a copy of *Leaves of Grass* "after three months of trying." A Pennsylvanian announces, "I for one want a book to last so that another generation may enjoy American literature." A Louisianan residing in a war veteran's home is "most anxious to secure these volumes to leave to my four grandchildren, who otherwise might well miss a beautiful part of their heritage." An Ohioan living "far from the Book Stores" wants to replace his copy of *Uncle Tom's Cabin:* "I had the Uncle Tom Cabin years ago. But was stoled. Please let me know if I could Buy one." Do these people constitute a substantial or untapped body of the reading public? It's hard to say. Until the readership of the Library is systematically analyzed, we can only guess its potential size and composition.

But enough evidence is at hand, it seems to me, to discount the intimation that this undefined public consists of a small number of nonreaders momentarily gulled by a sales pitch. Not surprisingly, the Library appeals to teachers and librarians. Professional people, especially doctors, also show strong interest in the series, some of them quite possibly out of nostalgia or national pride or pursuit of status or for investment purposes. Simply regarded as objects, the books are handsome. Yet I wonder if the favorable response to the Library hasn't a less crass explanation. Might it not indicate that more than a few doctors, lawyers, merchants, chiefs, are looking around for books they had no time or inclination to read during their brief exposure to the humanities in high school and college? A good many intelligent readers, I have come to believe, find so-called serious contemporary writing often too ephemeral for the difficulties it poses (as well as remote from their concerns), and a lot of "popular" books, including best sellers, either jejune or trashy. For them, perhaps, the Library of America promises literary fare more substantial and entertaining.

This is all pure supposition, of course, but I feel on firmer ground in proposing that the gulf between serious writing and a broad sector of the public is probably wider now than it was fifty years ago—and this despite the paperback "revolution" and the fact that a far greater percentage of American youth now attend colleges and universities than at any time before the end of World War II. To spell out that observation, I offer the following hypothesis, in the form of a sketchy historical detour—so bear with me.

"Serious" readers, I dare say, never made up a sizable percentage of any population, but before the advent of modernism in this country, works of "high culture" were well within the range of the educated minority. American writers in those days, many of whom ministered to their audiences as secular priests, seldom strayed far from the common culture. Longfellow may be taken as the preeminent example. Too readily patronized in our time as the Bard of the Bourgeoisie, it is important for my argument to see him as a poet in tune with the large and admiring audience he entertained, reassured, and instructed. Today we prefer the writers in his generation and the next who were less comfortable in the America of their times, those who tried to escape the deadening supervision of the "spiritualized" literary authorities and flew the coop. Yet even these writers "belonged" to their society in ways that contemporary writers do not. Their books had a national purport: to speak to, admonish, and satirize a sprawling nation, and provide it with persuasive symbols of its identity. Emerson's *Essays, The Scarlet Letter, Leaves of Grass, Moby Dick, Walden, Huckleberry Finn, The Portrait of a Lady,* are at once private and public declarations. Henry James's remark to his brother William, "I know what I am about, and I have always my eyes on my native land," might apply to the majority of other nineteenth century American writers, no matter how cryptic their utterances, how remote the landscapes of their books. If they chafed at editorial restraints or lamented the inhospitable literary climate, the facts of American life (and very likely their own inner reticences) compelled them, often with great reluctance, to adjust themselves to the going codes.

The genteel men of letters who enforced these codes between roughly 1865 and 1915 have been faulted on a number of scores: for their unshakable adherence to the ancestral culture of England in all of its aesthetic, political, and ethical ramifications; for propitiating the gods of the New England pantheon; above all, for closing ranks against literary experimentation and social heterodoxy. These charges, although vitiated by being lumped into a single category, are largely deserved. Even so, by insisting on the centrality of style, structure, form, clarity—on the craft of writing—the self-appointed priests did their best to raise the level of popular taste. They really believed in and practiced the gospel of literature that they preached to their admittedly restricted congregations, and kept them in touch with the world of books.

With the undermining of the genteel Victorian's authority early in the twentieth century, the evangelical and hygienic emphasis gradually faded. The cordon sanitaire that they had set up against what they deemed to be a deleterious foreign and local contagion was breached, and writers heretofore quarantined in a "literary" Ellis Island were released. Image-smashing Menckenians and other critic-journalists who flourished between 1915 and 1930, among them the leading explicators of European modernism, had fun at the expense of the old guard, who, Mencken charged, lacked "aesthetic passion" and spoke for "a primitive and timorous society." But the irreverent rebels, too, were freelance writers. They earned their livings largely by contributing to an array of newspapers and journals for which there is no contemporary counterpart. The best of them were also generalists able to gather and predigest assorted learning, and to dispense it to a widening audience hungry for random enlightenment.

This free-wheeling and diverse little company, according to my scenario, kept its consumers abreast of current literary movements until the onset of the 1930s, when it began to fall apart. I suspect that during the lean years of the Great Depression, the folding of many magazines and newspapers not only deprived journalist-critics of an important source of income, but also considerably narrowed their scope. What is more, as political issues subsumed a great part of American intellectual and cultural life, literature itself became politicized to the point where ideological affiliations and party loyalties absorbed a large portion of the literary community. The war and the subsequent turning of literary critics from social to personal concerns tended to distance them from a class of readers they had once been paid to address.

The effect of this disengagement on the book-buying, magazine-reading part of the population, together with the general decline in the amount and quality of informed book reviewing in the national press, has never been, probably cannot be, assessed. But certainly, readers who had once looked to magazines as diverse as *The Dial, The New Republic, The Nation, Harper's, The Atlantic,* and *The Saturday Review* to alert them to new writers, new literary trends, and the like, had fewer equivalent sources available to them in the post-World War II years. Contributors to these periodicals (Edmund

Wilson, Kenneth Burke, Allen Tate, Lewis Mumford, Malcolm Cowley, Conrad Aiken, Gilbert Seldes, Joseph Wood Krutch, Henry Hazlitt, Bernard De Voto, to name a few) formed a disparate and contentious republic of letters. They had discussed and debated a wide range of subjects in their books and articles and reviews, not simply fiction, poetry, and the arts, but history, philosophy, politics, and popular culture as well. What Allen Tate called "the illiberal specializations" had not yet completely taken root; the experiments of an avant-garde culture incubating in the "little magazines" imperceptibly filtered into the books and periodicals of larger circulation. By the end of the 1940s, however, a literary generation still believing in its mission to enlighten and guide, without compromising its artistic standards, no longer had the will, or enjoyed the conditions, to achieve it.

Edmund Wilson, the Founding Father of the Library of America, might serve as its exemplar. In many ways a social and cultural conservative, he managed with considerable success to instruct an audience still puzzled by the literature of modernism, if not downright hostile to it. And although he accepted cultural hierarchies and never expected to see great works of literature devoured by millions, he wasn't all that far from Emerson's Scholar or Man Thinking. For both, the vocation demanded a degree of devotion and sacrifice: not a retreat from society, but rather an active participation in it and an imperviousness to worldly blandishments. It placed disinterested curiosity above religious or political absolutes. It enlisted the man of letters in the fight against what Wilson called "the gulf of illiteracy and mean ambitions."

Wilson lived long enough to see the migration of the literary interpreters to university sanctuaries, the further polarizing of high and commercial culture, and the fragmenting of the "middlebrow" element in his constituency into a series of subcultures, each with its specialized and circumscribed territory. By my reckoning, this process took place as the arts (and the critical vocabulary contrived to explicate them) were turning private, technical, and hermetic, and as students handicapped by a lack of a common culture poured into the institutions of higher learning. Regimented into large courses, assigned packaged texts to be collected in the college bookstore supermarkets, and initiated into the arcane strategies of interpretation, it doesn't surprise me that a good many found the study of literature forbidding and joyless—a "discipline" indeed.

We shall have to wait until the long-term implications of the university role in setting cultural standards become a little clearer. Scholars, creative writers, and critics currently attached to colleges and universities, it's fair to say, pretty much dominate the literary scene. It is not to discount their manifold contributions to ask whether they have effectively supplanted the cultural middlemen who operated outside the academy. And given the prevalence of classroom teaching that turns the reading of fiction and poetry into problem-solving, and removes ideas, history, and life itself from anesthetized texts, one wonders if the benefits derived from a university-nurtured school of literature as it now exists are likely to seep down to the public-at-large.

These reflections bring me back to the Library of America and what it signifies. Is it a flash in the pan or a straw in the wind? Can it help to gather in a dispersed readership at a time when most of the purveyors of high culture have moved to the campus and write for a selected clientele? As one close to the Library, I merely note that we seem to have struck a popular nerve. Sales of the first four volumes (over 80,000 copies between May and November 1982) and the thousands of prepublication orders for the next set, in my opinion, can't be attributed to advertising "hype." There's been comparatively little of that. At least a segment of the population (how large or cohesive it is still too early to say) has welcomed the idea of recovering and preserving American books of literary merit.

To repeat, I can't account for this response. It may have something to do with the times, the "recession," to be more exact. During the 1930s, thousands of Americans looked backward to a "usable past," partly, perhaps, to clutch at reassuring and threatened "basic values," and partly to find out when and where the nation had made a wrong turn. Then again, the very title of the series may contain a clue to its popularity. Incidentally, we debated a long time before we hit upon "Library." We wanted a name that sounded inviting, that carried ingratiating connotations of friendliness and fellowship. We chose "Library" instead of "Literary Classics" because the latter seemed to our ears too marmoreal and fenced in.

We hope to dispel that chilly association. We envision (with what justice, it remains to be seen) a body of readers of undetermined number whose cultural wants have not been met. We propose to accommodate a variety of different tastes without denaturing or vulgarizing the Library offerings, and we seek to attract a broad cross-section of bookbuyers, from the "fans" of Raymond Chandler to the "disciples" of Henry James. Finally, we hope to see the sprouting of intelligent and curious-minded potential subscribers of all ages, background, and occupations, conceivably a good many of them uninformed about "Literature" and a bit in awe of it, largely ignorant of, or bored or put off by, esoteric commentary[1] in the reviews and quarterlies, but receptive, when given a chance, to books they've scarcely heard of.

If the Library manages to survive long enough to complete its planned series, the public will eventually be introduced to authors and titles not ordinarily mentioned even in cultivated literary circles—to volumes of nature writing, travel, exploration, philosophy, history, biography, autobiography, social theory. It will discover in some of these works themes and subjects infrequently dealt with by contemporary writers, particularly novelists and poets, but still speaking to the lives and conditions of modern readers.

One long-term test of the Library's success will be the extent to which the acquaintance of the American literary past quickens the interest of these readers in current writing and enhances their desire and ability to understand it, judge it, and enjoy it. I like to think that the very presence of the Library volumes in private and public places will affect popular reading habits and make new writers as well as preserve old ones.

Daniel Aaron

ENDNOTE

[1]The Library of America volumes have no introductions. Readers are released from bondage to claimed (and usually dated) critical authority.

Al Silverman

The Fragile Pleasure

B ESSIE WELLS lives in Toledo, Ohio. Anyone else in this time of video games, quartz heaters, stationary bicycles, and the Cuisinart might feel dislocated snaking through a six-room apartment furnished mainly with books, almost 6,000 of them. Bessie Wells is eighty-seven years old, blessed with reasonable health and amazing grace, and as active a reader today as she was when she first joined the Book-of-the-Month Club. "When was that?" I asked her.

"It started in 1926, didn't it?" she said testily. "Well, that's when I joined."

Mrs. Wells, a widow who lives alone, has read all her life. She grew up, she said, in the raw countryside around Defiance, Ohio. There was not much to do, and her parents were very strict. "My father had quite a few books—Shakespeare, Robert Burns, *Decline and Fall of the Roman Empire*. I still have them. He wouldn't let me touch them when I was young. I think it was a scheme of his to get me to *want* to read them."

The scheme worked; if not that, something else did. Bessie Wells became a reader. I asked her what she was currently reading. "Right now it's one of your latest books," she said, "*Flambard's Confession*. I'm enjoying it, but pretty soon books are going to be as large as Webster's dictionary. It hurts my lap."

Flambard's Confession is a 775-page historical novel set in England on the eve of the death of William the Conqueror. It centers around the Archbishop of Canterbury, Tanulpl Flambard, described in the Book-of-the-Month Club *News* as a sensualist "in pursuit of worldly power." The book was written by Marilyn Durham, who had one success ten years earlier with a Western novel, *The Man Who Loved Cat Dancing*. The publisher of *Flambard's Confession* had reasonable expectations for it, enough to print 25,000 copies. Published in the fall of 1982, it never made a best-seller list. The Book-of-the-Month Club printed 5,000 copies, and 3,200 members ordered it. Bessie Wells was one of them. Bessie Wells, who owns 6,000 books, wanted to read *Flambard's Confession*. She is an oddity, of course, as exotic a creature in this country as the whooping crane. But she is also a restorer of the faith.

In its early years, the Book-of-the-Month Club commissioned the Gallup organization to conduct surveys regularly of the book-reading habits of the American public. These probes were abandoned a dozen years ago, perhaps in fright. When George Gallup interviewed readers in 1937, he found that 29 percent of all adults were reading books at that time. In 1955 the percentage had fallen to 17 percent. Apparently nobody wanted to know what it was in 1970.

The newer executives of the club, it appears, decided that public opinion polls of reading habits were to be trusted even less than public opinion polls on politics. It is too easy to be conned by "the reading public." There is nothing a "reader" likes better than to inflate the cultural values of America's tastemakers by offering answers to questions that bear no resemblance to reality, but that they know the questioner wants to hear. "Did I read *Gravity's Rainbow*? Well, of course. I stayed in bed all summer to read it. It's my favorite book since *Finnegan's Wake*."

I encountered some of this gamesmanship last summer when I served on a jury in a case involving a house burglary. The prosecuting attorney, trying to find just the right jury for this case, asked every potential juror: "Name the last book 'or novel' you have read." Of the twenty-five panelists, four or five had the strength of character to say they didn't have time to read books. We ended up with a jury consisting of readers of *Shogun, Noble House, Ball Four, The Hotel New Hampshire, The Dollmaker* (large-type edition), and *The White Hotel*. The prosecuting attorney evidently got what he wanted: a literate jury that voted guilty on all counts.

The Gallup organization made one other interesting study in the early fifties. A group of college graduates were asked to name the authors of *An American Tragedy, Babbitt, The Canterbury Tales, Gulliver's Travels, Leaves of Grass, The Old Wives' Tale, Utopia, Vanity Fair, Origin of Species, The Wealth of Nations, The Rubaiyat of Omar Khayyam,* and *Tom Jones*. Nine percent could not name the author of any of these books; 39 percent could name no more than three. One identified a person named "Longsworth" as the author of *Origin of Species*. I suppose we shouldn't be surprised. Young people nowadays, readers and nonreaders alike, tend to block out the past like a magician palming an egg. It's not easy to make readers out of existentialists.

Of course no one needs a Gallup poll to know that we are not a nation of readers. That phrase, incidentally, came up a year ago when Daniel Boorstin, the Librarian of Congress, asked the Book-of-the-Month Club to co-sponsor a dinner of Very Important People at the Library to kick off a book exhibit that would run through the summer of 1982. The theme was to be "a nation of readers."

"Isn't that kind of wishful thinking?" I asked Boorstin.

"Yes," he said, "but it's something to strive for, isn't it?"

Most certainly, especially when we seem to be going the other way. Since the 1950s, according to a UN study, the United States has dropped from the eighteenth most literate member of the 158 member nations to forty-ninth. In addition there are now 60 million Americans who are either totally or functionally illiterate. To these must be added a strain recently discovered by social scientists, the "aliterates," those who know how to read but won't.

I have always envied other nations of readers. Ole Werner Thomsen, chairman of the Nordic Book Club of Scandinavia, an organization of book clubs from Denmark, Norway, Sweden, and Finland, told me recently that the total membership of all the book clubs in these countries was 1.1 million—or almost the size of the Book-of-the-Month Club's U.S. membership. But those four nations have a combined population of 23 million.

Another Nordic country, Iceland, has a 99 percent literacy rate. I talked about that with Amalia Lindal, an Icelandic expatriate who raised five children in Iceland, and after divorcing her husband, brought her family to Toronto to live a decade ago. She publishes a short story quarterly, *Reader's Choice*, and perhaps because the Canadian literacy rate is not that of Iceland, is having a difficult time finding readers. The tradition of reading in Iceland, she says, comes from stories and fables and fairy tales of the Land of the Midnight Sun handed down from generation to generation. Children become enthralled; they listen to the stories, and then read them for themselves. The habit sticks. So it is not just those long, cold winters, or the fact that, with only one television station broadcasting a mere three hours a night, TV-viewing is limited. In Iceland, Mrs. Lindal says, "either you have big families or you read."

Has the habit of reading fallen on hard times in this country? Polls or no polls, my feeling is that, on a per capita basis, there are probably no more book readers in this country today than there were back when Gallup was taking the pulse of the reading public. But there probably aren't any fewer readers, either. And the quality is up. Unlike steel and automobiles, reading is not a "sunset" industry. The futurists claim that the book as we know it will disappear, like that magician's egg, and that it will be replaced by "electronic data retrieval" through our home computers. But I doubt that this will happen, at least to the extent predicted, because reading, as we know it, the eyes fastening on the printed page, is a sensual experience. It feels, as Rilke put it in another context, "like a ringing glass that shivers even as it rings."

"You can't sell books to people who aren't readers"—or so they say. But the effort goes on, as it should. The enormously successful German publishing company, Bertelsmann, is today testing a new book club, American Circle, in two of our Western cities, and doing it the German way, the shop-at-home club. The shopping, however, is not done alone. Bertelsmann seeks its members by selling door-to-door, a method that has been remarkably successful in almost every other country in the world infiltrated by the Bertelsmann missionaries. The idea is a simple one: if the salesperson can get a prospective customer to open up that front door, he (or she) can persuade people who have never bought a book to join their club.

A while ago I had lunch with a group of senior Bertelsmann executives involved with the American operation. They wore stiff, correct clothes; at lunch, they drank white wine, like every other American publisher; and their talk was as stiff and correct as their wardrobe. They had no desire, they said, to compete with the great American book clubs. Rather, they would, by God, transform nonreaders into readers. And someday these Born Again readers would graduate to the big leagues—to membership in the Book-of-the-Month Club.

They told me what it was like to enter these households at mid-morning—that is, when law-and-order Americans allowed them through the door. First was the shock of the blue light hitting them in the face. Edmund Wilson once wrote a play called *The Little Blue Light*. His was a death ray, the ultimate weapon. Television's blue light, of course, is the ultimate pacifier: the screen glowing all day long in an empty house, the occupants paying only desultory attention to the varying levels of intensity emanating from the tube.

Except for an occasional Bible or Reader's Digest Condensed Book volume, there was not a single book to be seen.

And yet the Bertelsmann pioneers are full of hope, despite the difficult burdens they lay on prospective members. To join the American Circle you must first put down $5, a membership fee. You then have the privilege of buying whatever you want from the sales catalog, a catalog full of books for adults and children, lots of self-help, lots of Victoria Holt-type romances, mild-mannered sexual fantasies: "powerful sagas of love, hate, greed, and wealth." The new member must purchase something from the catalog and must continue to buy at least one item from each new catalog, which is delivered by the salesperson four times a year.

That the operation will be as successful in the United States as it has been in France, England, Italy, Brazil, and many other countries, the people at Bertelsmann have no doubt, because they believe in the underpinning of their concept: the promise of hope for the future. What the Bertelsmann salespeople tell the citizens of the world, the readers of tomorrow, is this: if the books are in the home, there will be a better life.

I am almost exactly as old as the Book-of-the-Month Club. In my early years, my Aunt Rose lived with us. Aunt Rose was considered a spinster then, though she was beautiful, intelligent, and popular. She finally did marry at the age of thirty-four, which was considered slightly unfashionable in those days. But Aunt Rose was always ahead of her time. She was a high-school teacher in my hometown of Lynn, Massachusetts. She taught typing and shorthand and the practical skills that young people would need to make it through the depression. My parents could never afford to buy books. Aunt Rose could and did. She had the same feeling as the Bertelsmann people—that books in the home were the symbol of a better life ahead. But Aunt Rose also liked to read books, so she joined the Book-of-the-Month Club.

The first book that I can remember her receiving was *The Forty Days of Musa Dagh,* by Franz Werfel, an immensely popular novelist, though not a writer with "finish." My Aunt Rose loved *The Forty Days of Musa Dagh,* and the books from the club just kept coming in until she got married and left us.

I never read *The Forty Days of Musa Dagh*—I was eight years old and mostly into the *Book of Knowledge,* where I sought refuge from a world that seemed too complex for me to handle, and a bit nasty, too. I was a floundering sort of student, and it was my third-grade teacher, Miss Moriarty, who called my mother into a conference to see what could be done about me. The best my mother could say on my behalf was that I did like to look at books. So Miss Moriarty suggested to my mother—as a last-gasp possibility—that she take me to the library to get me into the habit of reading. My mother did, and it became a weekly ritual with us to walk to the Parrot Street branch of the Lynn Public Library to drop off books in exchange for a new batch. I will never know whether it was those weekly treks to the library or those books coming into the house from the Book-of-the-Month Club that made a reader out of me. In hindsight, I suppose I favor the Book-of-the-Month Club because, after all, that's where I ended up earning my living.

But of course neither organization was responsible, nor was it any one book. The reading experience was activated by people who cared—in my case, my mother, my aunt, my third-grade teacher. Later, it was the writer—certain writers—who changed my perception of life. I was lucky in any case. The encouragement of reading in this country, which should be an urgent priority from the beginning of education, is mostly missing today. And so a small, elite corps of readers develops in this country, and the rest—the illiterates, the aliterates—get away from us, and are lost forever.

But watch out for what is meant by "elite" here. A person whose job it is to see that a large reading public gets the books it wants has to be without intellectual bias. The Book-of-the-Month Club is full of serious book readers, men and women who read books seriously—not all of which have to be serious books. Recently I overheard two grande dames with Viennese accents conversing in the library of the large resort of Mohonk, a Bavarian castle located—incongruously—ninety miles north of New York City, and leafing casually through the books on the shelves. One pulled a paperback detective story off the shelf. "Sometimes I like junk," she said half apologetically. Her companion quickly moved to reassure her. "There's nothing wrong with junk."

American intellectuals make an issue of what they perceive to be the conflict of popular culture versus serious culture, unhappy that the popular forever dominates the serious. But that is true in Iceland and everywhere else in the world, not just in the United States. It is always going to be so, and to strain for an elitist palace guard within the elite reading society only stifles the joyous totality of the reading experience. There will always be that gulf between high art and popular entertainment, but there is that bridge thrown between the two, and people can walk back and forth as they wish.

G.K. Chesterton said there was a great difference between the lively person wanting to read a book and the tired person wanting a book to read. The challenge that we have always faced at the Book-of-the-Month Club, where we read 5,000 trade books a year, is in trying to serve both constituencies as best we can. It's not easy. As the critic-novelist Edmund White once wrote, "Sometimes it seems that writers who can write can't tell a story and those who can tell a story can't write."

White was talking about fiction mostly. His concern was for the state of serious fiction in this country, "formally inventive and linguistically splendid" but unable to claim the reader's attention because of its coldness, because "it seldom compels the reader to read on." My own feeling, after ten years of dutifully reading contemporary novels, is that American fiction is in better shape than it has a right to be. The storytellers whose books you can't put down are very much out there, as always—Robert Ludlum, Stephen King, Judith Krantz—the Franz Werfels of our day. Serious novelists who do not receive such acclaim, but who write at clean white heat and do often tell a story that sweeps you along, are out there, too, writing better than ever. It is not nearly as bad as one impressionable young critic said to another in 1980 upon hearing of Sartre's death: "There is no great writer in the world"—to which the other fellow mumbled Beckett's name and let it go at that. But the living are with us, Bellow, Updike, Malamud, Gordimer, Naipaul, Handke, Marquez, Anne Tyler, and other splendid young novelists are coming up in the ranks. I believe there are more important serious novelists being published today than there were twenty years ago. And it may be just for the reason stated by Don DeLillo, a still-young novelist of vast potential, in a recent interview: "Maybe it's not writers alone who keep the novel alive but a more serious kind of reader."[1]

It has become trendy to jump on the book publishing industry for its failures, especially its alleged failure to honor the book. Book publishing *is* different from what it was twenty years ago. Only a handful of private houses remain. Most of the others have allowed themselves to be taken over, without a shot being fired or a voice raised in protest, by massive, multitentacled corporations. Some of these giants have done so to their sorrow, discovering only later a Vietnam in their conglomerate mix. Some have carelessly misused their adoption rights. As one victim said to me—after watching his publishing house being nibbled away by an American industrial giant—"They had such a batch of people looking out for the money that no one was looking out for the author." Yet most of these industrial "aliens" do leave the professions to the professionals—and that presents another problem.

Professionalism in book publishing today is as scarce as is an understanding of the business by the corporate owners. Editors don't edit anymore! It's a cry heard more and more from some of the wisest people in book publishing. Too many editors don't edit. Too many editors don't care enough about their authors. Imagine an editor today working with an author the way Kurt Wolff did with Kafka. In a *New Yorker* profile on Helen Wolff, Herbert Mitgang quotes from a letter Kafka wrote Wolff in 1917: "I do hope that you, dear Herr Wolff, will not quite desert me, provided, of course, that I halfway deserve your kindness. In the face of all the uncertainties of the present and the future, a word from you at this point would mean so much to me." Wolff replied immediately: "Most sincerely and most gladly I declare my readiness to give you, now as well as after the war, continuous material support."[2]

The wonder, then, is that the novel is as abundant as it is today, that writers continue to write. Can it be, as John Updike said, that this urge to write "arises out of the mad notion that your society needs to know what only you can tell—needs the truth that only you can deliver"? That must be part of it, especially today when so many of us live broken lives, on the edge of nightmare. But support is still needed. Writers today may not have a Kurt or Helen Wolff behind them, but these nonediting editors we talked about do respect, appreciate, sometimes admire, our serious writers. The truth is that anyone who can write a decent first novel today will probably get it published.

The squeeze comes when the first-time novelist, who is not expected to make money for the company, but not lose too much, also loses money on the second novel, and then the third. This is when the species becomes endangered. But this was ever so, even when book publishing was known, falsely and for all the wrong reasons, as a gentlemen's business.

But now help is here for the novelist into the third or fourth book, the novelist who finds it difficult to get a hardcover house to take the next one. Trade paperbacks, softcover books in hardcover size, printed on good paper, in readable type, durably bound, are proliferating. Trade paperback publishers are beginning to publish original middle-range novels that the mass paperback houses, because of economic woes, can no longer afford to acquire, and are developing their own audience for the serious novelist. Eight years ago we started a new book club, the Quality Paperback Book Club, and though it was a struggle in those early years, we're glad we did. Trade paperbacks are clearly the wave of the future. Their effect on the novel can only be salutary, for they offer the serious novelist reasonable assurance that it is worthwhile to plod ahead, as we feel our way around the minefields toward the twenty-first century.

While the novel flourishes, as novels always have, in a very small way, the problems are more complex in nonfiction. We can't find enough books on history and biography to satisfy that part of the Book-of-the-Month Club audience that tugs strongly toward nonfiction. Years ago we could count on a pool of old reliables to deliver a steady stream of works of substance—Carl Van Doren, Samuel Eliot Morison, Walter Lippmann, Charles and Mary Beard, Van Wyck Brooks, Marchette Chute, William L. Shirer, Catherine Drinker Bowen, Winston Churchill—a list that is none too easy to match today. That, incidentally, is why long historical novels now receive such attention. James Michener is read more for the mass of information he brings to subjects as varied as the South Pacific, Israel, the Chesapeake Bay, South Africa, or the space program than for his skill as a novelist. Other novelists, like James Clavell on Japan, Anthony Gray on Vietnam, Marilyn Durham on Flambard and his time, are writing enormous novels that give the reader the feel of history's sweep. They are filling a void left by the defection of the historian.

Where are the young historians in our colleges and universities who can write? They are probably perfectly good teachers, but apparently cannot transmit their knowledge on paper. We read scores of works at the Book-of-the-Month Club that turn out to be Ph.D. dissertations in disguise—dry, formulaic, unstimulating. Too many historians cannot write, and the few who can, lack the background, the discipline, or the tradition to open up the world of the past to us.

There are exceptions, of course. Last summer at the conference that laid the groundwork for this issue of *Daedalus*, Richard Poirier mentioned the biography of Walter Lippmann by Ronald Steel. Elizabeth Hardwick said she was sure that Steel worked for years on the book, "which is not a thing that people are willing to do." But some are. Edmund Morris, a young Englishman now living in the United States, has published, to critical acclaim, one volume of his two-volume biography of Theodore Roosevelt. When he finishes the second volume, he will have spent almost ten years on the project. Similarly, Robert A. Caro, who wrote a brilliant biography of Robert Moses that took seven years of his life, has just had published the first volume of his projected three-volume biography of Lyndon Johnson. When completed, this work will have consumed a decade of Caro's life. There are other young historians writing with dedication today, but, sadly, not enough.

The one exception to this discouraging trend in nonfiction is in the field of science. Never before have we had such a group of graceful writers of science—Lewis Thomas, Stephen Jay Gould, Robert Jastrow, Timothy Ferris, among others. They are a product of a world increasingly discouraged by the possibilities of our future, who are turning to science for explanations, and comfort, if possible.

Science, which opens up the future, lives, but the past languishes. And without writers to tell us about the past, or reveal it in new dimensions, there will be no readers to care about it. This is one of the reasons the Book-of-the-Month Club is reissuing classics as part of a series called "The American Past." We are republishing in fine editions books that are either out of print or mostly unread today—printed on quality paper, with seam bindings and archival illustrations, slipcased and with new introductions. So far we have published Catherine Drinker Bowen's life of Oliver Wendell Holmes, *Yankee From Olympus; The Peabody Sisters of Salem,* by Louisa Hall Tharp; *Benjamin Franklin,* by Carl Van Doren; *A Stillness at Appomattox,* by Bruce Catton; and *John Brown's Body,* by Stephen Vincent Benet.

In his introduction to our edition of *John Brown's Body,* Archibald MacLeish speaks of the consequences of the Civil War, about a nation caught in a terrible moment when its conception of itself is challenged. "To read the book now at the end of this tragic century," MacLeish writes, "in a generation which has lost its sense of itself, its sense of purpose—to read it as it was meant to be read—is to turn the mind around and face it forward." That is what history can still do. That also is the essence of what is called the reading experience—the continuity it offers in a life of discontinuity, the continuity between the writer and the reader.

Last August I received a letter from George Thompson of Halifax, Nova Scotia. He wrote to tell me that he has been a member of the Book-of-the-Month Club continuously for fifty-one years. Mr. Thompson keeps pretty good records; he sent us a copy of his accounts with the club from 1931 to 1936. In one month—October of 1933—Mr. Thompson received the following books from the club: *Looking Forward*, by Franklin D. Roosevelt; *Culbertson's Contract Bridge for Auction Players*, by Ely Culbertson; *Anthony Adverse*, by Hervey Allen (for $3); and a Dual Selection—*The Woods Colt*, by Thomas Williamson, and *Flush*, by Virginia Woolf. And Mr. Thompson still belongs. Continuity.

The book club business has changed over the years since Mr. Thompson joined, in ways I find encouraging for the future of reading in this country. The number of members we have today is not much larger than when I started at the club in 1972, but the quality of the membership has changed considerably. For many years, the Main Selection, the book of the month, was just about the only book taken by our subscribers. Under the principle of "negative option," a member must do something *not* to receive the Main Selection—he must return the reply form and check the box that says, "No, I don't want the Main Selection this month." Otherwise, he gets it. Negative option is the hub of any book club's business. Without it, book clubs probably couldn't exist because of the expense involved in recruiting members.

We had a lot of passive members in the first twenty-five years of the club's existence, the acceptance rate for the Main Selection averaging over 50 percent—that is, 50 percent of the members did nothing, and thus received the Main Selection. As we gave members more and alternate possibilities (thus the word "Alternate," now a generic book club term to describe all other books except the Main Selection), the acceptance rate of the Main Selection began to drop. In 1962 its gross average acceptance rate was 26.8 percent. In 1972 it was 17.7 percent. For 1982 it will be around 15 percent. But more members are buying a variety of Alternates on their own initiative. We think it is healthier that book club members are choosing books they truly want, rather than just accepting the Main Selection. But that's because book club members are more sophisticated, more knowing about books, more secure in their tastes than any previous generation of book club subscribers. On the wall behind my desk there is an old (June 13, 1959) *New Yorker* cartoon in which two young women are sipping espresso, and one says to the other, "He belongs to the Book-of-the-Month Club. I mean, how can you reach someone like that?"

That member has been transformed by our society from one of intent reader to intent viewer. Books are made into films or television series, and that sometimes inspires viewers to become readers, at least for the occasion. When "Brideshead Revisited" was shown on public television last winter, we reoffered the novel to our members (it had been a Main Selection when it was published in 1946), and it had a nice renaissance. We sold 20,000 copies in hardcover and another 14,000 in paper through our Quality Paperback Book Club.

Books today obtain more exposure than ever before on television. Authors are interviewed on Johnny Carson, on the "Today" show, on talk shows, and on other programs all over the country. And the authors, having learned from Truman Capote, the master of them all, are hustling as never before. No book achieves its purpose unless it is read, and this is a dictum most writers take with the utmost seriousness.

No one is immune when the bitch goddess moves within striking distance. Well, almost no one. In 1951, when J.D. Salinger's *The Catcher in the Rye* was chosen as the Main Selection, Harry Scherman, president and founder of the club, worried about its ambiguous title. At a luncheon honoring its author, Scherman asked him if he would consider a change in the title. Salinger replied, "Holden Caulfield wouldn't like that." And that was that.

Adding to the reader's awareness of the book today is the proliferation of bookstores. But this is a mixed blessing. In the past ten years, the number of bookstores in the United States has doubled from 10,000 to 19,000. Bookstore chains like B. Dalton and Waldenbooks are responsible for this increase. They can be found in shopping malls all over the country; and in cities and towns, they have often displaced the old personalized bookstore, gone now the way of the corner grocery. These giants help publicize books. They advertise extensively in daily newspapers, trumpeting the latest potential best seller. Best sellers are what they're after. These chains are highly computerized, so they stock up on the books that they think will sell. But just try to find a "small" book in the store, one of the second or third novels I talked about earlier. The homogenization of American culture has moved into the book business. A look at any best-seller list at any time of the year will tell you that.

At the Book-of-the-Month Club we have tried to counter this trend by becoming, as we have suggested in some of our ads—perhaps not too delicately—"America's Bookstore." We try to bring our members, an eclectic crew for the most part, a variety of contemporary books, many of which will never become best sellers. Our in-house readers, the people who help us decide which books to take, liked *Flambard's Confession*, so we bought it. It pleased Bessie Wells and 3,200 of our other subscribers. Fair enough. We believe with Chesterton: there ought to be books for the lively person wanting to read a book and for the tired person wanting a book to read.

The trick, I have always felt in selecting books for a veritable army of serious general book readers, is not to keep abreast of them, but to march out a half-pace ahead of them. It is akin to what the jazz pianist and composer Mary Lou Williams said about her art and how she treated her public. "I . . . keep a little ahead of them, like a mirror that shows what will happen next."

If I could have one wish about the relationship between the book-seller and the reader at whatever level—storekeeper, librarian, book club operator—it would be for us to all act as mirrors for our readers. That would be an expression of faith, the kind of faith that has existed between the writer and the reader since the writer began to weave words into magic.

In the last few months, many of us at the club have been telephoning members, trying to learn more about them, their interests, their needs, their wants. Who are these people who have come together with us in this odd and uncertain fellowship for the singular purpose of reading? What do they want from us?

Well, of course, they are not Bessie Wells, who has belonged to the club since its birth; nor Mr. Thompson, a member for fifty-one years, who first joined when he was twenty. Most of our members—restless, transient, with fragile roots, like this society we live in—come and go. We have to replace 40 percent of them each year. (Most book clubs have a 50 percent annual turnover.) And there are those who come and go and come back again. Our most easily acquired members are our ex-members.

I talked to one recently, a high-school teacher who first joined the club eight years ago and joined again this year because he wanted to receive, as a premium for joining, the new translation of Proust's *Remembrance of Things Past*. He lives in a suburb of New Haven. He is in his fifties, a bachelor, and he teaches English. He has a number of friends, he says, who belong to the club. "I order one, they order one. We exchange them." He is a committed reader. "I ask my relatives to buy me books as gifts. I tell them I can buy my own clothes. I'd rather have them get me the Nabokov letters or a superb edition of Shakespeare's sonnets." But he also reads "spy things, mystery things," he told me. "My kids get hysterical when I tell them what I'm reading. I should be reading Henry James."

We talked a long while about books. I felt I was intruding on his time, and I prepared to hang up, thanking him for allowing me to ask him about himself. He told me not to thank him. He seemed reluctant to break off the conversation. There was a moment of dead air. I was embarrassed to say goodbye, but didn't feel I should encourage him to oblige me further. But it was a self-examination he was conducting. Suddenly, as if he had drawn his thoughts from deep within himself, he tried to sum up his own passion about reading. "God, without books I'd be dead. Books remain my stability."

The painting hangs in the Art Gallery of Ontario. It is a portrait by Gustave Caillebotte entitled "Eugene Daufresne, Lisant." Daufresne is a portly, middle-aged man, a man of the nineteenth century. He is sitting in a red velvet chair. His watch chain dangles off his accommodating stomach. He has a book in his left hand. He is reading. There is an expression of angry intensity on his face. It would not be good to interrupt him. A thin ray of light slices over the hand holding the book, the light flashing from the left side of his face onto his white shirt and cuffs, running alongside his bowtie. The light keeps Daufresne pinned to that faded yellow-stitched paperbound packet he is holding, and nothing can pull him away. Nothing. He has been transported. He is alone, but the landscape of his mind vibrates with the sensations he is picking off that printed page. Nothing else matters. He is reading a book.

Yes, illiteracy is worse than ever in this country. Yes, aliteracy now enters the vocabulary. Yes, good books are desperately hard to find. Yes, standards are lower in book publishing. Yes, authors have to work harder than ever to mate the reader to their vision. Yes, reading time is being squeezed by the visual sensations of the new technology. Yes, reading is an endangered institution, as it always has been. And yet the book endures, and finds its lover.

I am myself generally schizophrenic about everything, reading included. I am an optimist when I know things to be bad, and I am a pessimist when things are going too well. So I refuse to despair about reading in this country and about the future of reading. The good signs are out there, too. Young American writers—women especially—are keeping the novel alive with their skill and grace, their anger and sensitivity. Seasoned readers like Bessie Wells and John Thompson and our schoolteacher from New Haven are holding to their commitment to the book. And the young are also coming to the book. Readers, just like books, grow from strange soil, soil that sometimes is totally without nutrients. But something happens. The seed takes root. There is growth, and, once in a while, a small harvest. Even in this land of plenty, the fragile and enduring pleasure lives.

ENDNOTES

[1]*New York Times Book Review,* October 10, 1982.
[2]August 2, 1982.

Walter W. Powell

Whither the Local Bookstore?

IN MOST INDUSTRIES, cottage-industry characteristics and modern bureaucratic corporate features appear in historical sequence; in book publishing, however, they commonly exist side-by-side, although not always in harmony. The range of individuals and institutions involved in the distribution of books illustrates well this combination of practices. There are independent local bookstores that stock new hardbound and softbound books, and maintain as well some inventory of older titles. These stores compete with book departments in large department stores and with huge chain bookstores that carry a more limited range of titles, usually new hardcovers of general appeal and popular paperbacks. In between are college bookstores, specialty bookstores, secondhand dealers, and an array of paperback outlets. Yet, despite this seeming diversity, the prospective book buyer often finds it difficult to obtain a book that is not currently on the best-seller list.

Any analysis of book distribution must begin with a basic point: the hundreds of book publishing firms use a wide variety of marketing channels to reach the book-buying public. Some books, particularly scholarly monographs, are sold directly to the consumer. Most general trade books reach their ultimate buyers through the help of intermediaries, such as wholesalers and various types of bookstores. Some book buyers are supplied by book clubs. A sizable portion of the book industry's output goes to libraries, where it is then made available to the public. College textbooks are handled almost exclusively by college bookstores. The ubiquitous mass market paperback can be found in supermarkets, drugstores, newsstands, transportation centers, and bookstores. In contrast to the distribution system for hardcover trade books, mass market paperback publishers rely on distribution companies that handle magazines as well as paper-backs. The distribution network is geared to very rapid turnover. Last week's romance may be almost as dated as last week's *Newsweek*. In sum, there is no one method of book distribution; books reach consumers through a number of competing ways.

My focus in this paper will be on general trade books—predominantly hardcover, but also quality paperbacks, because so many original works are appearing with increasing frequency in this format[1]— and on the general trade bookseller as a key agent in the dissemination of culture. I will argue that the character of literary output, regardless of time, is determined to a considerable extent by the prevailing methods of book production, distribution, and consumption, and by the patterns of financial reward for publishers, booksellers, and authors.[2] The traditional methods of bookselling in this country are changing in a significant manner; in time, these changes will have a pronounced effect on authors and readers, and in turn will shape our culture in ways that few have anticipated.

Although the selection, publication, and promotion of books has never been a highly efficient and rational process, bookselling and book distribution were, until recently, characterized by a degree of complexity and inefficiency that other industries would find inconceivable. Most industries that are faced with complicated product and delivery problems have developed viable wholesaler networks to service their retail outlets. Alfred Chandler, the eminent historian of American business, has shown that, in the late nineteenth century, one of the first steps to be taken by expanding businesses that wished to improve distribution of their products was manufacturer integration into the distribution process.[3] During that period, American publishers and booksellers confronted the very same problems that burden them today. The bulk of their profits were earned on large printings of a few books; most titles failed to earn money. In 1901 *Publishers Weekly* maintained that of the 1,900 titles published during the preceding year, one hundred at the outside had sold more than 10,000 copies.[4] Best sellers and loss leaders were industry standards; backlist titles were not favorably received. Books, even successful ones, had a short life. As early as 1872, *Publishers Weekly* complained that "nine out of ten queries are for this year's books," and in 1904 it claimed that "even the best books would certainly be 'crushed to death' by the new books that were piled on top of them."[5]

Three factors—time pressures, lack of information, and transaction costs—explain why the distribution of books intended for a general audience is so cumbersome and ineffective. The publishing industry's growth in title output and sales over the past two decades has so exacerbated pressures on book distribution that most trade books seem destined to have a very short life. Certainly not all books merit otherwise, but the unique feature of the book as a medium of communication has been its relative permanence, particularly in comparison with other means of mass communication. Yet current methods of distribution threaten the preservation of books. Moreover, a harmful cycle is set in motion whereby the financial importance of new books becomes much greater as the life span of each book is reduced.

Time Pressures

The orchestration of a book's publication requires that copies be available in bookstores at the time advertising and book reviews appear. To accomplish this, publishers must ship copies to retailers and wholesalers a month in advance of publication. Since it takes several months for a publisher's sales representatives to cover their territories, salespersons and commission men must call on bookstores and take orders for a new book at least four months prior to its publication.[6] Sales personnel cannot feasibly be informed of new books on a title-by-title basis, so publishers have developed a time-honored ritual, the sales conference, to present new books to the sales staff.

Sales conferences are held at least twice a year—in May for the fall list and in November or December for the spring list—and their main purpose, besides presenting the next season's books, is to fire the enthusiasm of the sales staff.[7] They will be supplied with dust jackets, catalogs, and all sorts of other paraphernalia. The conference brings together people with markedly different expectations. Editors have high hopes for their books. The sales staff, in contrast, are skeptical. They know that, at the bookstore, they will have only a few minutes to present each book; they know, too, that their effectiveness depends on recommending titles that a bookstore can sell. At the conference, the sales force looks for clues to which books will sell, the key ones of which are the sales quota and the advertising budget for specific titles. These figures influence how much attention a salesman will devote to a book. Obviously, there is an element of self-fulfilling prophecy involved—higher expectations, more attention, and more time spent selling the book can influence how many copies a book-seller will order.

A successful editor can deftly summarize a book in a few sentences and provide the sales staff with a "handle," a sentence or two that captures a book's qualities and will attract the attention of booksellers. Over the course of several days, a sales force will hear presentations of dozens of new books. Commission men, who sell for a number of houses and therefore attend several sales conferences, may hear hundreds of presentations. The problems with book distribution are exemplified by the sales conference—editors and the sales staff attempt the impossible task of cramming sufficient information about many, many new books into a few short days. Pep talks by editors are common, as are the after-hours efforts by the sales force to fortify themselves with spirits so that they can face another day of presentations.

There is much to do in preparing for a sales conference. All the material for the catalog to be distributed at the conference must be completed at least a month in advance so that the catalog can be printed in time. This requires that jacket design, a description of the book, and some hard information—title, number of pages, and price—be available. Such tight scheduling requires that a book manuscript arrive at the house in early winter in order to make the catalog for the May sales conference. There are, of course, exceptions; some books have accelerated schedules, and announced titles are frequently delayed. Yet such exceptions are costly and only serve to illustrate further the considerable time pressures that accompany the publication process.

Once the sales conference is over, the sales representatives return to their territories. The size of their sales area depends on the overall size of the house's sales force and the volume of sales in a particular region. These salespersons, often called book travelers, will visit several hundred accounts at least twice a year, armed with a list of books to sell, perhaps galleys for a few especially important books, and the jackets and advertising copy for the rest. They may also call on libraries and wholesalers, but their primary stops are independent bookstores and small local chain stores. The travelers will also check a store's inventory of backlist titles. Bookstore managers and owners are busy people, and stores are usually understaffed, so a book traveler has only a few minutes to make the sales pitch for his wares. Hence the traveler cultivates the ability to describe new books in a pithy and succinct manner. The fate of a book is often determined in a few minutes. Of course, booksellers have seen ads and prepublication reviews in *Publishers Weekly,* and witnessed the promotional hoopla at the American Booksellers Association's annual meeting in May. Although booksellers can place orders for new books on their own, this happens rarely. Most book orders are the result of the short visit by a publisher's sales representative.[8] The visit frequently takes place at the bookstore, and interruptions are common. The bookseller must combine ordering new titles with the other tasks of running a store; he or she wants to keep the sales interview brief. Such time pressures naturally mitigate against informed decision-making.

Lack of Information

The time pressures associated with book distribution create an atmosphere of uncertainty in which reliable information is seldom available. From the publisher's standpoint, the purpose of the catalog and the sales conference is to convey some information about forthcoming titles, to give the sales representatives a "handle." It is not uncommon, however, for this promotional information to be written before a final manuscript has been read by anyone at the house and, in some cases, even before it has been completed.

Since the sales effort is directed at getting new books into the bookstore, not in selling them to the reading public, few salespeople will have more than a superficial knowledge of the books they are selling. In contrast, old-fashioned book travelers frequently were cultivated people who loved books and were willing to forgo high incomes in return for the sheer pleasure of handling books. They found excitement and gratification in touting a particular work that had caught their fancy. Bruce Bliven's lovely biography of a traveler who covered the American South is a fine example of the old tradition of bookselling.[9] These book travelers frequently chose their vocation after attempting careers as book reviewers or authors or in other branches of the book world. Bliven's account illustrates many of the tensions faced by book travelers. His informant, George Fabian Scheer, points out: "I'm under constant pressure. . . . If my returns are low, my publishers suspect me of underselling. If I sell too hard and returns are high, my accounts turn me off. It's a tightrope."[10] These pressures have intensified in recent years and are partly responsible for the decline of the old book-traveler style. Bliven also describes the strong and enduring friendships forged between his book traveler and bookstore owners. The demise of many independent general bookstores has further contributed to the decline of traditional book travelers.

The sheer volume of new books creates considerable uncertainty for bookstore owners. The book industry brings out some 40,000 titles each year, and at least ten times that number are currently in print. Some of these books are textbooks, scientific monographs, and reference books that are rarely found in bookstores. But many books are intended for the general public, and only a very small proportion of these titles can be displayed on a bookstore's shelves. The majority of stores cannot accommodate more than 5,000 to 8,000 books. Moreover, a bookstore owner will order books from several hundred different publishers in addition to several major wholesalers. Thus there simply is insufficient information to make informed decisions. The common risk-averse response of bookstore owners is to order only one or two copies of most new titles.

Booksellers also lack information about publication strategies. A publisher's advertising campaign depends on the quality of the reviews a book garners. Given the unpredictability of reviews, a bookseller will have little advance knowledge of a publisher's advertising plans. Nor will booksellers know in advance whether a publisher plans to remainder a book, to be sold, that is, at perhaps one sixth of the original price, or to release it in paperback. With growing price resistance among book buyers, many consumers defer purchase of hardcovers in anticipation of remainders or cheap paperback editions.

That booksellers typically know little about new books or their intended audiences further complicates the selling of a book. The salesman's "handle" has long since been forgotten by the time a book arrives. Most bookstore owners have only a vague notion of the type of books that will interest their local reading publics. Yet, even if booksellers possessed more information about their clientele, the potential book buyer need not go to a bookstore to obtain a new book. The new title can be found at a library, acquired through a book club, or obtained directly from the publisher, thus bypassing the bookshop altogether.

Owing to the uncertainty inherent in book distribution, most publishers allow booksellers to return unsold books. The returns policy was developed in the 1930s to encourage booksellers to sell unknown, untested new "products." Such returns, however, are not free; both bookseller and publisher pay a price. Booksellers have capital invested in their stock: books are paid for within thirty to sixty days; returns can be reimbursed or credited against future purchases from a publisher. With all the paper work involved, money can be tied up for months. In addition, shelf space is taken up, and postage on returns must be paid. Returns can be just as vexing for publishers who lack accurate accounts of how many copies a book has sold or how many remain to be sold. Gone today, here tomorrow, was Alfred Knopf's sarcastic commentary on the returns policy. This policy discourages clearance sales at the retail outlet. Unsold books, which are returned to the publisher, will ultimately be destroyed or remaindered. Estimates for hardcover trade book return rates range from 25 to 40 percent; for mass market paperbacks, as high as 60 percent. On a routine basis, almost half of the mass market paperbacks shipped out have their covers stripped and returned for credit. The books themselves are then destroyed—to the tune of 100 million paperbacks a year.

Publishers and booksellers ought to ask themselves why a book merits attention. Whether a book is intended for purposes of education or entertainment, it should not be viewed as an isolated, unique product, but as part of a larger forum of communciation. Yet bookselling is characterized by thousands of individual, discrete transactions, the costs of which are considerable.

Transaction Costs

The current system of book distribution imposes considerable costs on both the publisher and bookseller, not to mention the book buyer. The multiple exchanges between publishers and booksellers are administratively complex. Furthermore, these exchanges have the unintended consequence of transforming the high birth rate for books into an even higher mortality rate.

A publisher inevitably finds that the costs of covering numerous small accounts is quite high. With the decline of traditional book travelers, the negotiations between the publisher's sales representative and the bookstore owner have become impersonal transactions. Some publishers have even gone to selling by telephone. Others see in the rise of book chains a means of reducing administrative complexity through centralized buying. The costs of handling many small accounts leads publishers to lose patience with local bookstores. Publishers justify their lack of a service orientation by pointing out that most of their sales come from a small number of accounts. This leads publishers to the incorrect notion that sales costs can be lowered by giving serious attention to only those few accounts. Yet, from the book consumer's point of view, the key to finding a new book is not the availability of multiple copies in one store, but the number of different stores where a copy can be obtained.

From a transaction-costs perspective,[11] booksellers face a nightmarish situation. Booksellers listen to hundreds, perhaps thousands of presentations of new books each year. They process paperwork for thousands of individual orders from hundreds of different publishers. Each publishing house has its own policies and customs—a different discount schedule, a unique payment policy that may require obtaining permission in advance to return unsold books. The paperwork involved in processing thousands of orders is considerable, and a record must be kept on each individual title. An order from a publisher seldom arrives complete, thereby heightening paperwork costs. In short, under the current distribution system, bookselling seems to operate with an inverse economy-of-scale principle: the more books published, the less the available time and information. Thus the sales chances of any single title are considerably reduced. The overall process has a deadening effect that cheapens the value of books.

Booksellers can and do turn to wholesalers as centralized repositories of the titles of many publishers. Wholesalers can provide speedier service, but at a cost to the author and the publishing house, whose revenues are reduced owing to the higher discounts given for wholesalers' volume orders. Wholesalers have also assumed the role of supplying libraries, which are, in effect, a form of competition for bookstores. This is a peculiar type of wholesaling, since libraries do not resell books. The recent rise of book wholesalers, chain bookstores, and specialty bookshops can best be viewed as efforts to economize on transaction costs.

DRAMATIC CHANGES IN BOOKSELLING

The great German sociologist Max Weber averred that rationalization and specialization were the dominant forces in modern industrial societies. The world of modernity has been deserted by the gods, and man has made calculable and predictable what in an earlier era was governed by chance, by personal appeal, or by passion. For Weber, the question is not how this evolution can be changed, for that is impossible; these forces have a momentum of their own. The question, rather, is what will come of it? Recent changes in bookselling reflect Weber's thesis: bookselling has been profoundly altered by these developments.

Although independently owned general bookstores have become increasingly less profitable and are in decline, the large book chains have grown dramatically. The chains have moved away from cottage-industry practices to highly rationalized procedures. They enjoy the same advantages over individual booksellers that McDonald's or Howard Johnson's enjoys over a "mom-and-pop" cafe. This is not because the chains have moved into the same locations as independent stores. They have, for the most part, opened entirely new territory, mainly in suburban shopping malls where they can attract affluent clients. The shopping malls provide convenient parking and are open evenings and weekends. Chain ownership helps finance the purchase of prime real estate that an independent bookseller could never afford. A consumer buying groceries in a local supermarket will often find a nicely furnished, brightly lit chain bookstore right around the corner. The merchandising style of the chains matches that of the supermarket. The sales personnel in chain stores are not likely to be particularly knowledgeable about books, but they can certainly direct customers to the best sellers and to books recently discussed on television talk shows. As in the supermarket, the sales personnel are unobtrusive. Chain stores have greatly expanded the book-buying audience, particularly in areas like the South, the Southwest, and the Midwest, where historically there have been fewer bookstores.

Chain stores sell large quantities of best sellers and pay scant attention to the diversity of their book offerings. The economics associated with high volume sales are considerable; thus the advantages that chains have over independent stores are many. All major decisions are made at the headquarters of the chains; so instead of visiting twelve hundred separate accounts, a publisher need only contact the central office of the two largest chains. Centralized purchasing leads to very large orders, and publishers reward the book chains with better discounts. Centralized management reduces the need for local store management and allows the chains to spread administrative costs across a large number of stores. The expansion of the two largest retail chains, Waldenbooks (a subsidiary of Dayton-Hudson) and B. Dalton (a subsidiary of Carter-Hawley-Hale) has been extraordinary. Both parent companies are large, diversified national retailers. Estimates of the sales of these two bookstore chains vary slightly, but it can be safely assumed that they now account for about 20 percent of all book sales in the United States. For certain best-selling titles, the chain's percentage of total sales is much higher. The book chains have installed modern, efficient computerized operations that keep track of their stock on a daily basis, register the sales record of every title, and alert their national buyers when a book begins to take off and new orders need to be placed. Close tracking of a book's recent sales history enables chain stores to sweep slow-selling books from their shelves promptly.

Subtle coercive pressures are built into any large-scale, continuing exchange relationships. Exchanges of this sort are characterized by transaction-specific investments in both knowledge and equipment. Once an organization chooses a specific supplier or distributor for its parts or services, the supplier or distributor develops expertise in the performance of the task, as well as idiosyncratic knowledge about the exchange relationship. The organization comes to rely on them, and such transaction-specific investments give the supplier or distributor considerable advantages in subsequent competition with others. A situation of dependency can develop between exchange participants. In cases where alternative sources are either not readily available or require extra effort, the stronger party to the transaction can coerce the weaker party to adapt its practices to accommodate the stronger party's needs. This has become increasingly evident in the relations between book publishers and the book chains.

With their unbookish flair for merchandising, the chains have left their mark on the book industry. Heretofore, the relation between publishers and booksellers was largely a traditional market exchange, in which the bookseller chose the titles he wished to acquire but had little influence on a publisher's choices. The national merchandising force of the chains has given chain book buyers new powers over the destiny of individual books. Chain stores and publishers are now linked in a complex reciprocal dependency. For example, *Publishers Weekly*, the book industry's trade journal, has long lamented the inaccuracy of industry sales figures. In 1980 *Publishers Weekly*, while noting its openness regarding suggestions for better methods for compiling sales figures, decided to reprint Dalton's list of best sellers as the best available record of sales for that year.

Chain store buying policies can directly influence what a publisher decides to publish. If a buyer for a chain store believes a book has sales potential, the chain will order a large number of copies. Having made such a major investment, the chain stores will then promote the book heavily and thus increase its chances of making their best-seller list. Chain store publicists have become key figures in the making of best sellers, and they must be "stroked" by publishers, since the latter's success or failure may depend heavily on chain sales. The impersonal market of individual consumer choices has been preempted by the buying power of book chains. It is not surprising that some publishers now show manuscripts of forthcoming books to chain store buyers even before the manuscripts are set in type. And trade publishers may show less and less interest in those books, such as first novels, demanding works of scholarship, poetry, and short stories, that chain stores do not stock.

The expansion of chain stores has cut into the sales of existing bookstores. In an effort to survive, some independent stores have tried to emulate the chains. One strategy has been to offer a restricted range of titles at high discounts. As Alfred Kazin has noted, "The Columbia University bookstore is now another Barnes and Noble supermarket featuring paperbacks and best sellers."[12] On Berkeley's Telegraph Avenue, which used to be a veritable heaven for booklovers because of the wide variety of small independent stores, the number of stores has shrunk, and most of the survivors now resemble either the chains or discount stores. On Chapel Street in New Haven, directly across from the Yale campus, there no longer are any general bookstores. One bookstore has turned over half its space to a coffeeshop; another has turned to remainders and heavily discounted best sellers. The latter store is also overrun by used books, and the proprietors have no idea where one could find a particular book.

Nevertheless, the book chains and discount stores are by no means the only new developments in book distribution. Although the economic logic of mass production and distribution encourages centralization and homogenizes products, the relative affluence of postindustrial societies and their complex division of labor give rise to specialization and differentiated tastes. In addition, we no longer have a cohesive intellectual class in the United States. Instead, there has been a flowering of many discrete interest groups, each of which displays considerable sophistication within narrowly defined realms. The increasing specialization of our universities has a pronounced effect on reading and writing. Even in academic circles, little reading is done outside of one's immediate area of interest. In book publishing, small specialty houses, catering to particular professional communities or to specific interest groups, have proliferated. Moreover, with rising costs, challenging books, on topics as diverse as public policy, international affairs, and social anthropology, that in an earlier decade of lower prices could be sold to the general public are now marketed through the less risky and more certain methods of direct mail distribution.

Catering to specialized interests is one approach now being pursued by independent bookstores. Diversification has proceeded rapidly. In Manhattan there are more than seventy specialty bookshops catering to particular taste groups. A similar trend is underway in the nation's capital. And in the Boston-Cambridge area, where a number of Barnes and Noble discount stores have been opened over the last few years, many of the independent bookstores have turned to specialization to survive. Stores now deal exclusively in mystery books, cookbooks, science fiction, women's literature, rare editions, or Asian literature.[13] Such diversification, however, seems feasible only in large metropolitan areas. In smaller places, which hardly sustain a single general bookstore, such a strategy cannot possibly work.

How is our public culture served by these recent changes in bookselling? The chains do a superior job of selling the latest books about cats, diets, and sexual performance. The specialty shops, whether their focus is Latin American literature or political affairs, provide admirable in-depth coverage of their respective fields. A microeconomist interested in Japanese printmaking and industrial policy will be well-served by various specialty shops, as will a nuclear engineer with a passion for science fiction and cooking. Books on these subjects can also be obtained directly from a publisher. Many readers will not find their interests poorly served by recent changes in bookselling. However, through no one's particular fault, I suggest that if present trends continue, irreparable harm will be done to our public culture. If our nation's cities and college towns cannot support a locally owned, high-quality general bookstore,[14] we lose one more institution that through the years has helped to bind the social fabric together. General bookstores offer readers a means of staying in contact with public issues. As Edward Shils eloquently noted two decades ago: "A good bookshop blows the breeze of contemporaneity on one; it puts one 'in touch'; it permits first contacts and offers prospects of greater intensity."[15] Such a bookstore permits a sharing of newly fashioned works of literature and new ideas. Chain stores and specialty shops cannot replace the function of the general bookstore. The chains can provide immediacy, books on the latest fads and fashions. The chains inundate us with trends and information, but provide little knowledge. Specialty shops provide much greater depth, but they cannot contribute to widely shared knowledge. They do not allow for the creation of a public dialogue. In an age of specialization, book buyers know little about what is going on in areas of endeavor other than their own. Perhaps this is our fate. In his essay "Science as a Vocation," Max Weber cautioned that "a really definitive and good accomplishment is today always a specialized accomplishment."[16] If this is indeed true, independent bookstores are an endangered species. It is high time that we recognize this disturbing fact and develop new ways to insure the survival of high-quality independent bookstores. We must do this, for as the book traveler George Fabian Scheer observed, "Nobody else . . . [can do] what the dedicated bookseller does."[17]

ENDNOTES

This paper draws on research done with Lewis A. Coser and Charles Kadushin for *Books: The Culture and Commerce of Publishing* (New York: Basic Books, 1982).

[1] It used to be possible to distinguish quality trade paperbacks from mass-market paperbacks easily on the basis of price, but inflation has done away with that distinction. Mass market paperbacks are best known by their size, $4'' \times 7''$—designed for easy display on book racks—their glossy covers, and their brief life span. Quality paperbacks are larger, have better bindings, and enjoy a longer life. Quality paperbacks are distributed in much the same way as hardcover trade books.

[2] For a useful model and discussion of the various forces that influence the book industry, see Robert Darnton, "What Is the History of Books?" *Daedalus* 111(3) (Summer 1982): 65-83.

[3] *The Visible Hand: The Managerial Revolution in American Business* (Cambridge: Harvard University Press, 1977).

[4] Donald Sheehan, *This Was Publishing: A Chronicle of the Book in the Gilded Age* (Bloomington: Indiana University Press, 1953), p. 28.

[5] Per Gedin, *Literature in the Marketplace* (Woodstock, N.Y.: Overlook Press, 1977), p. 55.

[6] Most large publishing houses have their own sales force. Smaller houses may rely on either larger houses for distribution services or independent salesman who work on a commission basis for as many as a dozen medium-size houses.

[7] Spring and fall are the two traditional selling seasons for trade books. These periods were originally determined by the movement of ice in and out of the rivers that served as the transportation links between East Coast publishers and the nation's interior.

[8] Publishers estimate that more than 75 percent of bookstore orders are the result of the visit by the sales representative. Moreover, few titles, including those that have sold out, are reordered unless a sales representative makes an explicit inquiry as to a book's availability.

[9] Bruce Bliven, *Book Traveller* (New York: Dodd, Mead, 1975).

[10] Ibid., p. 49.

[11] Oliver Williamson, *Markets and Hierarchies: Analysis and Antitrust Implications* (New York: Free Press, 1975).

[12]Alfred Kazin, "American Writing Now," *The New Republic,* October 18, 1979, p. 28.

[13]Maureen Taylor, "Boston: A Lot of Literacy," *Publishers Weekly,* October 31, 1980, pp. 38-39.

[14]Many of the independent bookstores that do manage to survive are doing so with very narrow profit margins. A 1977 survey for the American Booksellers Association notes that "half of the . . . member stores reporting in this survey are not profitable when judged by a reasonable standard of financial performance." Adjusted net profit for the average bookstore amounted to 2.5 percent, while those considered moderately profitable showed an adjusted net profit of 2.8 percent (*Publishers Weekly,* February 20, 1978, pp. 98-102).

[15]"The Bookshop in America," *Daedalus* 92(1) (Winter 1963): 93.

[16]Max Weber, "Science as a Vocation," in *From Max Weber: Essays in Sociology,* edited by Hans Gerth and C.W. Mills (New York: Oxford University Press, 1946), P. 135.

[17]Bliven, *Book Traveller,* p. 62.

William B. Goodman

Thinking About Readers

A good book is a book that sells good.
        —Modern publishing proverb, usually attributed
            to R.P. Ettinger (Prentice-Hall)

*Axiom: hatred of the Bourgeois is the beginning of virtue. As
for me, I include in the word "bourgeois" the bourgeois in
overalls as well as the bourgeois in frock coat. It's we, we
alone—that is, the educated—who are the People, or, to put it
better, the tradition of Humanity.*
        —Gustave Flaubert to George Sand, May 17, 1867

*There is a public which is always fairly constant in any of the
arts. I do not know about its size. I do not imagine that it
either grows or declines very much in the course of time.*
                    —V.S. Pritchett, 1956

THE SUBJECT IS SLIPPERY and elusive. It will not sit still for
comfortable generalization. There are some statistics, some
kinds of information, but if what you're after are *readers*, or
readers-and-the-books-of-high-culture,[1] then something else is required, probably something anecdotal, chastening, personal, perhaps
even something beyond print. Still, the need to make the subject coherent and manageable leads inevitably to statistics, to that place where in
the face of the elusive, we confront the problem of the "statistically
insignificant" modestly marketable books of high culture.

Readers are what matter most in this subject, but before they are
lumped together and buried in statistics, readers are readers in the
singular. They read in their own privacy, and sort into readers in
isolated communion with a text, sometimes as part of an intimate
network of those they trust to tell them about new books or about

old ones they do not know, and into readers who, as writers, have left some record of their encounters with books.

Here are some autobiographical emblems, from early in their addiction, by four champions of reading:

—William Cobbett, grandson of a day laborer, a rebellious lad in the 1770s, running away from the oppression of his father's small farm in Surrey:

At eleven years of age my employment was clipping of box-edgings and weeding beds of flowers in the garden of the Bishop of Winchester, at the castle of Farnham, my native town. I had always been fond of beautiful gardens; and a gardener, who had just come from the King's gardens at Kew, gave such a description of them as made me instantly resolve to work in these gardens. The next morning, without saying a word to anyone, off I set, with no clothes except those upon my back, and with thirteen half-pence in my pocket. I found that I must go to Richmond, and I accordingly went on, from place to place, inquiring my way thither. A long day (it was in June) brought me to Richmond in the afternoon. Twopennyworth of bread and cheese and a pennyworth of small beer which I had on the road, and one half-penny that I had lost somehow or other, left three pence in my pocket. With this for my whole future, I was trudging through Richmond in my blue smock-frock and my red garters tied under my knees, when, staring about me, my eye fell upon a little book in a bookseller's window, on the outside of which was written: *"TALE OF A TUB;* Price 3d." The title was so odd that my curiosity was excited. I had the 3d., but, then, I could have no supper. In I went, and got the little book, which I was so impatient to read that I got over into a field, at the upper corner of Kew Gardens, where there stood a hay-stack. The book was so different from anything that I had ever read before: it was something so new to my mind, that, though I could not at all understand some of it, it delighted me beyond description; and it produced what I have always considered a sort of birth of intellect.

I read on till it was dark, without any thought of supper or bed. When I could see no longer I put my little book in my pocket, and tumbled down by the side of the stack, where I slept till the birds in Kew Gardens awaked me in the morning; when off I started to Kew, reading my little book. The singularity of my dress, the simplicity of my manner, my confident and lively air, and, doubtless, his own compassion besides, induced the gardener, who was a Scotsman, I remember, to give me victuals, find me lodging, and set me to work. And it was during the period that I was at Kew that the present king and two of his brothers laughed at the oddness of my dress, while I was sweeping the grass plot round the foot of the Pagoda. The gardener, seeing me fond of books, lent me some gardening books to read;

but these I could not relish after my *Tale of a Tub,* which I carried about with me wherever I went, and when I, at about twenty years old, lost it in a box that fell overboard in the Bay of Fundy in North America, the loss gave me greater pain than I have ever felt at losing thousands of pounds.[2]

—Jean-Paul Sartre, a child becoming bookish, before the First World War, in his grandfather's library:

For me the Larousse Encyclopedia took the place of everything: I would pick up a volume at random, behind the desk, on the next-to-last shelf, A-Bello, Belloc-Ch or Ci-D, Melo-Po or Pr-Z (these associations of syllables had become proper names which designated sectors of universal knowledge: there was the Ci-D region, the Pr-Z region, with their flora and fauna, cities, great men, and battles); I would set it down laboriously on my grandfather's blotter, I would open it. There I would take real birds from their nests, would chase real butterflies that alighted on real flowers. Men and animals were there *in person:* the engravings were their bodies, the texts were their souls, their individual essence. Beyond the walls, one encountered rough sketches which more or less approximated the archetypes without achieving their perfection: the monkeys in the zoo were less monkey, the men in the Luxembourg Gardens were less man. In Platonic fashion, I went from knowledge to its subject. I found more reality in the idea than in the thing because it was given to me first and because it was given as a thing. It was in books I encountered the universe: assimilated, classified, labeled, pondered, still formidable.[3]

—Irving Howe, his family struck hard by the Great Depression in the early 1930s, in the East Bronx:

At the age of thirteen I caught scarlet fever, then a serious disease, and stayed in bed for six weeks. I sent my father to the local library to bring me the collected poems of Milton, Wordsworth, and Keats, names that had been mentioned by a teacher I admired. The librarian must have stared at my father, but perhaps she knew something about . . . immigrant Jews and their crazy kids. Lying in bed a little feverish, I read through the entire work of these poets: the clipped eloquence of *Samson Agonistes* and the candied richness of "The Eve of St. Agnes" remaining for decades in memory. Exactly what this was all about I am still not certain: some monstrous craving, some eagerness for cultural appropriation drawn from deeper sources than myself. In any case, stuck now in the East Bronx, I begin to cultivate—this is not a rare combination—both a heightened social awareness and an adolescent cultural snobbism. Later I would tell myself, trying to make it all a joke, that I had a kinship of sorts with American writers like Hawthorne and Melville, who had also known the shock of suddenly reduced circumstances.[4]

—Richard Rodriguez, a Mexican-American immigrant child in Sacramento, California, in the 1950s, learning to master English in a parochial elementary school:

OPEN THE DOORS OF YOUR MIND WITH BOOKS, read the red and white poster over the nun's desk in early September. It soon was apparent to me that reading was the classroom's central activity. Each course had its own book. And the information gathered from a book was unquestioned. READ TO LEARN, the sign on the wall advised in December. I privately wondered: What was the connection between reading and learning? Did one learn something only by reading it? Was an idea only an idea if it could be written down? In June, CONSIDER BOOKS YOUR BEST FRIENDS. Friends? Reading was, at best, only a chore. I needed to look up whole paragraphs of words in a dictionary. Lines of type were dizzying, the eye having to move slowly across the page, then down, and across. . . . The sentences of the first books I read were coolly impersonal. Toned hard. What most bothered me, however, was the isolation reading required. To console myself for the loneliness I'd feel when I read, I tried reading in a very soft voice. Until: "Who is doing all that talking to his neighbor?" Shortly after, remedial reading classes were arranged for me with a very old nun.

At the end of each school day, for nearly six months, I would meet with her in the tiny room that served as the school's library but was actually only a storeroom for used textbooks and a vast collection of *National Geographics*. Everything about our sessions pleased me: the smallness of the room; the noise of the janitor's broom hitting the edge of the long hallway outside the door; the green of the sun, lighting the wall; and the old woman's face blurred white with a beard. Most of the time we took turns. I began with my elementary text. Sentences of astonishing simplicity seemed to me lifeless and drab: "The boys ran from the rain. . . . She wanted to sing. . . . The kite rose in the blue." Then the old nun would read from her favorite books, usually biographies of early American presidents. Playfully she ran through complex sentences, calling the words alive with her voice, making it seem that the author somehow was speaking directly to me. I smiled just to listen to her. I sat there and sensed for the very first time some possibility of fellowship between a reader and writer, a communication, never *intimate* like that I heard spoken words at home convey, but one nonetheless *personal*.

One day the nun concluded a session by asking me why I was so reluctant to read by myself. I tried to explain; said something about the way written words made me feel all alone—almost, I wanted to add but didn't, as when I spoke to myself in a room just emptied of furniture. She studied my face as I spoke; she seemed to be watching more than listening. In an uneventful voice she replied that I had nothing to fear. Didn't I realize that reading would open up whole new worlds? A book could open doors for me. It could introduce me to people and show me places I never imagined existed. She gestured toward the bookshelves. (Bare-breasted African women danced, and the shiny hubcaps of automobiles on the back covers of the *Geographic* gleamed in my mind.) I listened with respect. But her words were not very influential. I was thinking then of another consequence of literacy, one I was too shy to admit but nonetheless trusted. Books were going to make me "educated." That confidence enabled me, several months later, to overcome my fear of the silence.[5]

One thinks of other gifted children: Henry Adams as a boy in his father's library at 57 Mount Vernon Street on Beacon Hill, that

accumulation of eighteen thousand volumes, by far the largest private collection in Boston, which pre-empted the finest room in the house, a sunlit oasis in an otherwise somber dwelling. Here Henry made endless forays upon the long ranks of well-entrenched authors. . . . Here also as a boy he first beheld the labor of the file when he patiently held copy for his father's edition of the works of his great-grandfather;[6]

William Dean Howells, with his famous barrels of books in antebellum rural Ohio;[7] and Vladimir Nabokov, at about eight—it's 1906 or so—at the family estate at Vyra in the province of St. Petersburg, already intoxicated by butterflies, finding in an attic storeroom a cache of books to instruct his nascent lepidopterism.

Other books I found . . . there, among herbariums full of alpine columbines, and blue palemoniums, and Jove's campions, and orange-red lilies, and other Davos flowers, came closer to my subject. I took in my arms and carried downstairs glorious loads of fantastically attractive volumes: Maria Sibylla Merian's (1647-1717) lovely plates of Surinam insects, and Esper's noble *Die Schmetterlinge* (Erlangen, 1777), and Boisduval's *Icones Historiques de Lépidoptères Nouveaus ou Peu Connus* (Paris, begun in 1832). Still more exciting were the products of the latter half of the century—Newman's *Natural History of British Butterflies and Moths*, Hofmann's *Die Gross-Schmetterlinge Europas*, the Grand Duke Nikolay Mihailovich's *Mémoires* on Asiatic lepidoptera (with incomparably beautiful figures painted by Kavrigin, Rybakov, Lang), Scudder's stupendous work on the *Butterflies of New England*.[8]

These young readers shine with appetite and optimism, but taken together, they make no sum. Still, if these accounts are encouraging, it is because of the connection through time they suggest, of the passing fusion between particular readers and particular books. It is the essence of time's passage, as well as proof against it, that we can read what they have read, or will have read before they disappear. And it is the generic genius of the book itself that allows us to repeat their transits over pages, sometimes in the very copies or editions they handled—which is charming, reliquary, and sometimes scholarly, but which is also evidence of how readers reading carry some books forward and so, in ways not well charted, modify the culture. The history of reading is not the same thing as the usual practice of intellectual and literary history and happily now has its active advocates.[9]

II

To get to readers in the plural, you have to pass through the terra incognita of "the reading public." This familiar term is one of those mildly delusionary phrases that, when used by writers, editors, and book publishers, signals more hope than dependable response. It is notoriously imprecise, yet belief that it represents a large group of probably interested readers is widespread. Those professionally concerned bat the phrase back and forth as if it were more than a piety or necessary fiction. When some professional reader, a literary historian, critic, or journalist, uses the term, it has both the ring of reality—the voluntary readers "out there"—and the congratulation of an honorific—the self-selected few capable of cultural recognitions. Still, it is hard to know how to get at what is actually represented by the term.

Some light is cast on the reading public if we look at the circulation figures for some of the periodicals serious readers buy. While this will not identify the actual readers of books, it does disclose the pool of those who may be expected to buy and read them. In the United States, from 1872, when the population was 38 million, to 1954, when it was 150 million, the following periodicals, many still with us today, moved in circulation as follows: *The Atlantic Monthly*, from 35,000 to 201,000; *Harper's Monthly*, from 130,000 to 154,000; *The Nation*, from 6,000 (1880) to 31,000; *The New Republic*, from 26,000 (1926) to 30,000, *The Dial*, from 7,000 (1921) to 10,000 at its demise in 1929; *Poetry*, about 3,000 throughout; *Time*, from 544,000 (1934) to 1,747,000; *The New Yorker*, from 205,000 (1944) to 377,000; *Life*, from 1,841,000 (1939) to 5,400,000. Two intellectual quarterlies, *The Virginia Quarterly Review* and *The American Scholar*, had about 3,000 and 5,000 subscribers respectively.[10] Beyond the modernist *Dial*, the period also included the brief lives of a number of low circulation and financially weak maga-

zines—*Little Review, Seven Arts, Camera Work, Hound & Horn,*
and *Twice a Year* are good examples—important for the welcome
their pages offered to new European and American artists, poets,
critics, and writers of fiction. What I would emphasize in the circulation figures for the years 1872 to 1954 is not that the popularly
conceived periodicals skyrocketed in circulation, but that the circulation figures for those with serious intellectual and literary programs
declined in relative terms, or, like *The Dial,* could not sustain themselves and ceased publication.

When we move to the present, where the population has increased
to 230 million, the situation repeats itself, but with some increase in
the number of magazines with editorial programs like *The Dial* or
The Nation. Today, *The Atlantic Monthly* and *Harper's* claim circulations of 350,000; *The Nation* has 48,370; *The New Republic,*
96,606; *Poetry,* 7,000; *Time,* 4,476,504; *The New Yorker,* 504,428;
The Virginia Quarterly Review, 4,500; *The American Scholar,*
30,000. To give a larger sense of the current situation, circulations
for the following periodicals help fill out the picture: *Antioch Review,* 5,000; *Commentary,* 52,000; *Daedalus,* 36,000; *Dissent,*
8,000/9,000; *Encounter,* 18,000; *Kenyon Review,* 15,000; *The Massachusetts Review,* 3,000; *The National Review,* 100,033; *Partisan
Review,* 10,000; *Ploughshares,* 3,000; *Salmagundi,* 4,800; *TLS*
(*Times Literary Supplement,* London), 38,000 (worldwide); *Tri-
Quarterly,* 6,000; *The Yale Review,* 5,000.[11]

The meaning of these numbers? The relative decline in the capacity
of serious literary and intellectual magazines to survive and flourish
continues, or is at best only marginally better today than it was in
1872-1954. No such magazine could begin now, much less survive,
without direct subsidy, from whatever source, or without intermittent patronage to meet emergencies. Doubtless this is a fair description of the situation of two new and promising journals, *The New
Criterion* and *Grand Street.* Editors of such magazines spend a great
deal of their time raising money to meet pressing bills. It is the disparity between population growth and the fate of publications with the
general program of *The Dial* or the perspectives of *Hound & Horn*
and *Partisan Review* that should not be missed. Moreover, it is that
continuing disparity which bears out R.P. Blackmur's rueful conclusion in his essay "The Economy of the American Writer"—from
which I've drawn the circulation figures for 1872-1954—that the
"market system" has steadily eroded "high aesthetic value" and undercut decent standards of literary and intellectual work.

There are, to be sure, more popular magazines than most of the current ones listed above. *McCalls,* for example, has a circulation of 6,206,424; *Reader's Digest,* 17,875,545; and *TV Guide,* 18,084,966.[12] These magazines shift the pursuit of the reading public to different ground, to material designed to be useful to women, as its editors understand their "needs"; to material deliberately light, entertaining, and patriotic; and, in the case of *TV Guide,* hardly to sustained reading at all but to the weekly television program listings. *TV Guide*'s 18 million copies per week, however, make it the most widely read or consulted magazine in the country. If its success is arguably beside the point where the fate of the books of high culture is concerned, its overwhelming circulation raises the question of what many believe is the pernicious influence of television on reading.

Seventy-eight million American homes have television today. More than a third of that number have more than one set. This is a fact of large cultural significance, and though the cultivated often hold television in superstitious dread for its presumed negative influence on reading and what reading represents, its importance as a clear and present danger to reading is exaggerated. Confirmed readers, it turns out, especially those whose reading habits were formed before 1950, when TV began to be ubiquitous, know how to read around television. Those born in the television age may have had a more difficult discovery of books. The superstitious dread of television as an absolute threat to reading books, however, is an unfounded fear. The fact is that "on the average, book readers spend as much time watching television as do nonbook readers."[13] In the early expansion of television-viewing, there was a good deal of rhetorical and actual resistance to television among the cultivated and the respectable. They feared, or said they feared, exposing themselves and their children, particularly their children, to the presumed opiate of television, but this has largely disappeared, though there are still some few who continue to resist and will not buy sets. A more common continuance of these attitudes is a defensive apologetics about television habits and, as if to confirm television's power to ruin reputations, sets in such homes are quite discreetly placed.

The competition between television and books for the same audience is clear enough. What that competition means, however, is not whether one shall exclude the other but how leisure time shall be apportioned between them. At the same time, what is not clear, where the extension of reading is concerned, is whether enormously popular television mini-series based on good books produce extensive bookstore and library borrowing carry-over responses. The splendidly acted TV costume drama made from Evelyn Waugh's *Brideshead Revisited* produced a national sale of the paperback edition, made available at the same time, in excess of a half million copies; but whether this attention to Waugh was transferred by his new readers to his better novels in anything like comparable numbers is not open to question. It did not happen. Moreover, similarly ambitious series, even when done as well as the sequence from Trollope's Palliser novels, do not uniformly succeed in prompting readers. A special edited version of the Palliser books failed in hardback, and a reissue of all of them limped in paperback. Interesting and sad, but it is worth noting that these series share a heritage with the history of reading. In the nineteenth century, in the great days of confident bourgeois culture—from Balzac's day through that of Trollope and Twain—when, by and large, there was no absolute differentiation in the reading public, novels, whether by Balzac, Dickens, George Eliot, Thackery, or their inferiors, were serialized in magazines or the periodical press—and everyone read them. In the United States in 1885, for example, in the *Century Illustrated Monthly* (with a circulation then somewhat more than 200,000 when *The Atlantic Monthly*'s was around 35,000), three novels—William Dean Howells's *The Rise of Silas Lapham,* Mark Twain's *Huckleberry Finn,* and Henry James's *The Bostonians*—were serialized at the same time. No American magazine since has been able to match that miracle. If English social life in the 1960s came to a halt till it had adjusted to the weekly program schedule for the television adaptation of *The Forsyte Saga,* something similar occurred in the nineteenth century with the serialized work of many novelists—notably in the familiar case of Dickens, where anguish over the fate of Little Nell convulsed in grief, it seems, all who could read English or understand it when it was read to them. So much for the echo of a golden age.

How do readers now know what books to read? Forty thousand trade books of all kinds are published in the United States each year. The publishers of this indigestible number attempt to get them into the bookstores, get them noticed and reviewed, get them to readers by whatever means possible. None succeed uniformly with every book they publish on their seasonal lists. In truth, they do not expect to succeed with every title, and they do not; and in spite of a rhetoric ritually invoked to reduce the annual number, it remains virtually the same. This productive persistence in the face of experience suggests that since they cannot be sure in advance which of their books will succeed, trade publishers, however reluctantly, are gamblers. An ungenerous way of acknowledging this condition is to say that either they do not know quite what they are doing or they are their own worst enemies. Perhaps; but it also says the best thing about them, which is their permanent hunger for new work. If this is often bad for their businesses, it is good for the culture. The best books, after all, swim in an undifferentiated sea of print, paper, and binding, and swim, moreover, in ways not known to water. The efficacy of that motion—not all books remainder, not all remainders sink—sustains the miracle of their ability to make themselves known somehow to readers.

Since only a small portion of the annual production of trade books is reviewed, the importance of reviews is difficult to exaggerate. In reviewing, moreover, nothing is more important in the initial reception of a book than the appearance of reviews at or near the publication date. For this, newspaper and weekly magazine response is the sine qua non. Here, the commanding place is held by the *New York Times Book Review,* which is part of the Sunday edition of the paper (circulation 1,461,673)[14] and which also may be subscribed to alone. Its circulation among those concerned with books is virtually nationwide. Major newspapers in Boston, Chicago, Los Angeles, San Francisco, Washington, and some other cities have Sunday book review sections. Some, like the *New York Times,* also run daily book reviews. To such reviewing must be added that done in *The New Yorker* and in the political weeklies and biweeklies—*The Nation, The National Review, The New Leader, The New Republic*—where book reviewing is taken seriously and given pride of place. Then there is the intellectual biweekly, *The New York Review of Books,* circulation 118,000,[15] which is almost wholly devoted to book reviews and where reviews of nonfiction books predominate.

Some readers read the reviews in one place or another and find that their appetites are not whetted nor their interest aroused. Sometimes three or more reviews of the same book will tell the reader all he or she wants to know about that book. When a book and a reviewer come together well, however, readers may actually go out and buy the book. It is, of course, quite legitimate to use reviews as news reports, winnowing the new books of any given week to decide which are worth looking at. Such inspection must be done fairly quickly, however, since the bookstore shelf-life of new trade books is remarkably short—in most shops, three months—and this becomes particularly important in the case of general and literary monthlies and quarterlies, which often review books *after* they have, in all likelihood, disappeared from the shops. To find a new novel, for example, in the average chain or personal bookshop six or even three months after publication is difficult, if not impossible. The same holds true of most new books by writers less than famous, and true enough for the average best seller. Everything in the economics of bookselling encourages this brief shelf-life. The bookseller who permits a slow-selling book to linger on his shelves does so at his peril. The better he knows his business, the more quickly he will respond to the publisher's returns policy.

In this light, the increasing importance of public libraries becomes comprehensible, for it is on *their* shelves that these quickly disappearing books will be found.[16] With current budgetary restraints, however, it is no longer certain that public libraries will always be able to purchase a copy of a first or new novel, or another work of nonfiction of whatever quality.

Book advertising, while psychologically important to writers—it confirms the existence of their books, after all, and expresses their publisher's commitment to them and their work—seems to make little sales difference. Few readers credit their initial interest in a book to an advertisement for it. Moreover, few readers, if any, can recall what books were advertised in the newspapers or periodicals they habitually read.

There is another elusive fact: not all who buy or borrow books manage to read them. Books are thought by many to confer cultural credit, and the more books, I suppose, the more credit: they fashionably furnish a room, are passports to being *au courant,* and give their owners an ambiguous prestige.

One last word (or set of statistics) on "the reading public." In 1978 the survey research firm of Yankelovich, Skelly, and White prepared for The Book Industry Study Group a comprehensive report entitled *Consumer Research Study on Reading and Book Purchasing.*[17] They found that out of the total U.S. population, for a six-month period in 1978, 30 percent had read from one to nine books and 25 percent had read ten or more. In numbers, the book readers totaled 119.7 million. It should be noted that half the readers obtained books from public libraries. The authors add: "Those who do use libraries rely *heavily* on this source of books. [In the period of the survey] library users . . . obtained an average of twelve books from libraries," or roughly *double* the average number of books purchased in bookstores in the same period.[18]

Trade publishers and booksellers necessarily view with skepticism the numbers and percentages such surveys produce. Survey research, to be sure, can be refined to provide market information for improving product development where *little* is offered to *many*—as in soaps, soups, cosmetics, and most other consumer lines—but in trade book publishing, where too much (so *many* titles) is offered to too few (*small* numbers of book buyers), any refinements, however theoretically possible, will fail to come to grips with the intractability of the sales situation. Where the books of high culture are concerned, it is the dynamics of the probable life histories of such books that survey research usually misses in its study designs. This does not mean that a more efficient study design could not be devised, only that it would be uneconomic for publishers to ask that it be done. Such titles by their very nature take more time to find their destined readers/purchasers than the seasonal publishing cycle permits. To make matters worse, it is difficult, if not impossible, to know whether presumed books of high culture are in fact such—every season has its intellectual fads, its hyped masterpieces—until the culture itself, in its own time, talks back to the publisher and tells him so. When this happens, and if copyright has not reverted to the author, and if the culture talks loud enough and steadily enough in back orders, the publisher reprints. This may be called ratifying literary history, or perhaps making it.

III

Although it is characteristically American to assume that a law of steady annual increase applies also to the audience for books, where the books of high culture are concerned, it is naive and dangerous to do so. Publishers bitterly understand the folly of overestimating the size of first printings needed to meet the unknown demand for the "literary" books they publish. I doubt that the percentage of the population interested in "serious" books is any larger today—if, in fact, it is as large—than it was on October 7, 1929, when Faulkner's *The Sound and the Fury* was published. The first printing was for 1,789 copies, a number, it was estimated, that would satisfy "all demand for the book for nearly a year and a half."[19] "The tiny readership for good books," Elisabeth Sifton, Viking's editor-in-chief, explains, has remained fairly constant for decades, even as our population grows and, with it, the number of first novels published. Bennett Cerf said forty years ago that selling 8,000 copies of a book should make any publisher proud, selling 80,000 was cause for celebration in the streets, and selling 800,000 was a positive miracle. That was true 140 years ago, too, and it's about the same now. There is a natural limit on the readership for serious fiction, poetry and nonfiction in America that ranges, I would say, between 500 and 5,000 people—roughly a hundred times the number of the publisher's and the author's immediate friends (Sifton's Law).

Her next point underscores the dark side of American exceptionalism where books are concerned.

Interestingly, these statistics apply to other countries as well. When a Swedish publisher tells an Italian or Brazilian or American publisher that he hasn't done as well as he had hoped with so-and-so's first book, he means just about what the other three would mean: he means he sold only a few thousand copies. But *he* sold his few thousand in a country of just a few million people, and America [in 1970] is a land of 220 million souls. The American publisher would have to sell 50,000 copies to reach the same pitiable proportion of the population reached routinely by his Swedish colleague.[20]

Sifton's analysis, which every trade publisher, marketing manager, and editor will credit, is the crux of the cultural situation. There simply are not enough copies of most books of high culture sold to pay their way on their publisher's lists, let alone sustain their author's lives. For the writers of such marketplace failures, it often means reconsideration of the uses to which their talents shall be put, something far easier to consider than to do.

Trollope thought of writing as a "second profession,"[21] his point being that it was idiocy to expect from writing an income sufficient to sustain him and his family during the years it would take to establish himself. He thought his chances—or anyone's, for that matter—of breaking through to financial solvency, much less conspicuous success, were worse than any sane gambler would risk. He spent thirty-three years working full days in the British postal service (after a daily writing stint that began at 5:30 in the morning and lasted for three hours on the average) before he resigned—and then reluctantly.[22] Faulkner could not live on the meager income his books produced when first published, and so wrote short stories for popular magazines while that market lasted, and worked on film scripts in Hollywood. It was only when Malcolm Cowley's critical acumen and editorial brilliance created the situation that produced *The Por-*

table Faulkner (1946)[23] that the reprinting of his books became a sound proposition. I use Trollope and Faulkner because theirs are normal and familiar examples of the writer's situation. Fortunate readers in the posthumous prosperity of their work should remember that only because both were somehow able to summon up the heroic strength needed to write their books are we able to enjoy them. Other writers, their lost contemporaries, some perhaps of comparable talent, are unknown to us. If E.M. Forster and Virginia Woolf had not been left small, but life-sustaining, legacies, we would not have *Howards End* and *A Passage to India,* and it is doubtful if any of us would know *Mrs. Dalloway.*

The social, economic, and cultural inventions that would overcome this situation have not been made. There have been salutary changes between the patronage system of Sam Johnson's London and the application routines in the United States today to private foundations and to state and federal arts and humanities agencies, as well as in the relations between writers and publishers. But the results fall far short of the obvious and probably impossible solution—an extraordinary increase in the number of Americans who demand good books and buy them regularly. Think of what it would mean to American writers and their publishers if their normal share of the audience were the Swedish cut. If the serious writer's situation in the twentieth century means anything, however, it means there is no chance for such a salvationary outcome, nothing at least anyone knowledgeable about "the culture of the West" would place anywhere near as high. Any publisher who set first printings on such expectations would be destroyed. Thus the already tiny audience for high culture will continue to shrink, while the national and world populations expand. Readers are stubborn, however, in what they need, and will not disappear, nor will the books of high culture; moreover, it is on readers—on what maintains and increases them—that everything turns.

IV

It takes a great deal, much of it unclear, to make readers. They cannot be force-fed. Colleges can do less for them than their implicit claims suggest. Real readers, like real writers, make themselves. They work in their own privacy, taking what signals they choose to take; sometimes trusting what other readers tell them, sometimes not; ignoring book advertising and most reviews; browsing in bookstores and in public libraries; always fending for themselves, yet responding

to some of what gets past their guard; and probably remaining un-
countable in ways publishers can use effectively. They are the vessels
of Flaubert's immortality, of Jane Austen's, of Faulkner's. And what
they do places on that obscure and slowly accumulating agenda of
the shifting permanent some writers of our own time to whom insufficient attention has been paid. Hugo Charteris? Paula Fox? Natalia
Ginzburg? Uwe Johnson? Howard Frank Mosher? Leonardo Scias-
cia? The poet Ruth Stone? If you think about readers and what their
reading means when it takes them past literate or not-so-literate pla-
cebos and time-killers,[24] you will have touched the mystery of what
will carry to the future. Here we stand at the edge of the elapsing
dark on whose border editors and critics light their candles, and
against which real writers work. If writers and their publishers are
lucky, readers will have created sufficient demand for their books, or
some of them, so that they will not be "out of print," or in the expir-
ing half-life of the "temporarily out of print," when their audience
widens beyond the happy few. It would be a decent act of the throw-
er of the cosmic dice if such renewed demand for a writer's work
were to occur either in his productive lifetime or during the fifty years
after his death, while copyright holds, so at least his heirs would
realize something tangible from what he has done. It would be a sign
of success in a mature culture if it could sustain not its publishers—
most Western cultures do that well enough—but its best writers, one
by one.

The overriding issue in the seemingly permanent book crisis is the
enigma of high culture and the near and far prosperity of its books.
Copyright finally lapses into the general welfare. It does so on the
assumption that ultimately readers have rights that exceed those of
literary property—which is fair enough, since what writers want in
the end are readers. And readers want to be left pretty much on their
own, with more good books at hand than they can read. Whether
these two expectations of the future will hold is questionable—or so
we are told by those persuaded of the inevitable dominance of the
new "information" technologies. Thus it is not clear that readers in
fifty years, the period usually suggested[25] for the phasing out of the
book "as we know it," will be able to enjoy that intimacy with the
portable book that is now taken for granted. Of the factors at work,
the most important is the least technological. Literacy for workaday
purposes everywhere is down; for the books of high culture, disas-
trously so.[26] Functional literacy makes "decoders," those for whom
successful written directions to get on with the daily work of the

world can be provided. Heightened, such literacy produces a certain kind of empiric or expert. Be that as it may, what information specialists tell us cannot be ignored. The book, they say, is inefficient; even its portable intimacy and variable pacing, which lets readers adjust to them as they will, is replaceable. Retrieval systems are so inherently perfectible, and new hardware and software so protean, that books and libraries will be transformed by screens and optional printout systems that will serve readers better. I believe it, insofar as much that is claimed by the informationists is in place,[27] but where the books of high culture are concerned, I cannot. The crux is what is meant by information.

The books of humanistic culture are not "information" in what distinguishes them, not in what database systems, however supplied, have been designed to store for maximally efficient retrieval. The difference is what is meant by literature. What makes the work of particular writers impervious to time, what makes some few books necessary, abides. The informationists smilingly say this is sentimental; worse, that it is wasteful of scarce energy and materials. But readers and writers have yet to agree. Publishers are worried and not so sure. For some of the kinds of publishing they do, database systems make sense, but for books of serious fiction, poetry, and nonfiction, the thrust of what the informationists say is at best premature. It is possible, of course, that this is a saddle-maker's mentality late in the age of the automobile, that those who embrace it cannot see the profound change going on about them. There are signs that the continuing breakdown of the old homogeneous reading public—which has so profoundly imperiled the first novel, for example—is so shrinking the audience for good books that the informationists may be right. If they are, it is for reasons outside their argument.

If new books of high culture are in trouble, it is not the sort of trouble that the informationist's technology can serve well. They are in trouble because less and less reading is being done, and because, at the same time, the economic structure that made books cheap enough for a broadly based readership is weakening. There is disturbing evidence that both conditions are accelerating. The total income of the American book trade in recent years shows annual dollar increase, but this reflects inflationary costs passed along in higher list prices, not an increase in the number of hardback trade books sold, which is down. Where does this leave readers and writers? In trouble, to be sure—and writers in deeper trouble than readers, since they have much unread capital—but not yet obsolete, because what they hold in common, a need and reverence for the creation and apprehension of written human expression, has not lost its redemptive importance.

There is this difference between our generation's burden and the one Matthew Arnold gave his: while we credit the idea of a self-selected saving remnant, this brutal century has so drained the remnant of its confident uplift, its thin salvationary ethos, so ruined its morale, that culture has been left, not in the disorienting hands of anarchy, but shorn of its Arnoldian mission. Auden makes the point unmistakably:

> Art in intention is mimesis
> But, realised, the resemblance ceases;
> Art is not life and cannot be
> A midwife to society.
> For art is a *fait accompli.*
> What they should do, or even how or when
> Life-order comes to living men
> It cannot say, for it presents
> Already lived experience
> Through a convention that creates
> Autonomous completed states.[28]

So, too, does Sartre: "I've given up the office," he says, at the close of his autobiography, "but not the frock: I still write. What else can I do?"

Nulla dies sine linea.

It's a habit, and besides, it's my profession. For a long time, I took my pen for a sword; I now know we're powerless. No matter. I write and will keep writing books; they're needed; all the same, they do serve some purpose. Culture doesn't save anything or anyone, it doesn't justify. But it's a product of man: he projects himself into it, he recognizes himself in it; that critical mirror alone offers him his image.[29]

It is a sufficient defense of a good poem or book to say that its value, as Blackmur said, "adds to the sum of available reality,"[30] which if it isn't quite enough, will have to do as it improves our capacities to become those on whom less and less is lost.

Envoi

The essential situation glossed in this essay is hardly new. Serious writers, editors, publishers, and critics know it in their bones, their scars mourn it, but their optimism, though continually undercut, holds. There's even a gaiety to it. When Orwell wasn't Orwell, when he wasn't, as V.S. Pritchett called him, "the conscience of his generation," what did Eric Blair do? It's scandalous. He collected silly postcards, some seaside, some not. He went to see a revival of *Chu Chin Chow* during the London Blitz and understood its appeal, kept a goat in the country, and, oh! sweet Lady of Correct Cultivation, took Somerset Maugham seriously.[31] Somerset Maugham! He saw, I dare to say, *The Out Station* for the adroit novella it is. Can't you just see Orwell, freed from his own New Grub Street, transformed to a triumphant Edwin Reardon, his eyes snapping, with Biffen gentle beside him, saying, "He's not a bad writer, you know, it's only that you've heard he was." So we're back to the personal, to "word of mouth," to that privacy where our snobbery and beleaguered elitism are let go. Why? Because in spite of the chaos endemic in the literary marketplace, we are sustained by a faith that some readers will find the best work, buy it or borrow it, and urge others to read it. Everyman, then, his own reader. Voltaire's garden grows.

ENDNOTES

A note of acknowledgment: This essay could not have found its present form had it not been for the spirited responses of David Staines, Prudence Steiner, and John William Ward to its first draft.

[1]"High culture" is not a popular term in a democratic society since it suggests superiority, that condition in which trained sensibility and thorough cultivation make necessary distinctions between "good" cultural productions and "bad." Any term that would function as well for "high culture" would soon acquire the same democratic defects. It is a vulgar error to suppose that all judgments are equal. Once that truth is understood, accusations of high and mighty elitism, while common, are beside the point.

[2]*Cobbett's Weekly Political Register,* February 19, 1820 (*The Life and Adventures of Peter Porcupine . . . By William Cobbett,* edited by G.D.H. Cole, Edinburgh: T. & A. Constable, The University Press, 1927, pp. 139-41). Also quoted, pp. 135-36, in *The Oxford Book of Literary Anecdotes,* edited by James Sutherland (London: Oxford University Press, 1975).

[3]Jean-Paul Sartre, *The Words* (New York: George Braziller, 1964), pp. 5-51.

[4]Irving Howe, *A Margin of Hope: An Intellectual Autobiography* (New York: Harcourt Brace Jovanovich, 1982), p. 7.

[5]Richard Rodriguez, *Hunger of Memory, The Education of Richard Rodriguez* (Boston: David R. Godine, Publisher, Inc., 1982), pp. 59-61. Used by permission of the publisher.

[6]Ernest Samuels, *The Young Henry Adams* (Cambridge, Massachusetts: Harvard University Press, 1965), pp. 7-8.

[7]William Dean Howells, *My Year in a Log Cabin* (New York: Harper & Brothers, 1893), pp. 26-30.

[8]Vladimir Nabokov, *Speak, Memory: An Autobiography Revisited,* revised edition (New York: Capricorn Books, Putnam's, 1966), p. 122.

[9]For this subject, nothing is as promising as the emerging field of the history of books. See Robert Darnton, "What Is the History of Books?" *Daedalus,* Summer 1982, pp. 65-83.

[10]R.P. Blackmur, *The Lion and the Honeycomb* (New York: Harcourt, Brace and Co., 1955), p. 57.

[11]The numbers are drawn from *'82 Ayer Dictionary of Publications* (Bala Cynwyd: 1982), and from *Ulrich's International Periodicals Directory* (New York: 1981 and 1982). Some are audited circulation figures and others are supplied by the publications themselves. The reliability of all these figures, therefore, is not uniform but what can be obtained from the standard trade directories.

[12]Ibid.

[13]Yankelovich, Skelley and White, Inc., *Consumer Research Study on Reading and Book Purchasing,* prepared for the Book Industry Study Group, Inc. (New York: October, 1978), p. 61.

[14]*'Ayer Dictionary of Publications; Ulrich's International Periodicals Dictionary.*

[15]Ibid.

[16]It is impossible to exaggerate the depth and quality that the public libraries have added to American culture. Nothing in the history of American philanthropy exceeds the democratizing beneficence of Andrew Carnegie's magnificent library program. Between 1890 and 1917, 1,678 public libraries were built in 1,412 communities at a cost of $40 million. George S. Bobinski, *Carnegie Libraries: Their History and Impact on American Public Library Development* (Chicago: American Library Association, 1969), pp. 3, 22.

[17]Yankelovich, et al. *Consumer Research Study,* p. 18, adjusted to include the report's definition of readers and nonreaders and their numbers.

[18]Ibid., p. 212.

[19]Joseph Blotner, *Faulkner, A Biography,* vol. 1 (New York: Random House, 1972), p. 633. "The book also had a number of enthusiastic reviews, and it also had enough readers to carry it after two years [despite the catastrophic stock market crash twenty-two days after its publication] into an extremely modest third printing" (Malcolm Cowley, *The Faulkner-Cowley File,* New York: Viking, 1966, p. 4). Total copies in print in October 1931? Probably no more than 3,000, and that may be a touch high.

[20]Elisabeth Sifton, "What Reading Public?" *The Nation,* May 22, 1982, pp. 628-29.

[21]Anthony Trollope, *An Autobiography* (1883), edited and with a preface by Frederick Page (London: Oxford University Press, 1950), p. 118.

[22]Ibid., pp. 278-84.

[23]See Cowley, *The Faulkner-Cowley File,* for the history of this astonishing anthology.

[24]Detective fiction is conventionally put in this category, even by those who cherish it, or who, like Jacques Barzun, would protect it as a private pleasure against the withering touch of academic institutionalization. The implication is that it is not quite respectable for a "cultivated" reader to be seriously interested in such fiction, since, in truth, it is no more than a mild recreation for the isolated housewife and her tired businessman husband or for Justice Holmes, Franklin Roosevelt, and Eudora Welty, after hours. Sartre says, "Even now [i.e., in full career], I read the Serie Noire [a detective series] more readily than I do Wittgenstein" (*The Words,* p. 76). For Friedrich Dürrenmatt, oppressed by the deformations of modern literacy and literary scholarship, there is this feeling on which he has acted: "Perhaps the writer can best exist by writing detective stories, by creating art where it is least expected" (*Plays and Essays,* edited by Volkmar Sander, *The*

New German Library, vol. 89, New York: 1982, "Problems of the Theater," p. 261). Detective fiction in its several kinds is read by every class of reader from low to high. No genre is more popular. Robin W. Winks in *Modus Operandi: An Excursion into Detective Fiction* (Boston: David R. Godine, Publisher, Inc., 1982) makes a personal case for the importance of detective fiction.

25Priscilla Oakeshott and Clive Bradley, editors, *The Future of the Book, Part I— The Impact of New Technologies,* Studies on Books and Reading, no. 8, UNES-CO (Paris: 1982), pp. 23, 24, 27.

26"There is no doubt that in the past decades [readership in this country] has been declining and that the general culture is thinning out. Literacy as a phenomenon of growth and modernization is a thing of the past. Until recently, this was a country of readers: people of all trades and professions and habits of mind read books. Now only students read, and that rarely, just as they are only barely made to write. Teachers, of course, don't read at all. You can tell that from the way they boast that they're too busy to, and when they commit a book to paper themselves, it is likely to be unreadable. Lastly, the actual teaching shows that they have little interest in encouraging students to be competent in, much less enthusiastic about, their language, their literature and their minds. Our college salespeople regularly report on the declining enrollment in courses about modern fiction. We hear of professors of women's fiction who haven't read Iris Murdoch, Maureen Howard, Shirley Hazzard, Nadine Gordimer, Alice Adams, Anne Tyler or Muriel Spark—much less newer writers. And few literature courses celebrate novels as creations that might still be alive and worth reckoning with: on the contrary, the critics freeze-dry literature—reductive is not a sufficient word to describe their efforts." Sifton, "What Reading Public?" p. 629.

27See Oakeshott and Bradley, *The Future of the Book,* Oakeshott's Appendix, "Electronic Publishing: An Introductory Guide," pp. 1-23, for a comprehensive current "state-of-the-art" account of the new technologies.

28"New Year Letter, Part 1." Copyright 1941 and renewed 1969 by W.H. Auden. From *Collected Poems,* edited by Edward Mendelson. Reprinted by permission of Random House, Inc. (New York: 1945), p. 267.

29Sartre, *The Words,* pp. 253-54. "No day without a line," I am told by Beatrice Gottlieb, is a proverb derived from a passage in Pliny's *Natural History* (35:36) about the Greek painter Apelles. Apelles is said never to have let a day go by without painting at least a line. If the exact reference is to another art, writers have taken the proverb as their own. See Trollope's use of it in the last chapter of his autobiography (Trollope, *An Autobiography,* p. 365).

30Quoted by John Bayley, *Times Literary Supplement,* August 27, 1982, p. 919, in a review of James Fenton, *The Memory of War: Poems 1968-1982.*

31"The writers I care most about and never grow tired of are Shakespeare, Swift, Fielding, Dickens, Charles Reade, Samuel Butler, Zola, Flaubert and, among modern writers, James Joyce, T.S. Eliot, and D.H. Lawrence. But I believe the modern writer who has influenced me the most is Somerset Maugham, whom I admire immensely for his power of telling a story straightforwardly and without frills." In *The Collected Essays, Journalism and Letters of George Orwell,* vol. 2, edited by Sonia Orwell and Ian Angus (New York: Harcourt, Brace and World, 1968), p. 24.

Samuel S. Vaughan

The Community of the Book

THE COMMUNITY OF THE BOOK, it seems safe to assume, consists of those for whom the written word, especially as expressed in printed and bound volumes, is of the first importance. Nothing else may be safely assumed, including the question of whether it is, in fact, a community.

The community's major elements, its ethnics, are authors; editors and publishers; booksellers, librarians, and wholesalers; literary agents and literary critics; book reviewers and book journalists; translators; educators; and—not least, though often omitted from full partnership—readers. Other groups are functionally, economically, or spiritually involved, though in a less obvious way. These include newspaper and magazine people, papermakers and printers, binders, bankers, television talk show hosts, motion picture story editors, artists and designers, and others. They are the community's uncles, aunts, and cousins.

I propose in this paper to offer observations on the issues confronting, supporting, or undermining the community of the book, and several reassessments, reconsiderations, and possibilities for future work. These notes necessarily focus on only a few sectors, neighborhoods, so to speak, rather than the entire landscape. One objective is to challenge some of our favorite assertions.

Book publishing, for example, tends to be spoken of as if it were largely general or "trade" books. (*Trade* as applied to books further contributes to the confusion. Trade books in the main are for general audiences, designed to be sold through the book trade, i.e., booksellers, whereas trade magazines are meant for specialized audiences.) Instead, general books constitute one of the smaller sectors of book publishing, an industry that, by conventional standards, is small,[1] though insistent arguments stress its "bigness." And the confusion is widespread. Recently, Curtis Benjamin, retired chairman of McGraw-Hill, told an otherwise able reporter who had been covering publishing for the *New York Times* that his paper's reports on the "publishing industry's" deep recession were in part inaccurate. Benjamin's point was that, yes, a number of general book publishers and mass market paperback houses were in difficulty, but that professional, scientific, and technical publishers, textbook publishers, and other significant segments of the industry were not. Indeed, some were having their best years. The reporter replied that his beat was to cover trade publishing, not the whole industry, and it did not seem necessary to him to make this distinction repeatedly in his reports. To Benjamin, it seemed less than likely that even one tenth of the *Times'* readership understood this difference when stories about the health of the "book publishing industry" were run.

Do such differences of opinion matter? Yes. Slipshod reporting affects the motivation and morale of authors and of those in publishing, the opinions of bankers and other backers, of industry suppliers—compositors, printers, papermakers—contemplating expansions of capacity (or otherwise), and politicians, academics, reviewers, and teachers whose judgments have a bearing on books.

Chronic misrepresentations about the nature, makeup, process, and profitability of publishing plague the community of the book. Those who care about books also care deeply about what goes with them: reading, writing, literacy, freedom, prestige. But they must also learn to care more for facts. There are, admittedly, too few facts available, but one is that our curious community is rife with rumor, riddled and rattled by speculation and assertion passed off as truth, and oversupplied with false issues that make all but impossible real confrontation with genuine ideas.

Misunderstandings about the community are causing malfunctions. If a good general-assignment reporter approaches a story about Big Steel or the Department of Defense, he is apt to dig thoroughly, because he knows he is not a specialist in the steel industry or in military matters. If a reporter approaches a story about book publishing, it is usually with the conviction that he knows the answers even before he asks the questions. He is, after all, a writer, sometimes with published books to his credit. If a corporate executive in steel or an army officer makes a public statement, he is apt to do so with a measure of sensitivity about his community. When a publishing executive pops off, it is often straight from the hip, shooting out the lights.

When it comes to books investigating big business, writers and publishers are tough-minded, fact-minded, all from Missouri. About ourselves, we are softhearted, soft-minded, and lazy. Our too few facts are too often misunderstood, misapplied, or garbled. Much of our industry's "data" is unreliably obtained, casually examined, and delivered as gospel. As in other areas of our national life, speculation is passed off as information. The rumor mills of America, it seems, are the only ones operating at capacity.

From all corners come the cries and the claims: publishers are pillars of greed, grasping, inept, insensitive, unethical, powerful. Authors are grasping, greedy, neurotic, paranoid, disloyal, insensitive to all but their own egos. Librarians are timid, ultraconservative, unconcerned about protecting the rights of writers, readers, or publishers. Teachers are inept and indifferent, incapable of maintaining order, increasing knowledge, or simply teaching people to read. Big bookstore chains swallow up big books and small bookstores, and they are, of course, grasping, greedy, insensitive to sensitive books. They attempt to dictate publishing practices. The small bookseller is besieged, beleaguered, a frail reed. The American reader is disappearing—or never existed in the first place. Our children don't read anymore; television is sapping their will and preempting their time. There are no good book reviews.

With each argument, new alignments form. Authors and publishers condemn librarians; booksellers and authors rail against publishers; the small bookseller joins the "small" author to inveigh against the big bookstores. Publishers mutter that authors demand too much. Wholesalers complain that publishers do not give them a sufficient discount. Librarians say books are too cheaply made. Publishing employees protest that the pay scale is absurdly low. Authors lament that book publishers do not spend enough money on advertising. So do the newspapers.

I have become an injustice collector. My thick file of what otherwise responsible people have said about publishing is an amusing dossier of damnation, but its long-term consequences are damaging, and not just to the well-being of publishers.

The community is full of those who would police it. We need constant vigilance—but do we need vigilantes constantly? Some would stamp out certain practices; others, certain kinds of books or authors. (The latter group is made up not only of self-elected censors but of authors themselves.) Some of this carping is traditional and is merely part of the cultural static. But individual issues deserve comment. For example:

CHARGE: *Big publishers dominate the industry, imperiling the small publisher and the small bookseller alike. Small is Beautiful. Subtitled: Big is Ugly.*

Not so. One industry specialist, Paul D. Doebler, wrote recently: "Small publishing is exhibiting robust health."[2] And it is growing. *Publishers Weekly* reports that "the world of smaller publishers is numerically huge and getting bigger all the time. According to R.R. Bowker, 12,845 publishers have books in print and most of these are, by any definition, small publishers. Perhaps 200 firms can be considered large, well-known companies with sales in the millions."[3] And these are not, by any means, all literary publishers. Richard Morris, who edits the newsletter for COSMEP (Committee of Small Magazines/Press Editors and Publishers), estimates that their current membership is roughly 40 percent "literary publishers, 30 percent self-publishers, and 30 percent commercially oriented." And, says Morris, "the number of people not primarily literary in orientation has been increasing."[4]

How are they doing? Very well, it appears. In its annual survey, Huenefeld, a small publishing consulting company, found that the sales of 192 small book publishers were up 12.5 percent in 1981 over 1980. These publishers were optimistic about 1982, predicting "an average growth rate of 19.3 percent." Furthermore, "nearly 74 percent . . . operated at a profit."[5] Few large publishing houses could match either this growth rate or profit picture. One finding is that 66 of the smaller houses categorized as "not-for-profit" outperformed their profit-minded counterparts.

What deserves closer examination—and celebration—is that one of the healthiest phenomena is the proliferation, growth, and geographical dispersion of small publishing enterprises.

CHARGE: *Conglomerates are taking over book publishing. Big publishers are buying up smaller ones. The end of literature is in sight.*

Understandable anxieties exist everywhere in the community, especially among authors, who feel underappreciated, and among publishers, who see books going down the drain instead of up the charts.

One of the most unreasonable fears, however, grows out of the automatic assumption that anyone not already in book publishing is therefore not fit to publish. When an executive from Western Pacific Railroad attempted to gain control of Houghton Mifflin not long ago, its authors rose up in a body and threatened to leave the company if this Ghengis Kahn from the West took over. From the authors' statements to the press, it was clear that no one knew much about the man. He is, perhaps, as cultured as any individual now heading up a book publishing company. But this is a possibility that authors in heat cannot conceive of, let alone entertain. Their elitism was extraordinary—and went largely unremarked.

Book publishers, after all, have to come from somewhere else at the outset. To be sure, several prominent publishers are descendants of publishing ancestors, inheritors of publishing companies and sometimes fortunes. But most people in publishing were not "in publishing" before they crossed the line. And not all of publishing's backing came from book sources to begin with. The initial funding for two of the most prestigious publishing houses in the country came from profits in steel and in girdles. But people spoken of as "nonbook" types are subject to prejudices that, if applied to religious groups, would bring out the shock troops of antidefamation leagues. A similar alarm, raised when American Express attempted to buy into a well-known publishing company, evoked the ludicrous image of a commercial "giant" gobbling up a pitiful little press called McGraw-Hill.

It seems to me that the real risk when "nonbook" people come into publishing is not that they know so little about books, but that they know so little about money. At no time has general book publishing ever contributed profits consistently to its mother company that could measure up to conservative investments in safe securities—money that could be earned without work and with relatively little risk. Their shortsightedness as investors, as businessmen, should characterize their unfitness, not their supposed lack of culture or assumed inability to read intelligently or to understand editorial talk (which can be difficult to translate at best).

The big buying trend is over, but the contradictions linger on. There is virtually no mention of the publishing houses and imprints that would simply have disappeared without the intervention of larger and more successful companies. Antiliterary charges are duds. Random House bought Knopf and Pantheon, and this complex was in turn bought by RCA, which later sold it off. This seems to have produced nothing more notable than a flow of capital and, presumably, memos. Despite all fears, there is no documented evidence that the CBS ownership of Holt did any damage to the Holt list.

These comments are no argument that Big (or Different) is Beautiful. But one of the built-in contradictions for antibigness authors is that the best known of them require publishing institutions of some size to do precisely what the authors want done.

CHARGE: *The major problem is distribution.*

Intellectuals, even more than marketing men, love to focus on the "distribution problem." It is as if they were seeking a cure for cancer, as if cancer were one disease, rather than several. If only publishers would set to rights the distribution mess in their own houses, all problems would be solved.

Publishers, in fact, do *not* control the means of distribution. It would be a far more efficient business if we did, and definitely more dangerous, as it is in countries—such as Italy and France—where one or two major publishing houses essentially own the engines of book distribution. Publishers perform only at the front end of the distribution chain. We are, in terms used for earth-moving equipment (which is sometimes what the work resembles), only "front-end loaders." We move the books, in essence, toward the distribution channels, trying to get them through.

As a matter of fact, distribution *is* getting better, and we owe the improvements in part to machines—which are, of course, resisted by those who see themselves as creative or intellectual and who therefore must protest the depersonalization of the machine, when not otherwise looking to it for miraculous contributions.

CHARGE: *Bookstores are dying out. Big chains are grinding the good shops into the ground.*

Add to this the comment of the respected head of a university press: "Most books are being bought in this country by two computers." Given the fact that most university presses get their books into the bookstore chains only with the greatest difficulty, his frustration is understandable—but inaccurate. Computers don't buy books. People program them to provide information on book sales, levels of inventory, and the kinds of information bookstore owners have needed for centuries to run their exceedingly complicated businesses.

The same chains the director criticizes employ *dozens* of individual book buyers for special categories of books.

Yes, booksellers large and small (and publishers, including the university press director) use computers. The failure to bring in such tools to aid in the management of the book business would be a much greater "sin." As for the decline of the small shop, we can look first at the comment, "The new shops, and the healthiest survivors of the old, are not the well-stocked personal shops of the 20's." This was in the Winter 1963 issue of *Daedalus,* before the growth of the large chain bookstore operations.

The big bookstore chains, notably B. Dalton and Walden, have become imposing presences, and independent bookshops have felt the heat of their competition. Any poorly located or lackluster shop is likely to be damaged by the arrival on the scene of a bright, "well-merchandised" chain store. At the same time, any well-run, intelligently managed individual bookstore is not likely to yield its customers to what is seen as the impersonality of a chain branch shop.

Just as fiction is a perennial invalid, so too is the good "personal" bookshop. It has been disappearing since it first began. The small bookshop goes out of business for the same reasons that many new small businesses expire. Many shops that are poorly run and inadequately financed are owned by people who would rather buy books than sell them, who love books but do not love the gritty details of managing a retail business with hundreds of "suppliers," all offering different terms. Constant problems of inventory, turnover, cash flow, credit, and erroneous shipments compound the difficulty, and the results are, in good years, a modest profit at best.

The well-stocked bookshop, operated by a perceptive owner, is a treasure, and an asset to any community. There never have been very many of this kind. The jewel of a shop is just that: rare, precious, hard to find—and, often, expensive. Chains compete vigorously with such shops. Discounters, in particular, give them trouble, at least, when the discounter first opens up. But the best bookshops do more than survive. They compete effectively with the chains by providing what is uniquely theirs to offer: personal service and attention; well-chosen inventories of books, old and new; gift wrapping; amiable return or exchange privileges, and so on.

It is not as if the little bookshop presents no problems of its own; for one, the highly opinionated prejudices of its owner. If you share the same tastes, fine. If not, the selection of books on hand can be decidedly limited.

The bigger chains—Dalton, Walden, Crown—are sharply competitive and decidedly unsentimental in certain aspects of their operations. The pride of some of them in their computers, category buying, and advertising is excessive. Chains put pressure on publishers, in addition to other bookshops, as all big-muscle retailing tends to exert pressure on its "vendors." Whether there are illegal discriminatory practices underway has yet to be tested. (One has to stress *illegal*. Otherwise, that's what buying is—discrimination.) It is inaccurate to say that there are no "book people" in the chain stores. The chains still find themselves employing clerks who are more responsive to books than to systems. More than one manager runs a chain store as if it were a personal shop.

Unmentioned in the complaints about chains are the smaller or middle-sized bookstore groups: Kroch's and Brentano's in the Middle West; Doubleday, nationally; and others. These include some of the best bookshops in the country.

In any case, there are facts. The number of bookstores in the United States has nearly doubled since 1972. Bowker, publishers for the book trade, notes an increase in the number of retail book outlets from about 10,000 to around 19,000 in that period. Some are chain outlets. But the big two taken together number less than 3,000 shops. Thus, *thousands* of other stores have come onto the scene even as the chains have been undergoing their greatest growth. For years before large group retailing developed, threatening to bind us, as some see it, in chains, the call was for booksellers who could sell books, as one solution to the distribution problem. The chains, for better and worse, provide some of that. Hundreds of shops are open where none existed before. Considered as a plus, as extra sales situations, they are valuable. They represent a large share, but not necessarily the essence, of the business.

The inspired, informed, informal bookseller is a sometimes delicate, sometimes hardy plant to be cherished. But the healthy ones become so because they are smart, not just sentimental. They know books, and they know their trade. Can they compete? Yes, and they do. They compete with group buying and big backing by using their own trusted methods; with their knowledge of books, authors, and customers; by risk-taking; and, through guerrilla warfare, taking advantage of their speed, mobility, training, and, the strongest motive of all, their will to survive.

CHARGE: *There are 40,000 books published every year. Too many.*

Book people persist in using balloon figures. For years, people have been saying that 40,000 new books are published each year, and that this causes stillbirth, that stores cannot accept that many, that reviewers cannot cover them . . .

First, it should be noted that when the number of books published went *down,* as it did from 1979 to 1980 (from 45,182 to 42,377), no one seemed to notice. Sooner or later, however, the total will pass 50,000.

So what? Such numbers miss the mark and send up clouds of dust. Of the 40,000-plus books published each year, between 7,000 and 9,000 titles are not new books at all but reissues. Of the rest, over 5,000 are in science and medicine, and of these, most are not general books, by any stretch of the definition, but technical. The largest category published is in sociology and economics, more than 6,000 titles per year, and few of these are aimed at the general reader, reviewer, or bookstore.

Fiction has soared—from 2,313 titles in 1979 to 5,003 in 1981. But what are they, especially given the decrease from 1979 to 1980? Many are "genre" or "category" novels, new releases in the seemingly endless stream of paperback romances, with varying degrees of spice, ranging, as in a Chinese restaurant, from bland to hot. These do not compete for review space, they have increased the profitability of stores who sell them, and they constitute something more akin to magazine than to book publishing.

In addition, many of the other books in the numerical tallies are scholarly or other specialized monographs. No one knows, in fact, how many of the books published are aimed at the general reader, and thus beamed at bookstores and reviewers along the way.

One source separates "literary books" from "practical and professional books." In 1979 there were said to be 8,416 "literary books" and 22,777 "practical and professional" ones. In the period 1959-79, the number of practical and professional books very nearly doubled, while the increase in literary books went from a little over 5,000 titles to over 8,000.

In terms of allover U.S. book production, the United States produced 12,000 titles in 1914 and did not come up with this total again until 1956. Thereafter, the period of most rapid growth was 1960-64, followed by a slowdown in 1969-70.[6]

A steadily swelling stream of "too many books"? Wrong. Too many indifferent, insufficient, unsatisfactory, or redundant books—which the public often ignores or rejects. The marketplace is the final editor.

CHARGE: *Authors are poorly paid and live on the edge of poverty.*

To the New York, Washington, or Los Angeles newspaper reader, this would seem a curious claim, since the reader is treated occasionally to accounts of million-dollar contracts. He tends to see the author in the same category as rock or sports stars, as indeed a few are. The author, on the other hand, tends to see himself/herself as inadequately compensated, possibly cheated, and certainly working at below the minimum wage, especially reckoned on an hourly basis. Indeed, most authors would be better off if they *were* paid hourly—at *any* rate—because most writers are writing nearly all the time, one way or another.

The Authors' Guild constantly surveys publishers' contracts and authors' earnings, to the extent of their ability to determine these figures. The *New York Times* carried the following front-page headline—based on a survey made for the Authors' Guild Foundation by the Center for the Social Sciences at Columbia University—"Average U.S. Author's Writing Brings in Less Than $5,000 a Year."[7] Following which, an author, James Lincoln Collier, wrote a piece for *Publishers Weekly,* entitled, "Can Writers Afford to Write Books," charging that the publishing industry exists "only by the grace of subsidies provided by writers."[8] Curtis Benjamin responded to the *Times* story and raised a few questions himself. As he put it, "The Columbia survey was narrowly focused and hence misleading."[9]

Benjamin's first discovery was that the sample was "badly skewed because it included largely authors who were likely to write only Trade books. . . . Much larger categories of authors, such as those of educational and professional or practical books, were all but ignored." The sample, he said, was confined to 3,200 of the 5,000 members of the Authors' Guild, plus about 1,900 other writers "who had been invited to join the Guild but declined to do so," and got a 54 percent response. But the report claimed that the survey was "unmatched" in its number of respondents, "its intention to represent the full population of book writers in America," and so on. Benjamin asked: Approximately how large *is* the total population of American authors? The surveyors had to acknowledge that the size and composition of that population remained "largely a mystery."

Many authors are academics. Whether one teaches to subsidize writing or writes to enlarge the compensation of teaching is an individual decision. But candid academics point to the surprising range of rewards that can issue from the publication of even the least successful book—fellowships, grants, symposia and speaking invitations, travel, and opportunities for career advancement. Far from publish or perish, it is more apt to be publish and prosper, when everything is added in.

That there are undercompensated authors, as there are unrecognized ones, is all too plain. That every author should earn more is all too silly.

MISCELLANEOUS CHARGES: *Publishers want only blockbusters*. Wrong. Publishers want blockbusters, but they also want good books that will sell in the middle range, and we want interesting new authors to publish. Anyone who doesn't is not planning to be in publishing for very long. *Publishing is no longer an occupation for gentlemen*. Partly true. For one thing, women are exceedingly important throughout the business. For another, there is the question of whether it ever was. The first publisher was the Church, whose members might have been part of an aristocracy, but who were not, in the conventional sense, gentlemen. Subsequently, publishers grew up out of booksellers and printers, that is, tradesmen. The title of the English publisher's memoir, *An Occupation for Gentlemen*, was meant to be ironic, a nuance missed by those who cite it without having read the book. The fact that on occasion gentlemen and gentlewomen have participated in publishing makes for an interesting cultural and commercial footnote but not for a characterization of the whole business. *Fiction is dead*. Fiction is always dead or dying and, like the theater and the bookshop, remains one of our hardiest invalids. More fiction is published than any other category of book. *Nonfiction sells better than fiction*. Wrong. The word "nonfiction" identifies nothing, except books that are, or pretend to be, not fictional. Some of the biggest selling books every year are novels, and the mass market paperback and book club businesses are founded on fiction. It is when hardcover sales alone are used to compute the sales of fiction versus nonfiction that the deception sets in.

Next, let us look briefly at two of our common concerns—reading and, that neglected and maligned figure, the reader.

READING

If reading is done off a "green screen" as some pre-
dict will be commonplace in the 1990s, [Secretary
of Education Terrel H.] Bell said, that makes
the teaching of literacy "even more important."[10]
—Publishers Weekly

The "teaching of literacy" evokes considerable concern in the community—as well it should. Of the various forms of poverty, the worst are to be starved for food or love, to be denied the vote or voice, and to be unable to read. Recently we have learned to worry about "functional illiteracy." A number of our citizens are able to read, that is, able to make out letters and words, but they cannot make the imaginative leap toward meaning and comprehension. We have now begun to speak of semiliteracy—which can mean either the disinclination of "today's youth to read for their own enjoyment" or the tendency to be satisfied with "shallow interpretations of what they do read"—and of "aliteracy," knowing how to read but not wanting to. Townsend Hoopes, president of the Association of American Publishers, describes this as an indication of the "widening gap between the leadership elite and the general public."[11]

As a nation, we have the notion that we have been spectacularly unsuccessful in combatting illiteracy. Indeed, it appears that we have been more ingenious at inventing new forms of illiteracy than in curing the basic problems. And we are generous in awarding blame. No wonder: there is plenty to go around, with dozens of suitable scapegoats. Parents and college administrators blame it on the teachers, primary and secondary schoolteachers blame it on the parents, everyone blames it on television. We hear of the latest learning disabilities; we are suspicious of the oldest teaching inabilities. Authors and publishers worry, but most do next to nothing about it, except to use the widely debated "readability" levels and word lists.

Not nearly as easy as assigning blame is recognizing the genuine difficulties of learning to read in less than auspicious circumstances. We have the example of Abraham Lincoln learning to read by firelight for inspiration; there are fewer case histories of learning to read without books at hand. Robert Coles and others have shown that learning to read can be extraordinarily difficult when the student does not come out of "natural reading circumstances." But it is more entertaining and makes better copy to give short shrift to the complexities of reading and to decry public education, Archie Bunker-type home life, and "The Dukes of Hazzard." And the emphasis on grades and ritualized homework, along with assorted threats, makes reading and writing difficult even for the "advantaged."

In *What Was Literature?* Leslie Fiedler writes that, although he does so for a living, "it is an odd enough notion . . . to 'teach,' say, the plays of Shakespeare or the novels of Dickens and Twain, works written to move and titillate: to *require*, in effect, a pleasurable response from a captive student audience." (Fiedler adds: "The whole enterprise is a little like giving a course in making love."[12] In this, he is surely correct. A required response, even for pleasure, induces impotence.)

Meanwhile, the enormous advantage of the "new technology" is not the microchip but rather that video games teach children to associate the flickering green panels with pleasure. A voluntary commitment of time and learning gives them action, control, and reward. Just as many younger Americans have grown up feeling that the paperback book is not a hardcover, hardnosed, required textbook but a friendly, spontaneous, portable, informal, disposable device, so the new games are teaching kids not just to blow up planets and blow away enemies, but that there is joy in the interaction between hand, eye, and screen.

Parents, publishers, and writers are too quick to blame teachers when there is ample evidence that children who see and possess books and periodicals in their homes, who are asked friendly questions about their reading, and who are read to, are the ones who become lifelong readers. Teachers are too quick to blame parents when part of the problem, at least, is the unwillingness of teachers to assign writing projects and to mark them carefully and sensitively. We concentrate on "skills" when we could be offering love, fantasy, reality, escape, understanding, surprise—the eternal gifts of reading and writing, of self-expression, and the discovery of the lives of others.

Characteristically, the community sees disaster everywhere. Taxpayer revolts distress liberals, who fail to understand that decades of reporting only the bad news—especially the "news" that the millions of dollars spent on education over the years have produced only widespread illiteracy—is reason enough for taxpayers to demand a slowdown. Instead of recognizing that the news is not all bad, that each year millions of youngsters are transformed into readers, we unvaryingly forecast poor educational weather, with more to come. We could instead offer, as energetically as we do the bad news, the good news that free libraries and both public and private schools, trained and sometimes gifted professionals, book reviews and book chats, television and movie versions of books, and the increasing availability of the best in children's literature at attractive paperback prices, all conspire to create a climate for literacy that is unparalleled in human history.

There are, too, unrecognized or unstated appeals in reading. No civilized person loves pornography. Yet more than a few people have become enthralled by reading when they discovered that sexual excitement could be found in books. Certainly, this is not an injunction to produce porn, but it could open the way for the recognition that what some people see in books is what others have seen in photography and art. Erotic arousal testifies to the pleasure and especially to the *power* of the written word—a not quite respectable approach, perhaps, but worth consideration. There are unquantifiable qualities in reading that draw people to print.

Ours is referred to as a time that is becoming increasingly visual, as if this were uniquely an era of images rather than an age of print. Yet there never were eras wholly devoted to print, which has existed simultaneously with paintings, posters, engravings, Chautauqua lecturers, opera, radio, motion pictures, newsreels, and cave paintings and other graffiti. Do we live in a time dominated by pictures, by symbols, a semiotic soup without an alphabet? Words *are* abstract art, *are* symbols. We should stop looking back at a golden age that never was.

READERS

Americans simply "don't read books"; to others, slightly less apocalyptic, Americans don't read "enough" books or "good" books. The question of who reads and why involves a web of motives, the transmission of messages, intended or accidental, and atmospherics as well as education. The situation is not helped by the analyses of most surveys.

Such studies as we do have—and these, in the main, reflect jaundiced opinions—appear to argue that readers are declining or that new readers are not being created. Comparisons are made to the sales of certain leading titles of yesteryear, or yestercentury, but such comparisons fail to take account of the fact that many yesteryears were times when fewer titles were published, when there were fewer popular authors, fewer forms of alternative entertainment, and less competition for the reader's time and money (though no one need minimize the appeals of sex, whist, or weariness to absorb hours and sometimes cash).

On the other hand, when a respectable study *is* done, questionable use is made of the results. In 1978 the research team of Yankelovich, Skelly, and White made public the results of a study they had conducted for the Book Industry Study Group. As reported—and interpreted—by the *New York Times,* "Study Finds that Nearly Half in U.S. Do Not Read Books." The Library of Congress came to a different conclusion: "Contrary to popular opinion, over 90 percent of the U.S. population constitutes a reading public—a significant number of them readers who find time for ten or more books over a six-month period."[13] At about the same time, a regular Gallup poll, sponsored by the American Library Association, released its results. Among them: "Fiction was still the most popular reading," and "One-fourth of . . . [the] respondents said television influenced their book selection."[14]

All this was interesting, but none of it was new, nor, sadly, was the poll designed to elicit additional needed information. Most surveys conclude that just under half of all adult Americans read a book sometime or other. The differing interpretations are standard, too. Is the glass half full or half empty?

The book publishers and the library association, with the best will in the world, had underwritten studies that merely confirmed what every serious study has shown over the past forty years. Many people like fiction. Book reading tends to correlate with several characteristics, among them education and income. In 1974 a report "Books and Leisure Time," by the Newspaper Advertising Bureau, indicated that nearly six out of ten (58%) Americans over eighteen had purchased one or more books in the previous year. Among those with "some college or more," 83 percent were book buyers. A study done by W.R. Simmons and Associates in 1975-76 showed the relationship between reading, education, and income, as did a survey by the National Advisory Committee on Libraries in 1967 and a study of book-buying behavior in 1966 by the National Industrial Conference Board.

In 1963, in an article for the *New York Times Book Review,* I pointed out that Gallup had made the dismal discovery that "just over half of American adults did not read a single book all the way through in the past year," and noted that for some, this nourished the notion that we were a nation of nonreaders. But Gallup's findings also meant that as many as 40 or 50 million Americans *had* read a book in 1962, over twice the number who had seen a basketball or football game; that well over $1 billion had been spent on books and maps in that year, more than we put down in movie theaters or at parimutuel windows. At any rate, what few reliable data there are go back to Bernard Berelson's work in 1949 and are astonishingly consistent. Reinventions of the wheel have a certain charm, but they do not advance the cart or the art.[15]

If the community is to become better at diagnosing, prescribing, and pursuing cures for the several illiteracies, perhaps we had first better improve our own reading, including survey result that come to Galluping conclusions.

The survey done by the Book Industry Study Group did turn up a few promising leads. I had always assumed, for instance, that the higher incidence of book reading among the "educated" meant the college-educated, as indeed it does. But those with a high-school education show up remarkably well as readers. Why should this be so? Are high-school graduates continuing their education? Are they seeking self-improvement? Or are they less satisfied than college graduates with their jobs and thus reading out of the almost universal need to escape? Skeptical as I am of "motivational research," it is essential to learn more about the healthy reader if we are to help the person who does not or cannot read.

Further, if we are to use the kinds of statistics that we are deluged with, let us insist at least on their disciplined development. Reader studies usually measure book readers against the total population, sometimes against only the total adult population. Which of these studies recognize that 18 million, or 11 percent of our people, speak a language other than English at home, that 8 million speak Spanish, for instance?

If readership studies start with a total population of 226 million, and that number is reduced by those under age nineteen, we are at

154 million in a single step. If, in a search for the center of the matter, we deduct those people over seventy-five, the working number becomes 144 million. Subtract non-English-speaking people and the number becomes something like 126 million—not the 226 million frequently spoken of as "our" population. Then remove the blind and other handicapped who cannot read, or read easily, and factor in not just hardcover book sales but book club memberships, the readership of paperback reprints, books in other forms (magazine serials or excerpts, for example), books borrowed not only from libraries but from friends, and, in addition to complexity, a kind of suitability begins to bleed into the otherwise bloodless statistics.

What do we make of the factor of the greatly increased number of working women? Women have always been assumed to be the readers in this country, to the extent that anyone will admit that we have readers. Does their presence in the work force mean that they have more money to spend on books but less time to read? Or do they find time to read regardless of their limited leisure hours? The common assumption that women are the readers is supported by the gender evidence in book club rolls. Yet what are we to make of the study in 1979 which showed that the most frequent visitors to libraries (about once every two weeks, or more than twenty-five trips per year) tended to be men, aged eighteen to thirty-four?[16]

Why speak of television as a minus, a deterrent, or a drain, when almost every survey tells us that book readers are not passive or bookish, that their interests are not confined to books? Book readers watch television, go to movies and ballgames, eat "fast" as well as "gourmet" foods, play records, go to concerts, and in general use more time than they think they have.

America has a long way to go toward universal literacy. But underestimating or undervaluing what we are accomplishing is a waste of time and energy. For years, expenditures for books have increased while money spent for magazines, newspapers, and movies has decreased. The number of book publishers has grown markedly and at a much faster rate than the formation of television and radio stations, newspapers, or periodicals.

Despite recent declines in the unit sales of individual books, we are still doing better than we were in the fifties, and not just because of increased population. The last time I looked at a comparison of unit sales of similarly popular novels, Herman Wouk's *Marjorie Morningstar* of 1954 and Peter Benchley's *Jaws* of 1974, the former had sold a little under 2 million copies in its original hardcover, paperback, and book club editions, while the latter sold, in the same three forms, around 10 million. And these numbers do not include what magazine people call "pass-along" readership—the reading of one copy by more than one person.

The popular perception persists—there are not many book readers in America. By what measure can we count ourselves a "nation of readers" (in the phrase used by the Center for the Book at the Library of Congress)? One hundred percent of all Americans reading how many books per year? Eighty percent? Anything over fifty percent? What number would you use to designate "book people?" Five million? One million? One hundred thousand?

Many authors feel that they know more writers than readers. Publishers mutter that if all the people who write poetry would buy one book of poetry per year, the entire aspect of poetry publishing would change over the weekend.

Yet over 5 million books are bought in this country *per day.* To be sure, this includes schools, libraries, book club members, paperback readers, and the rest. But institutions do not diminish the implications of this number; rather, they increase it, because an institutional copy is apt to be read by more than one person.

Such numbers are not offered as proofs or puffs. They only underline the indisputable fact that the community worries but doesn't wonder enough; it criticizes energetically but investigates perfunctorily; threatened by unknowns, it issues pronouncements as if they were facts. The leading spokespeople for books, a group of at least some education, display dizzying naivete, gullibility, and credulity.

A report that S.A.T. scores are rising brings out the scoffers immediately. When there is clear proof that the regularly maligned American is reading a book, he (or she) is accused of reading "trash." They don't read what they "should," what is good for them, and surely they cannot be reading both popular literature *and* Literature. Literary people may like pizza and popcorn as well as *paillard de veau* and Corton Charlemagne, but they cannot believe that others do too. Such concessions could be upsetting. Just when you have them safely stereotyped, tucked away in categories, American readers are revealed as pigeons who refuse to stay holed.

A *Roots,* a *Godfather,* a *Garp,* a Hailey, a Wouk, a Uris, regularly reach readers in the millions. Instead of dismissing this fact as unrelated to serious book reading, those concerned with reading habits should ask: Why them? What does it take to rouse the reader? The evidence is not that ours is a nation of nonreaders. We appear to be a nation that can be excited by a book—but not easily.

Within the community, a deep and divisive schizophrenia exists about whether we want to select and sell only The Best, even if that means selling to the fewest, or bring out books for the many, with the understanding that the popular fare will help to subsidize some of the best and also might lead readers from one kind of book to another. Underlying the conflict is the issue of whether we really want all sorts of books for all sorts of people, or just books for Our Kind, Our Crowd. No amount of cultural overlay or the laying down of sophisticated smokescreens from on high can obscure the fact that the views of certain sectors of the community are not notably democratic.

Then, too, we cannot shift all problems to the reader or the non-reader or the teacher. Instead, we should go back to origins. One reason for what some fear is a diminishing or disappearing audience for books is perhaps not attributable to the audience itself. Poorly written, uninteresting books might well cause indifferent audiences. As Richard Poirier puts it, "Bad things may indeed be happening to books these days, including, one might add, much of the writing that is found in them."[17]

It could be that it is not so much a matter of the disappearing individual reader as the disappearing individuality of books. One of the publishing industry's rare, thoughtful, and studious analysts, Per Gedin, put it succinctly in his little-noted book, *Literature in The Marketplace*. Citing the Euromonitor Book Readership Survey of 1975, Gedin writes, "Books are becoming another form of mass media and entertainment and are losing their individual appeal."[18] If book reading has slowed, it might not just be a matter of Reaganomics or red-neck six-pack pleasures, but a decline of the book itself. Successful or not, some books are becoming faceless in the crowd. Perhaps, given the difficulties, diversions, disappointments, and depression, it is remarkable that people read at all.

The arguments are all old, familiar, and fatiguing. As with disarmament, everybody's right and everybody's wrong. Still, the problems will not go away. A number of automatic antagonisms ought to be reexamined, and others replaced. The times call for an end to easy assumptions. Books are good? Some books are. Good books are neglected? Not usually. Great books are rare? Great everything is rare. Let us confront a few newer notions, for ancient arguments only camouflage what could be more important matters. Consider, for example, these issues:

Television and Reading—It is time to set aside simplistic notions that television is the enemy of reading or that television must be enlisted to "save" reading. Reading is not an isolated experience; it is ailing or alive in the culture and gets substantial aid and interference from other sources. Television has a push-pull influence: it conceivably attracts some readers; claims for its own nonreaders who would not read even if there were no television; and takes others away some, but not all, of the time. Even more obviously, television stimulates interest in reading on occasion, through its several techniques, intended or accidental. People are driven to books by good television programs made from those books; people are also driven *back* to books out of boredom with the small screen.

We need to recognize and study the ecology of the media. Currents of attraction swirl among minds, competition for attention is intense, and there are notable as well as minor distractions and substantial or trivial differences in pleasures offered to the individual. Scholars searching for suitable subjects could find in media ecology, relatedness, independence or interdependence, much to chew on. One medium has an impact on another, and all of them react to all others. For the first time since commercial television began, the total viewing audience is not growing rapidly. Does book readership decline when television and motion picture audiences increase? Does the record business run parallel with book publishing—or counter to it? Should authors and publishers attempt to adapt to the world of fast-moving images—or stay with what books do best, what moving images cannot do? Television news was once broadcast in "ghetto" hours; now it is prime time entertainment. What conclusions does this suggest for books, which are in part a journalistic, news-bringing medium, and for the novel as "news," one of its classic roles? Television people devote a good deal of attention to slotting, the sequence of programs, to how one program feeds interest in another, and to the competition in the same time period. Publishing devotes little, if any, time to considering sequence, and knows next to nothing about what the competition is doing, except for the most obvious big, popular books coming up. Can one book feed another—or does one highly touted, but ultimately disappointing, book diminish the audience temporarily?

Part of our anxiety about television is a fear of what might be happening to print, especially when the argument enters the TV-versus-newspapers stage. Everyone "knows" that American newspapers are dying, that most Americans get their news from television, and so on. A recent article by Leo Bogart in *The Wilson Quarterly* shows that newspapers have better circulation ratios to population in cities where TV news ratings are high rather than low; that what kills off newspapers is not a lack of readers but a lack of advertising revenue to the number two paper in any market; that the birth of new newspapers has approximately balanced the death of old ones (twelve dailies stopped publication in 1980-81, he writes, and twenty-five new ones were started); that daily newspapers are now published in 1,560 American towns, more than ever before; that during the 1978 strike of New York newspapers, television news viewing went down, not up.[19]

Needed—A solidly based study of the incomes and economic support systems of writers, publishers, scholars, and others to disperse the dust of both old claims and new ones. The survey of writers' incomes cited earlier failed to take adequately into account many factors of considerable consequence, including (as noted) the total population of writers in the United States; the incomes of technical, scientific, textbook, or scholarly authors; patronage apart from publishers; and the fact that, for most authors, writing provides a second income. What can be considered fair compensation for those for whom writing is a second, part-time job, performed, in some cases, in a secondary manner?

Needed—A closer look at the several kinds of publishing so that its sectors can be sorted out, and textbooks, general books, monographs, and so on, no longer lumped together indiscriminately.

Needed—Educational projects to bring the young and old of publishing together—to give the young some sense of history and a knowledge of antecedents, so that they will not buy every bargain apocalypse offered them, and to encourage the older members to contribute reliably to a credible history of a useful and little-understood industry. Hundreds of publishing courses are taught to people hoping to get into publishing; meanwhile, many of the people in publishing know little of the history of the book, misunderstand and misuse the few facts they know of their work, and misreport unintentionally the process in which they participate.

The literature of publishing is sketchy, scattered, and simply appalling. In the main, it is written not by publishers, but by authors. Thus the "history" of publishing is seen by privileged and sometimes victimized participants. When editors, agents, and publishers do write their memoirs, they are usually a collection of boastful or trivial recollections, unreliable, and almost always disorganized and in desperate need of editing.

Barthes writes that "for a very long time—probably for the entire classical capitalist period, i.e., from the sixteenth to the nineteenth century, in France—the uncontested owners of the language, and they alone, were authors. . . . If we except preachers and jurists (enclosed moreover in functional languages), no one else spoke."[20] Most publishing history is still written by the "owners" of the language.

On Censorship, Book-Banning, and Book-Burning—All our energies are given over to stamping out fires. Time should be devoted too (as with crime and poverty) to uncovering the root or hidden causes of resistance to books—the desire, say, in some textbook cases, to have a voice in the education of one's children. Or to go on believing in the Bible. As Paul Cowan wrote of a textbook adoption controversy in Charleston, West Virginia, "It is not an isolated battle . . . it is nothing less than a fight over America's future . . . it is a holy war between people who depend on books and people who depend on the Book."[21] Or the chance for self-aggrandizement of some of the publicity-hungry censors. Some of those on the other side of the line, who see themselves on the side of the angels, are decent people, trying to do the right thing as they understand right.

Know your enemy. He could turn out to be a misguided friend. Further, to use the language of the intelligence community, you might be able to "turn" him.

And let us give up overestimating the opposition. Liberals eager to leap to a defense of virtue, including their own, and ever-eager to find new monsters to scourge, contribute to the power of right-tilted, media-minded evangelists who claim vast followings but do not always have them.

The issues of censorship, textbooks, and pornography go beyond mere distaste for red-neck opposition to Darwin or J.D. Salinger. How can we fight fire with fire but also with education, to help people understand that banning books usually means banning freedom, and that good books (by any measure) are inevitably burned with the bad? How can we celebrate the heroism of those who stand up for freedom or those who help calm the fears of their frightened neighbors, who don't always buy sophisticated versions of science, religion, or morality? Not everyone, after all, grew up nurtured on the First Amendment—for all they know, every Amendment is important (a point lost on some First Amendment "groupies," who are less concerned about the Sixth, say, as long as they are not on trial for their lives). Granted, we have to accept grotesque distortions of the First Amendment to go on enjoying its benefits, but those feeling dismay have no constitutional duty to remain silent.

Let us look for issues under or behind an issue, for "reticences and resonances of this society," as someone said. Are there legitimate inhibitions to publication? Should there be? What are authors' and publishers' self-imposed standards? Are there *any* limits worth considering?

On the Courts' Call for the Notes of Writers—Let us fight this at the same time we look for these issues beyond issues. If the recent interpretations of some courts are to be construed as law, the reporter's hasty scribblings are now to be taken as gospel. This is somewhat like issuing a subpoena for a person's mind, his or her free associations, rough drafts, privileged impressions, private thoughts, and harmless mistakes.

Public Lending Rights—When will we take this issue—the possible payment to authors and publishers for their investment, by tiny fees paid for books borrowed from libraries—to the public? They deserve to know both sides, the desirability of this payment from one point of view, and the respectable opposition to it from others, including the inhibition of free libraries and the necessary policing and paperwork by librarians at a time when they are strapped for funds, staff, and time. Except for an increasing awareness of the question of justice in the copying of records and videocassettes, this issue is not even in the public consciousness. Yet it is the public who will pay—or not—and it is our job to bring them into the act.

Relevant, Useful, Economical Technology—This brings us to the decades of technological backwardness in printing and papermaking. Despite the proliferation of calculators and computers, progress is glacierlike. Few devices, processes, or products have been invented in decades to affect materially the costs of "goods" produced. Offset lithography made easier the reproduction of photographs. The word processor is excellent for "keyboarding" reference works that need regular revision; for "typesetting" manuscripts into reproducible copy—perhaps especially—for short-run publishing, including scholarly monographs. (The author is already doing the work anyhow—i.e., composing—and the possibilities are said to be, as possibilities almost always are, endless. But there are as yet no universals, no established standards for the hardware, and, as with booksellers/wholesalers/librarians, and publishers, system-to-system matching remains a difficulty.) Excellent, too, are the potentialities for disaster, with instant erasure or deletion as possible as accuracy. The opportunities to save both time and money are real. But for the editing of books, in the sense of what happens between an author and editor, the word processor does not yet show many advantages, except for producing clean copies of the manuscript when the author revises after editing. But for too long, the basic costs—of paper, printing, binding—have not been reduced materially. The nation suffers a shortage of technical as well as social invention.

In 1976 I said that publishing is not suffering from Future Shock, the supposedly onrushing future that is overwhelming us with technological changes and improvements. Rather, it is hampered by a receding technological future. The technology of the past weighs us down. In this vein, Joan Manley, vice-president of Time, Inc., asked the Book Manufacturing Institute: Where are the "innovators and inventors who should be easing the weight of past technology? Are they not there in the numbers we need because we think we cannot afford them?" She reminded the manufacturers that technological breakthroughs do not come on the cheap, that other industries recognize the importance of research and development. The National Science Foundation, she said, reports that all industries spent in general about 2 percent of their gross receipts on R&D in a recent year, when printers and publishers spent only 0.6 percent on the same effort.[22] In the end, or in the future, it may not matter, for conventional printing is being overtaken in several aspects by electronic reproduction, and printers will find themselves, like coopers and blacksmiths, technologically obsolescent.

And we are still tearing down trees to make paper. Can our vaunted technological community come up with nothing better?

The Politics of Publishing—What are they, not just those of altered textbooks, responding to ethnic or market pressures (often at odds—too few black faces; not enough yellow or white ones; etc.), but the politics of "general publishing," where most lists appear to be predominantly left of center, and only one or two houses identified as on the right? Publishers profess to have no politics, but their lists belie their claim.

Why do we divide the world of literature into the two categories of "fiction" and "nonfiction"? What *is* nonfiction, after all? It includes poetry, which at its best is truth, but is not limited to the factual. It includes biography, history, belles lettres, religion, instruction, sciences (soft, social, hard, practical, theoretical). It includes, in short, everything that the word "fiction" does not. It is, in other words, "everything else." Thus nonfiction is an inept, inappropriate, inelegant, unuseful hybrid, a nondescript nondescription.

Who is responsible for facts, claims, charges, in a book? This unresolved debate flared a few years ago. The author alone is responsible, says the publisher; there is no way for us to know. The publisher, says the author; there is no way for me to accept full responsibility alone. (This issue is at the heart of contractual questions about who shall insure whom, when one party tries to hold the other responsible or tries to be held harmless.)

What of the increasing tendency to blur the lines that once delimited fiction, history, the memoir, journalism, biography? And should there be a truth-in-packaging law applied to authors and publishers? Can the public be protected about reckless claims or mislabeling, even if it cannot be defended against hyperbole? Not only a few cynically commercial publishers practice deception; university presses tend to put definitive titles on narrow gauge studies published in volume form. Publishers and writers, especially journalistic ones, enjoy the First Amendment freedoms designed for the reader, the public, and regularly abuse them. This is part of the reason for the rage expressed against reporters, writers, editors, publishers, and broadcasters from right and left.

This condition is aggravated by publishing's refusal to follow the prescriptions and proscriptions proffered by literary watchdogs, antiliterary vigilantes, and other counselors who push opportunities for narrowness or bankruptcy. We will never be above suspicion; we must try not to lose even more respect for our work, our wares, and ourselves. Those who flourish in freedom, unfettered by formal and fixed responsibilities, must be the most responsible people of all.

If the community of the book is to progress beyond its usual limits, we must challenge the usual assumptions—about reading and the reader, about the writer, the book, the publisher, and the bookseller, and other related people, practices, processes. If we are to raise the standards of performance, we have to set aside the standard presumptions—our elitism, defeatism, the mind-set of We Happy Few, the usual dizzy "data."

The assumptions that most need shaking are those we hold near and dear. One is the unhappy tendency to divide all issues within the community into "we" versus "they." Of the industry, those who are inside are considered "book people"; all others are not, and are, when they come close, beyond the pale, beyond consideration. Of publishers, there are said to be "good" publishers versus "commercial" publishers, "literary" or "serious" publishers versus all others. Within a publishing house, astonishing prejudices still exist, notably the conviction on the part of editors, reviewers, and some—but not all—authors that editors are the soul and substance of the business, a belief reinforced by agents, librarians, and others, when they are, momentarily, not inflamed over some editorial insufficiency. The editor *uber alles* reflects an underappreciation of what is done by sales, promotion, and business departments. Inventory management, that is to say, setting printings, is the third most difficult decision in publishing after the first two, editorial judgment and the publisher's decision about whether to publish or not. Nevertheless, the unfortunate assumption persists that "noneditorial" people in publishing are semiliterate and are at the service of editors, rather than publishing specialists in their own right, with their own rights.

To be sure, imbalance of any kind is a poor idea, no matter what direction a house may be tilting. When one executive arrived to take charge of the publishing division of a national religious organization, he found that they had more accountants on the payroll than editors. "Ah," said Werner Mark Linz, the new publisher, "I see we're in the accounting business, not the publishing business." Still, defamations of accountants are commonplace, as if all accountants must be minimally human, interested only in The Numbers and unable to read anything except balance sheets. In a healthy publishing house, many opinions are taken into consideration, if not taken as definitive, because each person's opinion is worth something—as reader, as citizen, as a member of the firm.

These "class" distinctions are at times well founded but more often are based solely on bias. Such attitudes constitute an unattractive form of occupational discrimination, the sort of prejudice that the prejudiced themselves find hateful when based on race or nationality.

Publishing is not an equal opportunity employer when one function or department—finance, sales, editorial, rights selling, administrative or managerial—is ascendant, dominant over others.

None of the arguments above are to suggest that the substitution of my opinions and examples for those of others has any importance. What could be important, and are vitally needed, are serious, substantial additions to our skimpy body of knowledge and insubstantial literature. Instead of the babble and the incoherence, we need more structured debates, more disciplined inquiries. We need more information and less opinion, and more skepticism about our own convictions. Not least, there is a need for the parties to come reasonably well prepared for discussion. We can serve the book in no better way than to read and think, to refuse to be glib, and not to allow one more unexamined "fact" to pass by.

We neither understand our successes nor successfully diagnose our illnesses when they occur. Not every slip is a landslide, not every miss a mile. What is needed are centers for the study of the book, reading, reproduction, and so on, and journals to publish the results—as we have in *Daedalus, Book Forum, The Wilson Quarterly, The Annals, Publishing History*—although we have no one journal to consistently publish the results of work in our several related fields. We need scholars and others to collate and sift and sort the results of research and other sources of information, not a series of separated fiefs. Perhaps we need a General Theory of the Book. What we do not need are facile declarations, the glimmering, glowering generality.

Where are we to get this information? From library schools, earlier studies, the associations of publishers and librarians, bookseller records, the studies done continually by newspaper and magazine publishers. Book club information is among the best and "hardest" in the business, and although closely guarded, some things can be extracted or shared. One book club expert said, for instance, that the members of a military book club are not heavily veterans of World War II. They are younger. The members of specialty book clubs, devoted to interests like cooking, science-fiction, mysteries, and so on, are not as "upscale" as members of general book clubs. What are the implications of this information? If there are more female names on book club rolls than male, are men underrepresented? Do women buy for men, sign the checks? Are men closet readers, who admit to reading biography or history but not fiction? We need limited and linked studies, done on a manageable scale.

Who is putting together the work of gifted teachers with the work of those dealing with reading and learning difficulties, with the work of researchers in optics, motor difficulties, ethnic and cultural considerations? Where is the center for more than just discussion of the book? What prospects are there for a center for advanced study of democratic reading and writing institutions?

Here and there, excellent research is under way. Robert Darnton, professor of history at Princeton, has written a publishing history of the *Encyclopédie,* and his article, "What Is the History of Books?" (*Daedalus,* Summer 1982) is a model inquiry, serious but not grim, especially his wonderful work on the trade records of one bookseller attempting to corner the new market in Voltaire.

Beyond study, we need a genuine sense of community. American writers sometimes lament their dispersal, as if it were displacement. American booksellers, librarians, and publishers see themselves as separate parishes. Lewis Coser and his associates found that editors spend less and less time with authors.[23] We are more preoccupied with the practice of publishing. The less we see of each other, the more misunderstandings arise.

Perhaps we are not a community after all; perhaps we merely populate Pluto's Republic, "each according to our own prejudices," as Sir Peter Medawar puts it. Pluto's Republic, Anthony Tucker says in a review of Medawar, is "the foggy intellectual underworld of misperception . . . the fuddled underworld we all inhabit from time to time," marked by an "absence of logic, philosophical philanderings and misconceptions, . . . failures to confront reality or sift order out of chaos." Within the Republic "are all thinkers who regard rhapsodic intellection as an adequate substitute for the process of ratiocination."[24]

It is convenient to think about ourselves as the Community of the Book. But perhaps we are destined to remain a series of separate states, warring factions, shouting imprecations at each other across borders, with occasional skirmishes and now and then a six-day war. I hope not. For we are bound up in common concerns and causes; we do need each other, and for the usual reasons—because we are mutually dependent. "The word community," writes Henri J.M. Nouwen,

expresses a certain supportive and nurturing way of living and working together. When someone says, "I miss a sense of community here; something should be done to build a better community," she or he is probably suffering from alienation, loneliness, or lack of mutual support and cooperation. . . . It is therefore not strange that for quite a few critical observers of the contemporary scene, the word community has become associated with sentimentalism, romanticism, and even melancholy.[25]

Nouwen writes of the Christian community, but such thoughts apply to the Community of the Book as well. A community exists or comes together for the purpose of sustenance, shelter, support, safety, convenience, comfort, shared values. Communities are based, writes L.J. Vaughan, "on blood, family, kin, clan, race, ideology, love, shared goals."[26] All communities have their factions and their problems, and we are not lacking in ours. The factions take up positions. Snipers are posted in the trees. We send out scouts. But our reconnaissance, our intelligence gathering, is faulty.

We are eloquent on our weaknesses and fail to recognize our strengths. We are so concerned with calamity that we cannot see continuity. It has often been said, Eric Larrabee writes, "that the struggle of American consciousness has been to reconcile independence with interdependence, the one with the many."[27]

The search for community is not new, as Charles Handy writes: St. Benedict praised the idea when he founded his first monastery in the seventh century: "a community in which all were equal yet each was different, a community where each person's effort contributed to some common task or mission . . . where privacy and mutual aid were both important."[28]

Ours is a community of sorts, a pleasant, if troubled, place. Without crisis we feel threatened. Our institutions are smaller than they seem, our total numbers larger and of more significance than we sometimes think. We have our centers, suburbs, ghettoes, lords of the manor, and houses on the hill. Most of our officials are self-appointed, including those who, like myself, issue armchair generalizations. Our time and talents are taken up, much of the time, with activities of interest and importance—the transmission of ideas and analyses, the telling of tales. The community has its attractions and its attractive people, and an ebullient optimism, coupled with a streak of fatalism, that is among its most appealing, foolish, and basic features. The mass of work done is middling; the overall conduct and character of the community is characterized, falsely, by what happens at the extremes. Here, the norm is no more interesting than elsewhere, and the good news is no news.

Where is this place? Some say it is a state of mind. At moments, it looks like a state of mindlessness. Sensitivity is everywhere, but sense is uncommon, and many of our outstanding citizens are brilliant but not smart. Indians are always thought to be circling out there in the dark, and around here, everybody sees almost everybody else as an Indian.

We like it here. Our frictions make possible, indeed are essential to, the community's light, heat, and warmth.

ENDNOTES

[1] The figures available always seem large. John P. Dessauer (*Publishers Weekly*, December 17, 1982) places "relevant 1981 domestic consumer purchases at 1.34 billion units, yielding $5.76 billion in retail level sales and $4.12 billion in publishers' revenues." But as Dessauer and other industry analysts often point out, total sales of all book publishing of all kinds often amount to less than the net profits of any one of a number of truly large U.S. individual *companies*.

AT&T and Exxon, for instance, in 1981 had net profits of over $6.8 billion and $5.5 billion (*Forbes*, May 10, 1982). Again, publishing industry sales are said to be big—but every company that made the *Forbes* "500" list had sales of over $1 billion, and 110 of them now have more than $5 billion.

The few publishing companies that make the *Fortune* and *Forbes* 500 lists are those which include other and more profitable activities—magazines, broadcasting, and so on; i.e., Time, Inc.; The Readers Digest; McGraw-Hill; Times-Mirror (and Doubleday, whose figures, as a private corporation, are not published).

What is more interesting is that book publishing's influence, reach, range, presumed power, and prestige, for greater or lesser good, are out of all proportion to its dollar-ranking as an industry.

[2] Dessauer sums up the "explosive growth" of small publishing houses (as had Doebler) in *Publishers Weekly*, December 17, 1982.

[3] See also "Small Publisher Power," by Judith Applebaum, *Publishers Weekly*, September 10, 1982.

[4] Ibid., pp. 24, 25.

[5] Ibid., pp. 25-26.

[6] "American Book Title Production," *Publishers Weekly*, October 1, 1982, p. 40. The fiction totals can be misleading, thanks to what Bowker's *Weekly Record* confesses is "a considerable undercount of mass market paperbacks" in 1979 and 1980.

[7] June 15, 1982.

[8] July 27, 1982.

[9] Unpublished version of a manuscript by Benjamin, later revised for *Publishers Weekly*.

[10] September 24, 1982, p. 16.

[11] *Publishers Weekly*, October 1, 1982. Also, Association of American Publishers *Newsletter*, October 1982. The gap between publishers' concern and action is footnoted in a summary of "The Year in Review" for the AAP: "A major initiative undertaken during the year was the effort to find a special niche for publishers in the widening war on illiteracy, low reading skills, and low reading motivation." After letters to President Reagan urging a "Business Committee for Literacy," and pledges by twenty publishers, "at year's end the committee had not been established and no pledged money had been collected or spent."

[12] Leslie Fiedler, *What Was Literature?: Class Culture and Mass Society* (New York: Simon and Schuster, 1982).

[13]Herbert Mitgang, *New York Times,* November 14, 1978. *Library of Congress Information Bulletin* 37 (46) (November 17, 1978).

[14]*Saturday Review,* "Trade Winds, America's Reading," Walter Arnold, January 20, 1979.

[15]Samuel S. Vaughan, "The Quest for the 'Average Reader' is an Endless Game of Fiction," *New York Times Book Review,* December 29, 1963. Bernard Berelson, *The Library's Public* (New York: Columbia University Press, 1949).

[16]Information on U.S. households where English is not spoken or is not the first language is from *American Demographics,* July/August 1982; on library use, from "The Good News about Library Visitors," pamphlet published by the American Library Association, based on a study for the White House Conference on Libraries and Information Services, 1979.

[17]Poirier quote is from *Raritan.*

[18]Revised edition, 1958, Faber & Faber, London, p. 7. First published in the United States in 1977 by Overlook Press.

[19]Dr. Bogart has written extensively on print, especially vis-à-vis television, in *The Wilson Quarterly* issue on media, 1982, and in *The Age of Television.*

[20]From "Authors and Writers," in *A Barthes Reader,* edited by Susan Sontag (New York: Hill and Wang, 1982), p. 185. Reprinted from his *Critical Essays.*

[21]Paul Cowan, "A Fight over America's Future," in *The Tribes of America,* chapter 4 (New York: Doubleday, 1979), p. 77; previously published in *The Village Voice.*

[22]Reported in *Publishers Weekly;* followed by a report, December 3, 1982, entitled "1982 Was a Year of 'Technological Restraint.' " See also, "Technology, Enterprise, and American Economic Growth," by Jordan D. Lewis, *Science,* March 5, 1982, abstracted in *The Wilson Quarterly,* Autumn 1982, to the effect that the United States leads in corporate R&D as a percentage of industrial output at 1.9 percent—but "Americans concentrate on products for the immediate future, while leading foreign companies look decades ahead."

[23]Lewis A. Coser, Charles Kadushin, Walter W. Powell, *Books: The Culture & Commerce of Publishing* (New York: Basic Books, 1982).

[24]Anthony Tucker, "Poor Pluto," *The Guardian,* October 14, 1982.

[25]Donald P. McNeil, Douglas A. Morrison, and Henri J.M. Nouwen, *Compassion* (New York: Doubleday, 1982).

[26]In a letter to the author, November 1982.

[27]Buffalo *Courier-Express,* August 10, 1980.

[28]Charles Handy, *Gods of Management* (London: Souvenir Press, 1978; reprinted London: Pan Books, 1979).

Dan Lacy

Reading in an Audiovisual and Electronic Era

WANDERING TRIBESMEN with tales of what lay beyond the distant range or river, old men with memories of their own past and of their fathers' and grandfathers' memories, prophets who professed knowledge of the future—all have from time out of mind helped to fill the hunger of men and women to escape the narrow scope and brief moment of their lives. But the living word, fixed in no enduring form, swirled and rearranged itself in myth, and mankind emerged from a fabled and dream-haunted past to live in a world where monsters and boiling seas and magic mountains lay only a few days' journeys away.

Writing, which fixed words in unchangeable order, made possible the creation of a reliable history and, within limits, a known geography. Thucydides and Tacitus, Strabo and Herodotus, were knowledge-bearers, not myth-makers. Until the invention of printing, however, this possession of real knowledge of what lay beyond men's own eyes and memories was confined to the literate few with access to precious manuscripts. The growth of science was greatly handicapped by the inability to generate and distribute uniform texts that could be relied on by investigators spread across a continent. Thus the leap of knowledge that came in the sixteenth and seventeenth centuries was both print-born and print-borne.

In the first two centuries of print, many other inventions enlarged the capacity of humans to transcend their immediate experience, among them, the telescope, the microscope, reliable time-pieces, and ships adapted for transoceanic voyages. The development of a more powerful mathematics, especially the calculus in the late seventeenth century, greatly enhanced man's ability to organize newly discovered data in meaningful patterns.

Print made possible rapid, wide sharing of the new knowledge. Reports of voyages to Asia and to the newly discovered American continents, describing their geography, flora, fauna, minerals, and human inhabitants, were read avidly, and became the impetus for further voyages. Equally valuable was the new ability of scientists to distribute widely, relatively quickly, and in a fixed form and uniform state the results of their observations. Man's ability to know distant lands, even distant planets, and to achieve a deeper understanding of natural processes was greatly enhanced.

So, too, was the ability to know the past. The world's documented past had existed precariously in few handwritten copies subject to loss and decay, and imperiled by errors in transcription. The enormous multiplication of copies of these works and the increased ability to compare copies made possible the technical skills of editing, verification, and textual analysis, and focused attention on the past. There was a renaissance of the knowledge of antiquity that gave its name to the era. Print also facilitated not merely the preservation and dissemination of knowledge, but also its rapid accumulation, as each new student could in turn command and build on the published works of those who preceded him.

By the late nineteenth century, the processes by which verified knowledge was established and transmitted were both professionalized and institutionalized. It became possible to earn a living as a physicist or historian or philologist, and hence to devote one's full time to the discipline. Learned societies organized by discipline gave a specific focus not found in prior general academies, and created professional corps with a sense of collaboration in a shared undertaking. Universities became centers of research as well as of teaching. Learned journals multiplied, and university presses were created to provide additional means of recording and disseminating the rapidly increasing outflow of the products of research. Libraries became the centers of universities, and public libraries were created to bring the broad resources of books to the people generally.

During the same decades, a series of concurrent developments greatly widened public access to the flow of print-recorded knowledge. Steam-powered cylindrical presses, stereotype plates, and paper mass-produced from woodpulp greatly increased the output and diminished the price of printed matter. By the end of the century, several hundred times as many pages were printed per capita as at its beginning. The invention of the telegraph and the laying of the Atlantic cable enormously enhanced the speed and efficiency with which the press could convey the news; and the completion of a rail network made practical the swift nationwide distribution of magazines and books. Nearly universal elementary education and widespread literacy opened a broad public market for this enormous flow of print. With the penny newspaper and cheap magazines and books, print became a mass medium.

Indeed, during the period that in the United States extended roughly from the Civil War to the First World War, print played—as it never had before and never would again—a dominant and exclusive role. Almost all adults in the United States (as in Canada and Western Europe) could read and, moreover, had access to an abundance of print at a cost they could afford. And print was the *only* means, other than word-of-mouth, by which they could learn of things beyond their personal experience.

It was during this era of total print dominance that our contemporary educational system took shape, with an elementary curriculum primarily devoted to teaching children the skills of reading and writing and the comparably abstract techniques of numerical manipulation. High school and college were devoted to the use of these skills to extract knowledge from the accumulated wealth of print and, at the postgraduate level, to contribute further to it. It is no accident that a popular term for education was "book-learning."

In the decades since 1920, two major waves of change have overthrown print's dominance. The first was the audiovisual revolution. It was based on the late nineteenth century inventions of the phonograph and the motion picture and the early twentieth century discovery of radio, but its more important social impact came after the First World War. By the end of the postwar decade, most Americans had abundant access to all three. The speeches of political leaders could be heard rather than read; news had a visual impact through the newsreel. Films rather than novels became the major means of suggesting what life in other times and places and among other social groups and classes was like. It became possible for persons outside large cities to hear great music professionally performed. A more direct access was provided to the range of experience beyond life's daily ambit.

The power of the audiovisual revolution was enormously increased when television became widely available after the Second World War. Within an amazingly few years, television could be received in more than 90 percent of the homes in America, and the average American was spending several hours a day before the screen. Daily, hundreds of millions of hours previously spent in other ways were transferred to television-watching. Probably never before in history had so massive a change in social habit been achieved in so very brief a time.

Some of the change wrought by TV may have been less important than it seemed. To a considerable degree, TV was simply a way to see movies more cheaply and without leaving home. Much of what was shown on TV did indeed consist of films previously shown in motion picture theaters, and much of what was created specifically for TV was very like the movies both in technique and in the recreational functions it served. But the amount of time devoted to the medium, even granting the similarity of the content, was so large as to be very important in itself.

Yet through its news and documentary programs, television emerged as a truly new medium. Radio had already imparted some of the instant availability of news as well as the sense of actual presence, as in Edward R. Murrow's wartime broadcasts from London or Roosevelt's fireside chats. And the newsreels and the rare filmed documentary had provided precedents for television. But the nearly universal attention to television as the principal source of news about events here and abroad, of information about politics and social conditions, about the nature of other cultures and about science, was quite extraordinary. In barely more than a decade, television replaced the newspaper as the principal source of news and, indeed, replaced print in general as the foremost means by which most Americans came to perceive reality beyond their daily experience.

In our own decade there is yet another revolution, that of the computer and its related technology of data communication. The dramatic decrease in the cost of computers has opened their use to people in general. It will probably become quite common to be able, in one's home or office, to call up almost instantly, from enormous banks of information, the particular set of data one seeks and to manipulate it and array it with extraordinary power. Texts and images as well as numerical data can be stored with incredible compactness on laser disks and recalled through the computer's extraordinary searching power, thus creating still additional possibilities. Enthusiasts for the new information technology believe that it will replace or diminish the role of a whole series of industries and institutions: the newspaper, the journal, the book, the library.

The two revolutions—audiovisual and electronic—provide a range of alternatives to communication hitherto carried by print, and promise as well the possibility of many kinds of communication not achievable at all through print: the sound of speech and music, the vision of motion and color, the perception of events as they occur, the instant conveyance of constantly changing data. The average American every week spends several times as many hours with the new media as he or she does reading. The exclusive role of print to provide the reality that lies beyond personal experience has been shattered forever.

How has this affected the role of reading, and what difference does it make? The sheer production of printed matter has been affected less than one would expect. The number of newspapers has declined sharply, and urban evening newspapers have been especially affected. Few cities can any longer support more than one newspaper, very few, indeed, more than two. Television is not only a far more widely used source of news, but a more trusted one. Mass circulation magazines directly competitive with television for audience and advertisers, like the *Saturday Evening Post, Life, Look, American,* and *Colliers,* have died. Yet surviving urban newspapers and a growing number of suburban newspaper chains are highly prosperous, and the magazine industry, with its myriad journals catering for special tastes and interests, is thriving.

The total number of books published annually has approximately quadrupled since television became generally available. Sales of books, as measured in copies rather than dollars, increased rapidly in the early days of television, though they have tended to level off in recent years. Library circulation has been flat or declining in recent years, but this may be reflective more of weakened community support, declining educational enrollments, and the availability of relatively inexpensive paperbacks than any public decline in reading.

None of these statistics gives any clear picture of the amount of reading actually done in our society, but a considerable increase— certainly no such decay as has long been prophesied—appears to have taken place. Our society is by no means ready to say, as in the title of Anthony Smith's recent book, goodbye to Gutenberg.

Yet the functions of print are changing. It is still the indispensable recorder and conveyor of research results and other scholarly activity. In fact, much of the increase in the number of books and journals published reflects the heightened level of such activity. Similarly, though there are marginal and, in some cases, growing uses of audiovisual materials and computers in the classroom, print is still the principal medium of formal education. Finally, there is a substantial increase in recreational reading of various kinds of subliterary novels, among them, romances, "Gothic" stories, suspense stories, and science fiction.

But for all these continuing strengths, reading is no longer the main, indeed almost the only, way of extending personal experience. Most people today decide whom they will vote for, what they believe about atomic weapons control or unemployment, how they perceive the issues of the Middle East, what they conceive China to be like, how they envision the history of man, much more from what they observe on television than from what they read. Beyond the bounds of our daily lives, we all react not to reality, but to an *image* of reality, created for us through the media of communication, and in the last generation, the nature of the media that create this image has changed fundamentally.

Does that matter? Is the image more clear? Less clear? Are our reactions more responsive and meaningful? Or are they being confused and made irrelevant? I suggest that it does matter, that the way we perceive external reality through the audiovisual media is a quite different process from that of perceiving it through the medium of print, and that the quality of our perception is now more important than ever before in our history.

That the quality of our perception of reality not experienced directly is important seems clear enough. In the simpler days of our national growth, the great issues we confronted were perhaps as demanding as those we face today, but they lay within the everyday experience of ordinary citizens: British versus local rule, taxation of the unrepresented, a strong or weak union, slavery or freedom, regulation of railroads or submission to their economic dominance. Issues today involve distant lands and peoples, complex economic and governmental issues, esoteric scientific questions. No ordinary citizen on the basis of personal experience alone can have a useful opinion about what our policy should be toward the Middle East—or toward Russia or China or Japan or the Caribbean—or the control of nuclear energy and nuclear weapons, or the reduction of unemployment. The more crucial the issue to public well-being or even to national survival, the more likely its sound resolution depends on knowledge that most of us can achieve only at second hand, through one medium or another. Moreover, a consequence of the increasing involvement of the total population in the flow of the media is the near-instant stimulation and impact of public opinion. Our Constitution was evolved during weeks of secrecy by a few dozen men, unvexed by public pressures; any such effort today would be harassed into impotence by unceasing public pressures. Public opinion narrowly limits the discretion of authority in every major policy question, so that those who govern us cannot be wiser than we are.

But the demands on us for comprehension of what lies beyond the daily sweep of our eyes is not confined to the demands of public policy decision. The extraordinary enhancement of the power of human observation by instruments ranging from the electron microscope to the X-ray telescope, and by techniques of chemical and physical analysis using spectrography, radioactive tracers, lasers, and other devices, plus the enormous achievements made in synthesizing intelligence, have made it possible, in the last century, to construct a perception of the universe utterly beyond anything suggested by direct experience: a universe of billions of galaxies, each composed of billions of stars and presumably of solar systems, lasting for tens of billions of years and perhaps for repeated cycles of compression and explosion, each extending over reaches so near to infinity that light itself may require billions of years to traverse them. At the same time, we have discovered that the human race is hundreds of thousands of years older than it was thought to be, and is linked with all other forms of life in a common flow of being. And our conception of the nature of the genetic and biochemical processes that determine the forms and processes of life, intelligence, and self-consciousness itself has been revolutionized.

The comprehension of all this total restructuring of the conceived reality of the universe, of life, and of man's relation to them can of course be achieved only at second hand, through the reception of messages through media of communication. In what ways, then, does it matter how—through which medium—our perception of reality beyond our direct observation is formed? To answer this, one has to begin with the function of words themselves. All words are necessarily abstractions, reaching into the swirling totality of experience and singling out a specific aspect for identification. To put a group of words together in a sentence is not merely to abstract a number of single bits of the surrounding experience, but to assert a structured relationship among them. Even the simplest sentence describing an ordinary event is an extraordinarily complex intellectual exercise, in which human meaning is imposed on a fragment of experience. This is true, of course, of speech as well as writing; but speech conveys more than the words say. Speech is a kind of action itself, bearing a freight of emotional overtone; and informal speech, in particular, may not represent a considered and digested conceptual organization of experience, but rather an instinctive reaction.

Writing distances the reader yet farther from reality than speech does the listener. An event is still described rather than experienced directly, but here the reader is removed from the writer as well as from the event. The overtones of pitch and cadence and gesture are gone; the words lie mutely on the page, stripped of their emotional penumbra.

Print lies at an even further remove. Intended for a large audience, and usually for indefinite preservation, the words are chosen and arranged with greater care. An impersonal formality takes the place of the casualness of, for example, the personal letter.

To convey meaning through print is a demanding enterprise. From an unbounded flow of reality, the author must abstract just those elements—an almost infinitely small fraction of the whole—that he will attempt to convey; must define each by selecting a particular word for each; must describe how he believes these elements relate to each other by arranging the words into sentences (and in more extended communication, such as print is commonly used for, the sentences into paragraphs, hence into chapters, and into the whole complex architecture of a treatise); and must encode all this into complex patterns of ink on paper. The reader, in turn, must decode these patterns, perceive a meaning for each of the words, and construct an image of the complex structure of conceived reality the author has created. It is simply impossible for any idea or information to be conveyed by print without both author and reader having *thought* intensively about the message.

This mode of communication—abstract, formal, and fixed—of course sacrifices much of reality as it may be conveyed through the audiovisual media. To read a description of a Mozart quartet is but a thin and desiccated experience as compared with hearing it by record or radio; to read a description of a sunset or of an El Greco painting is similarly but a poor substitute for seeing it on a slide or film, on a high-definition television screen, or in a color print (which is really an audiovisual rather than a verbal-print form). So, too, the reports of correspondents in earlier wars affected us far less directly and emotionally than the televised scenes of the Vietnam War. No description of a presidential candidate or printed text of his speech can quite convey the living sense of the man as we see and hear him deliver it on a television screen.

Yet the very distancing that separates the reader from reality described is the price paid for understanding and mastery. *Meaning* is a phenomenon created by the reduction of experience into words organized in sentences. The process of understanding is the very process involved in reducing an event to writing. A television documentary about El Salvador or Lebanon can help the viewer create an image more vivid and moving than any conveyed by print; but unless the documentary is accompanied by a spoken analysis—which is, essentially, print read aloud—the documentary will fail to give the auditor the kind of understanding, the kind of *meaning*, he would derive, say, from an article in *Foreign Affairs*. Reading is inherently a different way of constructing an image of reality than is viewing or listening. And it is an indispensable one when the purpose is to require a structured understanding, rather than an impression or an emotional experience, of reality.

There are two other rather obvious ways in which communication by reading printed matter differs from communication by watching or listening to television, radio, films, or records. One is simply the ability to present a substantial *mass* of information: the content of a single issue of the *New York Times* covers far more than a week's television news programming, and a book affords the only realistic medium for presenting an extensive, structured, and detailed treatment of a subject. The other is the almost infinitely wider range of choice of subject and treatment offered the reader as contrasted with the radio listener or the television viewer. The thrust of the broadcast media, by reason of their very technology, has been to assemble larger and larger audiences for fewer and fewer sources. A prime-time network television program with fewer than 10 million simultaneous viewers can hardly be sustained. In very recent years, this situation has improved substantially, as FM radio, cable television, videocassette recordings, and videodisks have greatly increased the range of individual choice. But there are thousands of magazines, catering to every interest; and the most meager of bookstores or the smallest public library offers incomparably wider opportunities to pursue inquiries or individual tastes than the totality of audiovisual media available at any one time.

The other alternative to reading that has developed in our time is the computer with its related telecommunications facility. In fact, the computer, by increasing the efficiency of editing and printing, providing powerful bibliographic and indexing services, and simplifying library services, does far more to facilitate than to replace traditional reading. But the growing use of electronic publishing and information dissemination does give emphasis to a concept of what it is important to communicate that is widely at variance with that of traditional reading. It is customary to describe a reservoir of knowledge to be disseminated electronically as a "databank" or "database." This is significant, for it reveals the assumption that important knowledge consists of an accumulation of discrete facts, and that the function of at least this medium of information is to select out of the accumulation and deliver the individual facts or collection of facts that have been called for. It assumes that the needs and mode of thought of an inquirer are analogous to those of someone who looks up a number in a telephone directory or consults a dictionary, not those of someone who reads a novel or a biography or a poem. And the oft-expressed conviction that the computer will make the book obsolete reveals a perhaps unconscious, but arid and constricted, belief regarding the nature of important knowledge and important communication.

This is not to question the major and very valuable social roles in communication—roles quite beyond the power of print and reading—that the audiovisual media and computer will play. The color, vividness, and immediacy of the audiovisual media have enriched the lives of all of us. And they have enormously increased the perceptive outreach of most people, for most of the time devoted to viewing or listening occupies hours that had been devoted not to reading, but to activities that did not extend beyond the daily round, and perhaps to inactivity. There can be no question that the audiovisual media have extended and enlarged, for untold numbers of people, an awareness of other lands, other times, other ideas than their own. So, too, has the computer given us powers without which modern society could not operate, and has enhanced immeasurably the capacity of human intelligence to analyze and organize experience.

But neither provides what reading offers as a bridge to the universe of experience beyond our daily ambit. The one can bathe us directly in the unexamined flow of experience, but without the processes of abstraction and organization that give it meaning. The other can give a command over discrete facts scraped bare of penumbral meaning, but does not provide the holistic gathering of experience or endow it with a human conceptual structure.

It is well for our society that the audiovisual and electronic revolutions have complemented print, not replaced it, and that reading vigorously survives as the means of establishing a bridge of meaning, both human and thoughtful, between ourselves and the totality beyond us: a bridge between our culture and other cultures, between ourselves and the infinitely vast and infinitely microscopic world of science, and between our present and the past and the future. Without reading, meaning and comprehension could dissolve into "feeling" or splinter into data, the awareness and integrity of individual identity and purpose could be but ill sustained, and Burke's sense of society as an all-embracing compact of the living with the dead and those yet unborn could not be achieved.

Benjamin M. Compaine

The New Literacy

*I believe books will never disappear. It is impossible
for it to happen. Of all of mankind's diverse tools, undoubtedly the most astonishing are his books. . . . If
books were to disappear, history would disappear. So
would men.*
                                        —Jorge Luis Borges[1]

Reading and writing will become obsolete skills.
                                        —Sol Cornberg[2]

O N ANY GIVEN WORK day, perhaps 7 million employed people are paid to spend their time in front of a television
screen. They are not watching "General Hospital," but
rather, are reading material produced by a computer. These people
are airline reservations clerks and travel agents, stockbrokers, newspaper reporters and editors, catalog showroom order-takers, and
customer service representatives at telephone, utility, and other sorts
of firms. Among the 7 million, there are secretaries and, to a small
but increasing extent, executives. They clearly have many different
jobs and levels of responsibilities, but they all share one trait: more
and more, they are using the computer for some portion of their
information storage and retrieval. And instead of using a computer
specialist as an intermediary, as they would have done only a few
years ago, they are interacting directly with the computer. This
means that much of what they read appears on a video display terminal—a VDT—instead of in ink on paper.

This essay is about the implications of the skills these workers are
developing. It is about the possible significance of the *$8 billion* spent
on video games in 1981—more than was spent on movie theater

admissions and record purchases combined. It is about the phenomenon of using microcomputers in elementary and secondary schools—often at the insistence of kids and their parents, before the curriculum supervisors know what's happening. It is about computer summer camps for kids. It concerns the wired university.

My objective here is to describe several of the forces and trends at work in society—only in part a function of technology—and the implications of these for traditional concepts of literacy. Central to this discussion is the role of the engine of this change, the computer, and hence "computer literacy."

In this essay, I do *not* predict the future. Nor do I advocate a course of action: I aim to neither salute nor denigrate the idea of a new literacy. But change is clearly in the wind. This essay, then, suggests that factors may impinge on future developments in reading and literacy, and that those who consider themselves to be educated and, above all, literate will want to take heed.

THE OLD LITERACY

We cannot talk about the future of reading or the book without reference to their fellow traveler, literacy. Each generation tends to assume literacy is static, petrified, as it were, in their moment of time. Literacy, however, is dynamic, a bundle of culturally relevant skills. The appropriate skills for literacy, moreover, have changed over time. Before the written record came into wide use (in England, starting in the last half of the eleventh century), the oral tradition predominated. To be literate meant the ability to compose and recite orally. In the twelfth century, to make a "record" of something meant to bear oral witness, not to produce a document for others to read. Even if a treaty was in the form of sealed letters, "both parties also named witnesses who were to make legal record . . . in court if necessary." Despite the existence of written documents, "the spoken word was the legally valid record."[3]

Furthermore, at that time, to be *litteratus* meant to know Latin, rather than having only the specific ability to read and write. To be sure, the vernacular replaced Latin for discourse. But even then, because of the difficulty of writing with a quill on parchment or with a stylus on wax, writing was considered a special skill that "was not automatically coupled with the ability to read."[4] The most common way of committing words to writing in twelfth century England was by dictating to a scribe, who was a craftsman and not necessarily himself able to compose. Thus, reading and dictating were typically paired, rather than reading and writing.

Although the basic skills of modern literacy—reading and writing—had become relatively widespread in England by the mid-nineteenth century, the literati of the period seemed to impose a greater barrier for admission to full-fledged literacy. It was not merely the ability to read, they said, but the reading of the "right" materials that separated the truly literate from the great unwashed. How, if at all, they asked, did the spread of the printed word contribute to the spiritual enrichment and intellectual enlightenment of the English nation? "More people were reading than ever before; but in the opinion of most commentators, they were reading the wrong things, for the wrong reasons, and in the wrong way."[5]

All this is grist for the notion that today's standards of literacy are rooted in the past, yet at the same time, should not be presumed to be the standard for the future. For example, at a recent meeting of "experts" convened to discuss the status of books and reading, several participants indicated that when they referred to the status of "the book," they had in mind great literature and intellectual enrichment. They were not referring to the 38,000 other titles (out of about 40,000) published annually that range from cookbooks and "how-to" books to Harlequin romances. Thus they were carrying on the tradition of the nineteenth century literati, who idealized their own past. They felt that things were far different—and infinitely better—in the old days.

Similarly, the library, today's bastion of the book and reading, has not always been held in such high regard by the literati. Free libraries for the common man in England were viciously criticized by the reading elite. Instead of encouraging "habits of study and self-improvement, they catered to the popular passion for light reading—above all, for fiction."[6] Indeed, one librarian told a meeting in 1879 that "schoolboys or students who took to novel reading to any great extent never made much progress in after life."[7] The irony of attitudes such as this should not be lost to the critics of video games as a corrupting influence on today's "schoolboys or students."

THE NEW LITERACY

"To describe our business as one that traffics in paper, ink, and type is to miss the point entirely. Our real enterprise is ideas and information." A quote from a futurist? Perhaps. This is the strategic outlook of W. Bradford Wiley, chairman of John Wiley & Sons, one of the oldest publishing houses in New York City, and publisher, in the nineteenth century, of Herman Melville, Nathaniel Hawthorne, and Edgar Allen Poe, and most of the first American editions of John Ruskin. Wiley adds, "Until now, our medium has been the bound book; tomorrow our medium will expand to include [computer-stored] data banks and video discs."[8]

What evidence is there that Wiley is onto something? First, he has recognized, at least implicitly, that Marshall McCluhan was off base. The medium, by and large, is *not* the message. The message is the content, and the medium is the way it is conveyed and displayed. *Content*—the ideas, knowledge, story, information, and so on—is the work of an author, a producer, a photographer. Technology, history, and even politics play a role in how this content is processed and the format in which it is ultimately displayed. *Process* incorporates the gathering, handling, storage, and transmission of the content; it may involve typewriters, computers, file cabinets; telephone lines, broadcasting towers, printing presses; and trucks and retail stores. *Format* is the manner of display—such as ink on paper, sound from a vibrating speaker cone, images on a cathode ray tube, light projected through a film, and so on.[9] Thus the content may be quite independent of the medium.

This article, for example, has been written at a standard typewriter keyboard. But instead of paper as the format, the letters appear on a green television screen. Although you are now reading this in a conventional ink on paper format, the process for creating this bound version may be quite different from that used only ten or twenty years ago. Computerized phototypesetting equipment has substantially replaced all the old Linotype machines that used to produce lead slugs for galleys. Moreover, there is no technological or perhaps even economic reason to keep subscribers to *Daedalus* from reading this article the same way it was written—on a video screen. It may be argued that someday it will be. The major barrier to this may be cultural: most of us have been brought up to read print on paper. Many adults would today recoil in horror at the thought of losing the feel and portability of printed volumes. But, as Wiley indicated, print is no longer the only rooster in the barnyard.

There are more solid trends that support Wiley's approach. One is the pervasive and perhaps long-run impact of video games. In short order, these have gone from barroom novelties to a worldwide phenomenon. In 1976 Atari's sales were $39 million; in 1981 they were

$1.23 billion, and may double in 1982 to $2.4 billion (about the size of Kellogg or Gillette). Americans may spend about $2 billion in 1982 on cartridges for home video games, and they will likely drop into video game machines this year considerably more than the 22 billion quarters they did in 1981. That money is coming from somewhere, most likely, from the implicit budget people have for other media and entertainment. This includes movie admissions, records, and, to some extent, books.

Even if the video game craze itself is a fad, it nonetheless may have considerable cultural significance, much as the dime novel or penny press had in earlier eras. For the first time, it has made the video tube into something other than a passive format for the masses. Heretofore, only a handful of specialists, mostly computer programmers and some designers, used VDTs as an interactive medium. The rest of the world sat back and watched on their television tube what others provided.

Moreover, while critics of video games decry the presumed ill effects of the video game parlors—much as their nineteenth century counterparts lamented the coming of literacy for the common reader—they may well prove to be myopic regarding the nature of the games themselves. As with much great literature, which can be appreciated on several levels of understanding, video games can be viewed on one level as simply entertainment. But in his book *How to Master Home Video Games,* Harvard undergraduate Tom Hirschfeld described these games as presenting players with a challenge. He notes that those who become the best at it are those who figure out the pattern programmed into the computer. The game players are becoming, almost painlessly, computer-literate. Without becoming computer experts, they may be intuitively learning the strengths and limitations of computer logic. The U.S. army, which must train large numbers of youngsters fresh from the video game rooms, understood the implications of the games almost immediately, and has already contracted for training exercises using video gamelike lessons played on microcomputers. The schools will no doubt follow.

The home video games are actually specialized personal computers. They have made consumers familiar with the concept of a computerized console that plugs into a video tube. All that a computer adds is a keyboard. Of the approximately 1.5 million personal desktop computers in use by the end of 1981, about 500,000 of these were in homes. With the Timex 1000, the retail price for a real, programmable computer has fallen to under $100. As a result, it is estimated that the number of computers in homes will triple by the end of 1982. Thus, unlike the situation in the 1960s when expensive computers in schools were imposed from the top—and computerized education failed miserably—we now see the development of grass-roots interests in having microcomputers in the schools. It is the kids and their parents who are often in the forefront of this effort, with local PTAs holding bake sales and the like to raise the money when school districts are pinched for funds. (In the past, some of that effort went to buying books for the school library.)

Thus, although educators are still concerned primarily with how students learn from print, young people today spend more time (about twenty-eight hours weekly by one study) using electronic devices, like television and electronic games, than with print (about twenty-five). Further, most of the discretionary time spent is with the electronic medium, while most of the time spent with printed material is involuntary.[10] Together with the video game trend, this suggests that schoolchildren of today are developing a new set of skills that may lead to a different standard for literacy.

But what about the 7 million or more adults working with VDTs as part of their daily routine? How will they approach the prospect of adopting at home tools similar to those they use in the workplace? Besides home computers, there are already a few such opportunities to retrieve and manipulate content, with a great many more in prospect. Services such as those offered by CompuServe Information Service and Source Telecomputing have already offered portions of newspapers such as the *New York Times* and the *Los Angeles Times* via computer to home terminals, in addition to a wide range of other types of information. Houghton Mifflin has produced an interactive videodisk version of Roger Tory Peterson's venerable bird identification books.

Three "videotext"[11] services, Oracle, Ceefax, and Prestel, have been commercially available in Great Britain since 1980. Prestel, the most ambitious, has been slow to achieve much popular interest, perhaps because of its cost, its strangeness, and the method required to access its voluminous information stores. Nonetheless, several videotext services that are in the prototype stage in the United States at this time may well be made available commercially by traditional publishing firms. These include Times Mirror Company (publisher of newspapers, books, and magazines), Knight-Ridder Newspapers (publisher of newspapers and books), and CBS Inc. (which, in addition to being the largest television network, also owns the publishing company Holt, Rinehart, & Winston and many well-known magazines). While the services offered by these firms are likely to tie together home terminals with large computers by telephone lines, the country's largest book and magazine publisher, Time Inc., has also tested a text-on-the-video-screen service to be delivered via cable.

That nonpublishers are getting into the act is a fact not lost on traditional publishers. Mead Corporation, one of the largest paper manufacturers, is also one of the most successful electronic publishers. On its NEXIS Service, it offers the full text of articles from the *Washington Post, Newsweek, U.S. News & World Report, Business Week,* UPI, Associated Press, Reuters news services, *Encyclopaedia Brittanica,* and scores of other publications. The company's LEXIS service is known by most lawyers and used by many. It provides nearly unlimited access to tens of thousands of laws and cases, at federal, state, and international levels, that often required days of work in a library. These services can be accessed by users who have received very little special training. Although the cost today restricts NEXIS and LEXIS to use in institutions, similar services may become as inexpensive over time as today's mainstream media.

The interest in "electronic publishing" is motivated by more than a mere fascination with technological toys. In part, there are some significant economic trends involved. The price of the paper used in book and magazine publishing has jumped substantially since the early 1970s, following years of only minimal increases. The cost of newsprint jumped 200 percent between 1970 and 1981, well over twice the rate of increase for all commodities. In large measure, these huge increases reflect the high energy component in the manufacture of paper. The physical distribution of printed material, moreover, especially newspapers, is highly energy-intensive. These cost trends contrast dramatically with the costs of computer-stored information, which have been declining at a rate of about 25 percent annually for the last thirty years. (Consider the magnitude of this decline: if the price of a Rolls Royce had decreased in proportion to that of computer storage, a Rolls Royce today would cost about $2.50.) The outlook for the foreseeable future is for continued similar decreases in cost.

As a preliminary indicator of the changing demand for new information skills in the workplace, Carolyn Frankel, a researcher with Harvard's Program on Information Resources Policy, surveyed the help-wanted ads in the *New York Times* for the same June day in 1977 through 1982. She counted all jobs or skills in those ads that mentioned some "computer literacy" skill, such as word processing, programming, data entry, and so on. In 1977, 5.8 percent of the want ads specified those skills. The percentage increased regularly to 1982, when 10.3 percent of the jobs listed required such skills. Perhaps of equal significance is the way these jobs were described. Earlier in the period, the ads were for specific jobs that implied a computer skill, such as "Wang operator" or "word processor." By 1982 conventional job titles such as secretary specified the required skills as "experience with word processing" or "knowledge of Sabre" (a computer system for travel agents). From this apparent trend, we can conclude that, as new technology becomes more commonplace and skills in it more widespread, the skills become incorporated into traditional jobs. When the power saw was a novelty, building contractors sought out "power-saw operators." But later on, when most carpenters were expected to have some familiarity with this tool, builders again began to seek out carpenters as such, carpenters who had, among other skills, knowledge of the power saw.

In 1977 none of the help-wanted ads for travel agents in the *Times* on the day surveyed mentioned any sort of computer skill; in 1980 one fifth mentioned a computer-related skill. By 1982, as a consequence of the implementation of computer reservations services by the industry, 71 percent required familiarity with such skills. Similarly, the number of bookkeeping jobs requiring computer-related skills doubled to 24 percent from 1977 to 1982; the proportion of secretary/typist want ads that required word processing skills went from zero in 1977 to 15 percent in 1982; and the number of jobs that were labeled "word processing" or that specified the ability to use a word processor, increased eightfold in that period, despite the recession in 1982 and a lower level of help-wanted ads overall.

The impact of all this in the workplace will be visible, if not profound. About $25,000 of capital is invested for every worker in a manufacturing setting, compared to approximately $4,000 for every office—or knowledge—worker, but that may change soon. In 1980 even an information-intensive company such as Aetna Life & Casualty Company had only one video terminal for each six employees; by 1985 they expect to have one terminal for every two employees. The ubiquity of these terminals and the increased familiarity workers will have with them may result in expanded application, such as electronically transmitted and stored "mail" both within an office and from remote office sites, including overseas offices.

Other indicies suggest that we are in the midst of a fundamental change in the way we receive and process information. A taxi service in Ottawa has eliminated the crackling radio heretofore used to dispatch taxis and replaced it with a video screen in the cab on which the messages flash. When the driver is called, a buzzer sounds and a fare's location is printed on the screen. Since no other driver gets that message, no one can beat him (or her) to the fare. The head of one cab company using the system likes it, he explained, because voice dispatching causes noise and confusion, not to mention slips of paper everywhere.

We now see centers of higher learning using computers in the liberal arts. Classics scholars at Princeton are studying Virgil with the help of a computer programmed to scan the text quickly, picking out passages that contain the same word used in different contexts. This reduces the drudgery, they claim, and allows them more time to study the meaning. Dartmouth applies similar analytical techniques to the Bible and Shakespeare. Apparently, students are integrating this technology into their academic lives as easily as they did the simpler calculator in the last decade.[12]

Even department stores and toy shops now carry computers so that consumers do not have to go into the threatening territory of a specialty store. At the same time, advertising campaigns by computer manufacturers are using well-known entertainers such as Bill Cosby and Dick Cavett in prime time commercials to further demystify their product.

COMBINING THE OLD AND THE NEW

Historically, the development of a literacy has gone through identifiable stages. Literacy starts with specialists, and then begins to have a wider impact on institutions, as it becomes the preferred medium of business, culture, and politics. Finally, it becomes so pervasive that even the masses are considered to be handicapped without it. We can trace modern notions of literacy from eleventh century England, in the movement from reliance on spoken words to written records, first in the Church and then in political institutions; to the introduction of the printing press in the fifteenth century; to the development of the newspaper and mass-consumed book along with popular education in the nineteenth.

History also suggests that one need not be fully literate to participate in literacy. One measure of changing literacy in twelfth and thirteenth century England was possession of a seal. In the reign of Edward the Confessor, only the king possessed a seal to authenticate documents. By the reign of Edward I (1307), even serfs were required by statute to have one.[13] In colonial times in the United States, signing one's name was skill enough to be called literate.

In the thirty-five or so years since the development of modern computers, we can identify trends similar to the much slower advance of traditional literacy. At first, computers were strictly for those who could read and write in the tongue of computer machine language, a "priestly" class whom all users of computers had to depend upon. As computers became more widespread and their application more pervasive, they began to have a greater impact on business and social institutions. The languages (COBOL, FORTRAN, BASIC, etc.) evolved into something closer to the vernacular, so that more people were able to learn to read and write computer language.

Today, we are perhaps at the threshold of an era where the computer is becoming so simple to use and inexpensive that the masses can use it without having to understand how it works. They can thus participate in computer literacy without necessarily being computer-literate. That may come in time, as the computer becomes as commonplace as the book. Yet, if we look at the computer as a tool, it may be no more necessary for the mass of people to understand how a computer works in order to use it than it is to understand the mechanics of the automobile's internal combustion engine in order to drive. (This suggests a nice parallel. In the 1950s, when the automobile was king, many boys were born "with a wrench in their hand." Today, we see kids who are barely teenagers playing around with RAM chips in much the same way.)

IMPLICATIONS FOR READING AND THE BOOK

It would be foolish, though perhaps fun, to speculate on the long-term societal impacts that may grow out of the trends I have described. As someone must surely have once said, "Predicting is a hazardous occupation, especially when it deals with the future." Moreover, while I have tried to identify some forces and trends relative to literacy and reading, there are other trends—cultural, political, and technological—that have not been included or even recognized as yet.

In the long term, it is possible, even probable, that the computer, combined with modern communications facilities, will be cited by historians of the future as a fundamental milestone for civilization, out of which many changes will be traced. What those changes will be cannot be foretold; it is difficult enough to understand the implications of our own historical antecedents. Elizabeth Eisenstein wrote: "It is one thing to describe how methods of book production changed after the mid-15th century. . . . It is another thing to decide how access to a greater abundance or variety of written records affected ways of learning, thinking, and perceiving among literate elites."[14]

In the near term, we might profitably think about computer skills as additional proficiencies in the bundle we call literacy. Note that I have referred to computer skills as additional to, not replacements for, existing skills. Reading and writing will continue to be essential; computer memory may replace some paper and file draws; but we will still have to compose sentences for a documentary format. And although the text may appear on screen, it must still be read and, of course, understood. Thus the written word must be taught and learned. Slightly further out, however, writing—meaning composing with pen in hand or fingers on keyboard—may become less necessary. Although still far from perfected, work on voice recogntion by computers is proceeding rapidly. Today, an increasing number of busy people dictate their letters, memos, and even books onto audio tape for later transcription by someone else. Ironically, this harks back to the Medieval era, when the educated composed orally to scribes, who made the written record. With reliable voice recognition computers, we could return to such an era of oral literacy.

There is an even greater likelihood of computer-generated voice synthesis; that is, the output from a computer in the form of a voice—like Hal, in the movie *2001: A Space Odyssey*—rather than as text on a screen or printer. Yet it is unlikely that voice synthesis will totally replace reading, since we can assimilate information much faster with our eyes than with our ears.

Even that assertion, however, is subject to question. The current adult generations, raised on print and the book, have a close cultural identity with both. We have *learned* how to use them, how to skim, how to use an index with ease, and so on. We associate certain pleasant emotions with the tactile sensation of the book. And, as one skeptic put it, could we imagine curling up in front of a fire with a Tolstoy novel on the video screen?

But these are largely learned cultural biases. The kids today playing Pac-Man are learning to assimilate great amounts of information rapidly from a video screen. They are learning to manipulate the information on that screen at an intuitive level, using keyboards or "joysticks." If the technology results in the development of video screens with twice the resolution of today's (possible now, but prohibitively expensive), and with ever lower electronic storage costs (perhaps using a videodisk), it may not be all that farfetched to expect tomorrow's youngsters to carry their thin, high-resolution video screens with them when they travel or to sit in front of the fireplace reading from them. And, conceivably, an "oral" generation may also learn to absorb content at a faster rate from speech, with greater skill—or literacy—and with enjoyment equal to our pleasure in reading words from a book.

Such speculation should not obscure the robustness of older formats in the face of new ones. Records, film, radio, and television have successively been feared as threats to print. Yet all have survived and thrived, though sometimes having to fill somewhat different functions. General interest mass audience magazines like *Look* and *Life* lost their national audiences to television, and as a result, magazines generally became largely a special-interest medium. Books, on the other hand, have shown remarkable resilience in the face of new informational and cultural formats. Indeed, new processes and formats frequently create opportunities for the older ones. Television spawned magazines such as *TV Guide*, and is widely credited with sparking interest in sports magazines and expanded newspaper sports pages. Cinema and television films based on books have increased sales of those books. In some cases, original scripts for films were later published as books. Examples range from *Star Wars* to *The Ascent of Man*. Computer magazines are thriving. And there are now books and magazines for video game enthusiasts.

There are few fears evoked today that were not previously heard during the Victorian era. Today, the enemy of reading is television. But the doom of reading has been falsely prophesied ever since the invention of the pneumatic tire, when it was believed that the bicycle would put the whole family on wheels and thus spell the end of fireside reading.[15] On the other hand, there is a certain validity to the pessimism of Samuel Johnson—who, had he lived today, could have had in mind Atari's Pac-Man—when he wrote: "People in general do not willingly read, if they can have anything else to amuse them."[16]

It is likely that we are on the verge of yet another step in the evolution of literacy. Yet we can feel confident that whatever comes about will not replace existing skills, but supplement them. Neither the printing press nor the typewriter replaced either speech or hand-writing. The electronic hand calculator has not replaced the need to understand mathematics, though it may reduce the need to memorize multiplication tables. The new literacy will likely involve a greater emphasis on the visual, but only as a continuation of the trend that has involved the improvements in photography, printing techniques, and television.

Above all, the new literacy, whatever it looks like, is not to be feared—first, because it will come about regardless of what we think about it; second, because for any threat to some existing institution or relationship, the new literacy will provide equal or greater opportunity; third, because change brought about in part by technology takes place incrementally, and adjustments by society and individuals will evolve naturally.

I remain haunted, however, by how a sixteen-year-old reporter for *Children's Express*, a newspaper published entirely by school-children, characterized the Fourth Assembly of the World Future Society in July 1982, whose theme was the new world of telecommunications: "I think the message was clear that it's really our [young people's] world. I was kind of laughing at the people here. This technology, all they talked about, they really couldn't grasp. This belongs to us."[17]

ENDNOTES

The author gratefully acknowledges the contribution of Harvard graduate student Carolyn Frankel for the research and analysis incorporated into this article.

[1] From *Horizon,* in an article about the importance of books in an era of mass communication. Quoted on the editorial page of *The Wall Street Journal,* February 6, 1982.

[2] Quoted by Alvin Toffler in *Future Shock* (New York: Random House, 1970), p. 144. Mr. Cornberg is a communications system designer.

[3] M.T. Clanchy, *From Memory to Written Record: England, 1066-1307* (Cambridge: Harvard University Press, 1979), p. 56.

[4] Ibid., p. 88.

[5] Richard D. Altick, *The English Common Reader: A Social History of the Mass Reading Public,* 1800-1900 (Chicago: University of Chicago Press, 1974), p. 368.

[6] Ibid., p. 231.

[7] Ibid., p. 233.

[8] Jack Egan, "Publishing for the Future," *New York,* August 16, 1982, p. 10.

[9] Benjamin M. Compaine, *A New Framework for the Media Arena: Content, Process and Format* (Cambridge: Program on Information Resources Policy, Harvard University, 1980), pp. 6-17.

[10]Fred M. Hechinger, "About Education," *New York Times,* December 15, 1982, p. C-5.

[11]"Videotext" (sometimes videotex) is a term used to describe any service that provides text and graphics on a video screen in a "page" format. That is, each screenful of material is identified like a print page and can be viewed in its entirety by the user. Videotext (in a version sometimes called "view-data") may be transmitted from a computer to the user by a telephone connection, by cable, or, conceivably, by other electronic transmission techniques. It is considered "interactive" because each user determines which "pages" should be sent by some type of controlling mechanism, such as a numerical keypad or a full typewriterlike keyboard. Videotext may also provide opportunity for ordering goods that are featured or advertised on the system, or even for certain financial functions, such as checking banking account balances or transferring funds. Teletext refers to systems that appear to be similar, but involve transmission of the video pages by cable or by broadcasting in a continuous stream. The user has a numerical keypad by which he can identify a particular page to view. The next time that page is transmitted (probably no longer than thirty seconds), it will be "grabbed" and held on the video screen until another page is requested. It is therefore not a truly interactive service, as the user never has access to the computer itself.

[12]"The Wired University Is on the Way," *Business Week,* April 26, 1982, p. 68.

[13]Clanchy, *From Memory to Written Record,* p. 2.

[14]Elizabeth L. Eisenstein, *The Printing Press as an Agent of Change,* (Cambridge, England, and New York: Cambridge University Press, 1979), p. 8.

[15]Altick, *The English Common Reader,* p. 374.

[16]Ibid., p. 373.

[17]"Time Tripping at a Convention of World Futurists," *The Boston Globe,* August 4, 1982, p. 55.

Paul Starr

The Electronic Reader

I
N THE LAST SEVERAL DECADES, new technology has greatly altered the production of the printed word without much affecting
how it is distributed or read. Computerized composition, phototypesetting, and word processors have changed the editorial rooms
of newspapers and the printing systems of nearly all publishers, but
readers can scarcely tell the difference. The development of electronics promises to change this pattern, to alter reading as well as publishing. At work and even at home, many people who never expected
to use computers are growing accustomed to reading and writing on
a computer screen controlled by a keyboard. "Software" publishers
offer an expanding selection of educational programs for self-instruc-
tion that supplement—and may, perhaps, substitute for—textbooks,
training manuals, and how-to guides. Commercial services provide
on-line access to newspapers, financial data, judicial decisions, and
references such as dictionaries and bibliographies. Encyclopedias and
even the Bible are now published in electronic editions for use in
home computers. Ten years ago, it might have seemed a fantasy to
expect that books, journals, and libraries would be available electronically. It is fantasy no longer.

The new medium has some evident advantages. As the on-line systems demonstrate, electronic texts can be distributed over long distances almost instantaneously, continuously updated, and called up
with a speed that no library can match. Texts in electronic form can
be stored with great compactness and rapidly searched for relevant
passages. The introduction of electronic retrieval and reading may
enlarge the capacities of readers not only to locate but also to create
knowledge, since computerized systems that provide access to data in

addition to texts allow readers to rearrange tables and other information to suit their own purposes.

Computers are so strongly associated with data in conventional understanding that their uses may be disparaged as limited to information-gathering, but this would be a mistake. The new medium has distinct capacities for graphic representation, such as for animated graphics, and unlike print, permits interaction between reader and text. Computer games and instruction take advantage of these features; so also could a serious electronic literature. Although the new technology is now used mainly for didactic, fact-finding, and entertainment purposes, it may stimulate the development of new intellectual and artistic forms that may be partly read, partly played.

Print, however, is not about to disappear, nor do I suggest that we are on the verge of a "cultural revolution," or that we shall all be obsolete in our professions if we do not become literate in computer languages. The printed page has such obvious advantages in ease of access and flexibility of use that there is no likelihood of its abandonment for most ordinary reading. Books can be conveniently carried to the beach, to the bathroom, and to bed. The printed page neither blinks nor malfunctions; and almost alone among man-made objects, it has never even been accused of causing cancer.

However, the new electronic medium, insofar as it carries texts, does not exclude production of printed copies. A primary use of the new technology will be to deliver printed texts more efficiently than before. The real question is what work will go in which of several possible printed and electronic formats. In addition, how will the new technologies affect the role and power of publishers, and their relations to writers, bookstores, libraries, and the reading public? How will reading itself change, and will the technology open up new possibilities in intellectual and cultural life?

Much of what I shall say about these issues is speculative and no doubt reflects the considerable shortcomings in my understanding of the technology. I approach the subject not as a professional in the field, nor as someone with a proprietary interest in its success, but rather as a sociologist and author, eager to learn about developments that may affect my culture and my craft. I confess willingly to a long-standing irritation with the organization of libraries and publishing that disposes me to look more favorably on the new technology than do many of my colleagues, who see it variously as a fad, a threat, or a nuisance. I am no computer buff or enthusiast, but I do believe that the technology now being developed will not merely simplify the handling of information, but change, mostly for the better, the work of all who work with words.

TEXT, TECHNOLOGY, AND THE SOCIAL SYSTEM OF PUBLISHING

Let me begin by assuming that most readers will continue to prefer conventionally printed texts; only gradually will I relax that premise. I want to ask first how the new methods for producing and distributing texts may affect the social and economic relations among writers, editors and publishers, booksellers, librarians, and readers. Then I will turn to the possible cultural impact of the new medium.

The new technology is now finding its way into every phase of the production of the printed word, but it is not yet integrated into a system. Even though many writers, or their secretaries, now use word processors, most still send their work to their editors and publishers in manuscript form, rather than transmitting it electronically. In the process of manufacture, the publisher usually has the work put back into digital form, but it is issued in print. Books and journals are not communicated electronically to bookstores, libraries, or households, though many of these now use small computers for other purposes. The impact of electronics upon the social system of publishing depends, in large part, upon the electronic integration of writer and publisher; publisher and bookstore; publisher, library, and reader; or perhaps even writer and reader without intermediary.

Electronic Integration of Writer and Publisher

Except in newspapers and other organizations that incorporate printing facilities, the electronic integration of writer and publisher has generally been blocked by the incompatibility of different computer systems. This difficulty is now being overcome in at least two different ways. Some book publishers are accepting "manuscripts" in machine-readable form (floppy disks, magnetic tapes); some even lend their authors word processors to ensure compatibility with the typesetting equipment used for their books. Here, the author provides an "electronic manuscript," which the publisher then has coded for the appropriate typeface and book design. A few publishers have gone further, contracting with authors to produce camera-ready "repro" (reproducible copy, the typeset pages from which books eventually are printed). These authors, however, are typically in computer sciences and have access to special equipment at the institutions where they work. In this case, the author has the pages produced according to previously agreed-on specifications and then transmits them to the publisher, who arranges for the book's manufacture and distribution.

These are, I should emphasize, still marginal developments in publishing, but they may augur broader change in the future. Authors who deliver their work in machine-readable or camera-ready form are taking on some of the functions traditionally performed by publishers. In return for the added value of their authors' labor, a few publishers have paid them an additional fee or given them a larger share of royalties, but this is by no means common.[1] The transfer of functions creates tensions over both money and control. There is a potential for conflict over the division of the financial benefits of streamlined production and the control of book design and style. Many publishers are extremely reluctant to have authors prepare books in machine-readable or camera-ready form, for fear of compromising their standards of editing and design. But once editors become proficient in revising books on word processors, these objections may diminish. Now, however, the new technology is strange and intimidating, and it threatens to disrupt the division of labor in book publishing (as it already has in newspapers).

During the spring of 1982, I had some first-hand experience with these problems in publishing a book, *The Social Transformation of American Medicine,* with Basic Books, a subsidiary of Harper & Row. Since I had written the last draft on a computer system at Harvard, I proposed using the computer to deliver the book in either machine-readable or camera-ready form. The idea aroused much skepticism and resistance. I was told that an earlier such effort at Basic had caused difficulties in production. Nonetheless, after confirming the practicality of the idea with an editor at Harvard University Press, which had published a book using the same computer system, I was able to persuade my editors at Basic to go ahead. However, an attempt to produce camera-ready pages with a firm in Cambridge did not work out, so the wizard who runs our computer transmitted a magnetic tape of the book directly to Harper & Row's compositor, along with the results of a program that converted the output of our system to a form acceptable to theirs. This tape produced page proofs (we skipped galleys) without any serious problems, eliminating not only the need to have 850 pages of manuscript "keyboarded" anew, but also the possibility of introducing further typographical errors. In effect, as I had written the book, I had set the type.

However, not all went well. I had expected that delivery of the book in machine-readable form would speed up publication. Though it might have cut a month or two, the publisher was neither confident of the process nor capable of exploiting it, and unrelated delays at the plant—a flood, not a metaphorical one of work, but a real one of water—resulted in a three-month postponement of the publication date. The final date was nearly seven months after the tape was delivered. In addition, the reduced expenditure for composition did not appear to make much difference in the list price of the book—$24.95 for a volume of 525 pages.[2]

Nonetheless, as word processing becomes standardized and the problems of "interface" are overcome, the electronic integration of writer and publisher should contribute to more rapid and less costly book production. The advantages, however, will be limited and apply primarily to scholarly and technical works rather than trade books. The longer a book and the smaller the print run, the larger the proportion of production costs that goes to composition—hence, the greater the savings from a method that eliminates resetting the text. For a university press book with a small printing, composition may absorb as much as 50 percent of production costs. On the other hand, for a trade book with a relatively large printing and a substantial advertising budget, composition costs are a minor part of the publisher's total investment. For academic writers and scholarly publishers, a machine-readable manuscript may make commercially feasible the publication of an otherwise unprofitable book for a specialized audience. Therefore, although the savings will be too small to make any major dent in book prices, they may help some serious scholarship find its way to publication.

Scholarly journals may also benefit by their contributors' growing use of word processors. If authors submit their articles to journals by electronic mail, or on a standard floppy disk that is compatible with the publisher's system, the articles can be edited and set on a computer entirely in-house and the services of a compositor dispensed with. In computer science, authors now routinely submit their articles in camera-ready form to publications in the field.[3] Professors in computer science obviously have skills and subsidized research facilities unavailable in other disciplines, but as the technology improves and costs go down, the practice may become more widespread and journals will be relieved of a significant expense.

New Forms of Publishing

Thus far I have been discussing efficiencies in production that may help to maintain the traditional forms of distribution and reading. But it is only a short step from the electronic integration of writer and publisher to the linkage of publisher and bookstore, or publisher and reader. If an author writes a book on a word processor, the possibility presents itself of storing his work in electronic form and printing it out at a bookstore when a customer asks for it, or transmitting it electronically to a reader, or selling it in a memory disk, chip, or cassette. Here are three major alternatives, each with variations, for the future of publishing: "on-demand" publishing, "on-line" publishing, and "electronic editions."

On-Demand Publishing—Book publishing is a magnificently inefficient industry. As Leonard Shatzkin, a publishing consultant and former Doubleday executive, points out, in no other industry do retailers regularly return to manufacturers about one third of the merchandise they receive. Further, of every two hardcover trade books sold, one is remaindered at or below cost; the very prospect of remainders, in fact, undermines sales at the original price. Most important, perhaps, the distribution of books is spotty and erratic. The high costs of inventory and space prohibit booksellers from displaying more than a small fraction of new books—let alone stocking publishers' backlists. In light of these limitations, key decisions affecting *which* books get into the stores are made months before publication and reviews, in thousands of individual meetings between sales representatives and booksellers—decisions that are often based only on the past performance of similar books and the kinds of books that are currently selling well. Even books that are well reviewed may be stillborn in the marketplace because of low advance sales. According to Shatzkin, surveys indicate that half of the customers who go into a bookstore looking for a book walk out disappointed. At the same time, the typical publisher holds in inventory as many books as the house will sell during the year.[4] However, the cost of unsold stock has risen owing to a recent IRS ruling that prevents publishers from depreciating inventory—a long-standing practice in the industry—and publishers are now more inclined to take books with low sales out of circulation.

The new technology may provide a partial solution for these problems by opening up an alternative method of production or, more accurately understood, a new line of business: on-demand publishing. This would logically begin with backlists that generate only limited income. Even books that predate computerized composition can now be transferred, at relatively small expense, into digital form by means of "optical character recognition"; new books could go directly into the memory banks. The publisher could then issue books, either from a central plant or local stores, as they were demanded, rather than printing them in quantity. Even if the facilities for publishing on demand were centralized, this would still permit a reduction in inventories of unsold books and improve the circulation of ideas by making it feasible to keep books in print indefinitely.[5]

On-demand publishing, however, would be even more valuable if customers could have the books they want printed up when they walk into a shop. In effect, the bookstore would have an additional line of business, in some respects analogous to photocopying. The text might be stored on videodisk at the store or transmitted long-distance via cable or telephone from the central computers of individual publishers or "electronic wholesalers." Thanks to facsimile transmission, national newspapers such as the *Wall Street Journal* now publish at several locations around the country. The bookstores might sell on-demand facsimile editions of books in softcover bindings, which would be to paperbacks what paperbacks are to cloth editions. Since they would be easily divisible in this form, books could also be sold in parts (for example, to students seeking chapters of books assigned in college courses). The bookstores would be automatically charged royalty payments by publishers, income that is now typically lost to publishers and authors when copyrighted material is photocopied. Publishers have fought the photoduplication of their books without success because they have had nothing competitive to offer; local on-demand publishing might change that.

The local facsimile-production of books would preserve the virtues of the printed page while allowing some of the flexibility of the electronic form—for example, continual updating of reference works. Its chief advantage, however, is that it would give readers immediate access to the full range of books in print instead of the much smaller selection now found in bookshops. Of all the various alternatives that I will mention, I believe this one holds out the greatest probability of satisfying the interests of readers in acquiring books, and of publishers and authors in generating income.

On-Line Publishing—While local on-demand publishing is still a matter for speculation, on-line publishing is already being used for newspapers (back and current issues), financial reporting services, and various references. These are collectively called "databases," a term that, unfortunately, does not convey their full variety. While some "information providers" (publishers, government agencies, and other organizations) offer bibliographic references, abstracts, or digests of information, others retrieve the full texts of documents and other publications. By mid-1982, 1,200 databases were available on-line in the United States, triple the number in 1979, and growing at a rate between 20 and 40 percent a year. To access these services, users connect their terminals via telephone either to individual on-line services or to one of the information "supermarkets" that sell a variety of products. Lockheed's Dialog, for example, offers 150 databases.[6]

On-line publishing permits access to a far larger volume of information than businesses and other organizations could expect to hold in their own files or libraries. Moreover, because of economies of scale, on-line services can more easily keep information current. These have been factors in the success of Lexis and Westlaw, two services that retrieve the full texts of laws, regulations, and judicial decisions. Through the use of key words, they first identify potentially relevant precedents, then display short segments of text to determine whether a particular source is appropriate, and finally provide the full text if necessary.

On-line services also provide a means of direct publication. So far I have discussed systems that abstract from or retrieve previously printed texts. But in computer networks now in operation, professionals use the networks' electronic mail service to broadcast messages and drafts of papers to other individuals with relevant interests. In specialized scientific fields where the readers are well defined, subsequent publication in print may be, to some extent, a formality, more necessary for certification and promotion than for scientific communication. Another means of dissemination, evidently popular among children as well as adults, are "electronic bulletin boards," where queries, compositions, and memoranda are posted and then viewed by interested subscribers. It has been suggested that refereed "electronic journals" might operate by the same means: papers could be submitted, reviewed, and announced as published, all within a computer network. But the time is not ripe for such journals, and for reasons of prestige and tradition, it may never come, at least not to leading publications.[7]

On-demand publishing, as I have described it, would be on-line in local bookstores, but the same book banks might be directly accessible to households with personal computers. The publisher might use such a system for promotional purposes. The potential book buyer, for example, might be allowed a certain amount of time without charge to peruse a volume on a screen at home to decide whether to order it from the publisher. Such a system could provide an alternative to browsing in the bookstore. Or, if facsimile printers became common components of personal computer systems, readers could just be charged the cost of making their own copies.

But if books could be perused on-line from publishers, why not from libraries? The relation of libraries to the new technology may raise some difficult questions. One possibility is for them to subscribe to on-line services that are primarily commercial, but the costs may be prohibitive. Another possibility is for the libraries themselves to develop electronic collections. In electronic libraries, more than one person at a time could read a book; thus books would never be "out." But precisely for that reason, publishers may claim that free, on-line library service violates copyright protection, unless such services are limited to books in the public domain. The libraries might also be asked to monitor and charge for use, and to pass on part of the fees they collect as royalty payments.

The new technology, therefore, may bring about a convergence between publishers and libraries. Both may distribute texts from their computers; the difference would be the publisher's ownership and promotion of books. In effect, the publisher would become an active electronic library; the library, a passive electronic publisher.

Electronic Editions—A third alternative is for publishers to sell memory disks or chips that carry texts to be read on personal computers. The *Random House Dictionary* and the King James Bible are now available in electronic editions. A disk or chip, like a book, is a one-time purchase, freeing the reader from the uncertainty of breakdowns in centralized systems, interference in long-distance connections, and price increases for on-line access.

Rather than thinking of disks or chips as replacements for books, it is probably more useful to conceive of them, at least for the foreseeable future, as additional forms of distribution. Just as recording companies now release cassettes as well as records, so might publishers release some books in both electronic and printed editions. But the electronic versions could be quite different from the printed ones because of the potential for interactive routines, graphics, and the mixing of music with text. For this reason, a literature might develop that had distinctive electronic editions (almost analogous to stereophonic recordings) or that would be available only in electronic form.

Today, electronic editions of books have a limited market because of the inconvenience of reading them on a computer terminal. The prospects for their use, however, would improve considerably if a book-size battery-powered computer, with a high-resolution screen capable of displaying libraries stored on a chip, were to become available in the price range of electronic calculators. With a small, durable electronic reader,[8] portability might count in favor of electronic editions, since it would be possible to carry around a much larger volume of material in disks and chips than in printed books. For the overburdened student, the book bag might go the way of the slide rule.

In the long run, the most serious drawback to electronic editions may prove to be the difficulty of controlling their reproduction. Photocopying, as I have mentioned, has already weakened the force of copyright protection. But photocopying is time-consuming and relatively expensive, and the product is usually less compact and convenient than a book. Electronic reproduction of floppy disks is extremely quick and inexpensive, and the copy is indistinguishable from the original. (Videodisks cannot be reproduced outside of a factory, but protection of the information they carry may still be limited.) These considerations may make publishers reluctant to release books in a form that might subvert their own proprietary interests.

Even if this obstacle were overcome, it is difficult to imagine many readers and *any* authors who would be satisfied with electronic editions alone. We are, many of us, attached to printed books as objects of art and sentiment. Even when their design and manufacture are of a low grade, books command more respect than do magazines or other, more evanescent forms of publication. People are surprisingly reluctant to throw books away. Books are presumed, perhaps ridiculously, to be especially lasting contributions to the stock of human knowledge. These attitudes affect how they are written and how they are read. Though our writing, like our speech, is much less formal than it used to be, the printed book often seems like the last refuge of public civility. Writing a book is still, in a sense, an occasion to dress up. Electronic publication may diminish this sense of ceremony. The electronic text will not be fixed, and it may not create the sense of a testament to posterity. It may blur the distinction between published and unpublished words that now encourages writers to adopt the public graces lost elsewhere in modern society. The illusion of permanence that the printed book gives, so necessary to its authority and to the vanity of authors, might be lost in electronic form. The art of letter writing vanished with the invention of the telephone; the all-too-apparent impermanence of electronic publication might have a similar baleful effect on writing in that medium.

Computers, of course, inspire respect, but they have more authority in the realm of numbers than in the realm of words. The great deficiency of the electronic book (the book published *only* electronically) is that, deprived of corporeal existence, it will be considered distinctly second class, particularly in the academic world, where conspicuous production is a professional imperative. Such considerations may favor retention of the printed book, no matter how well electronic editions serve the needs of communication.[9]

THE COMPUTER AS A CULTURAL MEDIUM

What difference does it make if we read texts displayed on a computer screen instead of on paper printed with ink? The computer certainly does not guarantee deeper comprehension, greater subtlety of mind, or a wider range of imaginative reference. The mediation of a computer, however, puts new powers at the disposal of intelligence. For one thing, the computer itself can do simple reading—as I have noted, it can "read" an immense body of literature in search of designated words. As anyone knows who has ever spent days in libraries in search of errant information, simply identifying relevant sources absorbs inordinate amounts of time in research. The objection may be raised that a search of texts by computer may block the serendipitous discoveries that occur while browsing in the stacks of great libraries. No member of the academy need fear that the use of a computer will keep him from the stacks, but browsing is, if anything, easier if texts can be called up on a screen in the serenity of one's chosen surroundings.

The great deficiency of libraries, as we know them, is that while titles are catalogued, the libraries have no master indexes of the contents of books. Individual volumes, it is true, have indexes, often of inferior quality, but even the best indexes must be examined one at a time. The great advantage of an electronic library is that a computer could search and analyze its contents without proceeding volume by volume. As work in artificial intelligence develops, computer systems may also become adept at more complex tasks, such as summarizing texts, which has been accomplished experimentally.

Earlier I alluded to the interactive possibilities of the electronic medium. We have associated almost all of the new technology of twentieth century culture (the cinema, radio, television) with an increase in the passivity of the audience. However, the electronic text is different, since it enables the reader to respond, choose, and create. The new electronic literature may take advantage of this feature in works of nonfiction and fiction alike.

Let me give an example of electronic nonfiction from my own field, sociology. Among the contributions of the Chicago school of urban sociology were "community fact books" that brought together data about cities and their neighborhoods. These volumes provided useful background for community organizations and the local press, but they could present only a limited amount of information, and after lengthy preparation, were soon out of date. Recently, a sociologist at the University of Illinois, Harvey Choldin, described an "electronic community fact book" in progress for Chicago.[10] Unlike its predecessors, the new one can be continually updated with new information from census surveys and other sources, and it will allow the reader to create new tables by reanalyzing the data in the system. It will also take advantage of computer graphics to display information in more interesting formats. In addition, it will have an instructional sequence that will permit students to proceed through the material in an interactive fashion.

The artistic possibilities latent in the new medium will take time to exploit. One firm has already released a detective story in which the reader/player can follow up different clues and question witnesses and suspects. But electronic fiction of genuine literary interest may also emerge. Imagine, if you will, a twentieth century Lewis Carroll (Carroll was a mathematician as well as an author) about to write the contemporary equivalent of *Alice in Wonderland*. The computer opens up entirely new possibilities for a narrative game, with choices left to the reader and characters programmed to respond in certain structured but variable ways. Such a "book" could be both read and played in endless variations. A John Fowles would revel in it.

In this new medium, the author would have to combine traditional literary skills with an ability to program the computer imaginatively. Just as a composer does not fully anticipate or control the way his music will be performed, so would the writer of electronic literature create a work that would be open, not just to critical interpretation, but to the interpretation of different performances. Gimmickry, you may say, and that it will be, but it may be more.

I do not wish to overlook some drawbacks to the hypothetical developments I have been speculating about. The skills required to read a printed book do not vary from one book to another, as long as they are in the same language. Reading does not require any equipment. And we have a well-established tradition of public libraries that make books available for free to poor and rich alike.

On the other hand, the skills required to use a personal computer are more variable from one system to another. The cost of equipment may be dropping, but it is still a barrier to widespread access. On-line services are being developed commercially, and the role of public libraries in the electronic provision of information is uncertain. Where the federal government provides such services for free, private companies are making a concerted effort to restrict its role.[11] The result may be to make access to the electronic medium more restricted than access to the printed medium.

On-line publishing also has some sinister possibilities. In the hands of a totalitarian government, it could be used to monitor what citizens were reading. When it suited the regime, the texts of past newspapers, journals, and books could be permanently altered. In her study of the invention of printing and its impact, Elizabeth Eisenstein points out that one crucial difference between manuscripts and print was "typographical fixity."[12] Manuscripts had been constantly revised in the process of transcription; with the invention of printing, texts finally acquired a fixed form. This fixity might be lost with electronic publication.

My purpose here, however, has been neither to predict nor recommend a purely electronic system of publishing and scientific communication. There are risks and uncertainties, to be sure, in any new technology. The full course of the evolutionary process now beginning will probably take decades to unfold, and it is unclear what will be the pace of change, the intermediate phases, or the new equilibrium. The uncertainty derives partly from the unpredictability of invention. The microprocessor was invented only in the early 1970s, and it opened up radically new possibilities for the use of computers. Other developments, now unforeseen, may also change ideas and expectations. But even with what is now available or on the horizon, it is clear that the new technology can contribute significantly to scholarship, science, and the circulation of ideas, if we can put aside prejudices about computers and exploit their possibilities as a medium of culture as well as information.

ENDNOTES

[1]Among the publishers who have entered into more flexible contracts are Addison-Wesley, McGraw-Hill, and Computer Sciences Press.

[2]While the normal composition costs were estimated at between $8 and $10 per camera-ready page, the firm in Cambridge that offered to prepare repro would have charged about $3 a page, for a total saving of between $2,500 and $3,500. Basic's own estimate of the savings was initially $2,800, half to be paid to me directly (which would just about cover my word processing bills from Harvard) and half to be used to reduce the book's list price. But $1,400 spread over a print run of five to six thousand copies does not amount to much.

[3]My informant is Daniel Gusfield, assistant professor of computer sciences, Yale University.

[4]Leonard Shatzkin, *In Cold Type: Overcoming the Book Crisis* (Boston: Houghton Mifflin, 1982). See also Lewis A. Coser, Charles Kadushin, and Walter W. Powell, *Books: The Culture and Commerce of Book Publishing* (New York: Basic Books, 1982).

[5]On-demand publishing is already the method used for releasing a vast amount of scholarly and technical work. It is used by University Microfilms in "publishing" dissertations and by the National Technical Information Service in "publishing" government-funded research reports. University Microfilms also publishes out-of-print books on demand.

[6]Andrew Pollack, "Putting Out the Word Electronically," *New York Times,* August 27, 1982.

[7]Alan Singleton, "The Electronic Journal and Its Relatives," *Scholarly Publishing,* October 1981, pp. 3-18.

[8]It would probably be best if the device were called an "electronic reader" because of the misunderstanding that the term "computer" creates. One reason for the commercial success of word processors is that they seem to many to be nothing more than souped-up typewriters. Were they called computers, they would be far more intimidating. Furthermore, in many companies, anything called a computer has to be approved by the data processing department, whereas a word processor is just another office machine and can be ordered by any manager. Many people who might never consider buying a computer might buy an electronic reader, which would require only that they plug in a cassette and push a few buttons.

[9]For further discussion, see Irving Louis Horowitz and Mary E. Curtis, "The Impact of Technology on Scholarly Publishing," *Scholarly Publishing,* April 1982, pp. 210-28.

[10]Harvey M. Choldin, "Electronic Community Fact Books," *Urban Affairs Quarterly* 15 (March 1980): 269-89.

[11]For an account of one such battle, see Nicholas E. Davies, "The Health-Sciences Information Struggle: The Private Information Industry versus The National Library of Medicine," *New England Journal of Medicine* 307 (July 15, 1982): 201-4.

[12]Elizabeth L. Eisenstein, *The Printing Press as an Agent of Change* (Cambridge, England, and New York: Cambridge University Press, 1979).

Peter Conrad

The Englishness of English Literature

IN 1955 Nikolaus Pevsner delivered the Reith lectures on the BBC. His subject was "The Englishness of English Art." His account of the national characteristics evinced by art—pragmatism in Hogarth, "frank, naive" provincialism in Constable—found scant favor. The English have a blunt-minded hostility to the generalizing temper, especially when it presumes to generalize about *them*. Thus, when Pevsner had completed his peregrination round all the counties, personally inspecting every edifice for the two dozen volumes of his Buildings of England series, the English ungratefully joked that only a Teuton would have the obsessiveness to conceive of, and the compulsiveness to execute, such an enterprise. Pevsner's inquiry into Englishness in those lectures is indeed disappointing, because it retains too Germanic a faith in a racial spirit, a mystic mental disposition that begets the illogical, atmospheric, waywardly anticlassical art of England. I don't intend to make conjectures about national character. In transferring Pevsner's investigation to literature, I shall begin by considering the ways in which English writers reflect on their own Englishness, and from there, go on to hint at what seems to me the formal unity—the integrity and secret indwelling pattern—of English literature.

The comments from which I start are, oddly, not patriotic anthems but elegies: laments for the desacralization of English and, in one case, Irish terrain; farewells to absconding gods. From the first, English literature has been preoccupied by the impoverishment of its own locality, the deconsecration of its reality, the departure of divinity from places. Chaucer's Wife of Bath, that veteran marital campaigner, has an atavistic memory stretching back to the ancient days when "al was this land fulfild of fayerye" and the elf queen and her cohorts danced in the meadows. But since then, this indigenous population of spirits has been expelled by the friars, who go about

> Blessynge halles, chambres, kichenes, boures,
> Citees, burghes, castels, hye toures,
> Thropes, bernes, shipnes, dayeryes—
> This making that ther been no fayeryes.

That censorious blessing is the *un*hallowing of the land. Now, instead of a reality divinized by magic, there is only the dreary specification of the Wife's inventory of real estate. The cities, castles, towers, and barns are enumerated as nouns, without adjectives to enliven or inspirit them. The Wife herself is a diminished survivor from those magic days: an earth-mother whom her companions of the pilgrimage can only interpret as a salacious hag; a raddled and dejected goddess.

Spenser's *Faerie Queene* attempts allegorically to reconsecrate this depleted and defrauded reality, but cannot help admitting the incompatibility between its own god-frequented realm and the secular map of English geography. Some of Spenser's characters trudge on

> following Dee, which Britons long ygone
> Did call "divine," that doth by Chester tend.

The river's title to divinity is by now an antiquarian fable; its actual business is the drab one of flowing past Chester. Spenser's poem breaks off when the gods voluntarily and vengefully renounce the soil where he has tried to give them a local habitation and a name. Diana, offended by an impertinent subject, abandons her Irish pleasance, and

> There-on an heauy haplesse curse did lay,
> To weet, that Wolues, where she was wont to space,
> Should harbour'd be, and all those Woods deface,
> And Thieues should rob and spoile that Coast around.
> Since which, those Woods, and all that goodly Chase,
> Doth to this day with Wolues and Thieues abound:
> Which too-too true that lands in-dwellers since haue found.

The stanza's long final line extends itself to encompass and shake its head over the homely misery of what's left: the place where Spenser himself, exiled from the Elizabethan court, was writing the poem. The gods have levitated vertically; all the poem can do, in elegy and commemoration, is stretch out horizontally, as it does in those long end-lines ("And the faire *Shure,* in which are thousand Salmons bred"), computing the quantity of things remaining—salmon, wolves, thieves, the stock and random staffage of reality.

The literature of the English Renaissance contains a sequence of such unavailing propitiations of the gods: elsewhere in Spenser, Colin Clout's musical conjuration of the Graces, who desert him when Calidore intrudes; Glendower's offer in *Henry IV* to call spirits from the vasty deep, and Hotspur's rejoinder, "But will they come?"; Prospero's animation of gods who are no more than his obsequious stage props. At the end of the series is Milton's expulsion of the disgraced pagan deities in his poem "On the Morning of Christ's Nativity," and his pained desecration of his self-constructed paradise, which Adam and Eve lose but which he destroys, scorching it to a Libyan desert as the earth tilts on its axis. Thereafter, all English landscapes are paradises lost: Johnson's niggardly and denuded Scottish highlands, for instance, which Boswell fretted to replenish romantically with an emotion disallowed by Johnson (when Boswell enthused over a sublime mountain peak, Johnson insisted on the begrudgement of denotation, and called it merely a considerable protuberance); the mirroring vacancies of Wordsworth's lakes or moors, images of the mind's abstraction of itself from actuality; the ocean, which the Ancient Mariner curses as idle, pictorial, unhelpful, and undrinkable; and the desert island where Tennyson's Enoch Arden is sentenced endlessly to look without ever seeing the single object he longs for—

> The blaze upon the waters to the east;
> The blaze upon the island overhead;
> The blaze upon the waters to the west;
> Then the great stars that globed themselves in Heaven,
> The hollower-booming ocean, and again
> The scarlet shafts of sunrise—but no sail.

Or the lurid desert, a Dead Sea reconstructed in sandboxes in his studio, where Holman Hunt situates his scapegoat. Idyllic enclaves that remain are threatened, as is Oxford, in Hopkins's poem, by its base and brickish skirt. Wordsworth seems to speak for all his predecessors—and his successors, too—not just for himself and his own conviction of imaginative failure, when he demands

> Whither is fled the visionary gleam?
> Where is it now, the glory and the dream?

English literature considers itself a parodic epilogue to some preexisting state of vital and spiritual joy.

The lamenting discovery that Englishness means a reduced reality that demeans imagination continues throughout the nineteenth century, with Peacock's acknowledgment that "there are no Dryads in Hyde Park nor Naiads in the Regent's Canal," and Henry Tilney's reproof to the suspicions of Catherine in *Northanger Abbey:* "Remember that we are English, that we are Christians. Consult . . . your own sense of the probable. . . . Does our education prepare us for such atrocities? Do our laws connive at them?" Catherine is compelled to recognize that "in the central part of England," fantasy must submit to suppression. The Gothic novel belongs in "the Alps and the Pyrenees, with their pine forests and their vices." England is a region, not of moral extremes, but of the "unequal mixture of good and bad"—the territory of the entrammeling mediocre that George Eliot called Middlemarch, dismaying because middling. For the poets, the liability of England is its inhospitability to the gods; for characters in novels, the problem is its discouragement of those godlike deeds that would make them heroic. Catherine must forswear the heroic vocation she dreams of if she is to remain "among the English." Dorothea Brooke still hopes it might be "possible to lead a grand life here—now—in England," but the here and now obstruct her, and other George Eliot characters displace heroism elsewhere, to regions of subjunctively wishful geography: Maggie Tulliver assuring Tom that he's a hero and would rescue her from lions "if we were in the lion countries—I mean in Africa, where it's very hot—I can show you in the book where I read it"; Gwendolen Harleth imagining herself a queen in the east like Lady Hester Stanhope.

Connected with this recurrent complaint about the infliction of Englishness is another strange phenomenon of English literature: a declension from grand designs, a fatigued or deconverted aborting of structures. *The Canterbury Tales* begins with the ambition of integrating a society, but ends in that society's quarrelsome dispersal. Rather than convening a community of faith, the pilgrims have taken to scheming against or abusing one another; and at the same time, they reject the designs on them of Chaucer's poem. Often they seem reluctant to tell the tales assigned to them and prefer, like the Wife of Bath, to reminisce and editorialize. When they do consent to tell tales, it is to malign other pilgrims, not to celebrate, as the game proposed, an accord with them. Eventually Chaucer resigns responsibility, calls off the journey, and disappears behind the guileful, ironic conventionality of his retraction, asking to be forgiven for having authorized the calamity. Langland's allegorical quest in *Piers Plow-*

man founders and is twice resumed before it too is suspended. Spenser's messianic structure—the allegory that will terminate the long march of history and restore the cycling eternities of myth, that will redeem society and make it once more fit for the tenancy of gods or saints—is not so much angrily or despairingly halted, as are those of Chaucer or Langland, as suffered to trail off in endless postponements or deferments; until Spenser at last consigns himself to the temporary, temporal reign of mutability, which his poem had existed to oppose, and hopes for a visionary glimpse of distant paradise rather than arrival there. Though Milton at least attains completion, his ends are never triumphal arrivals. They too are exhausted and autodestructive. *Paradise Lost* falls apart into a merely human chaos, myth (in Adam's preview of the future) degenerating into the affray of history. Christ at the conclusion of *Paradise Regained* absents himself—slipping away through a gap created by the enjambment—from the festivities hailing his victory:

> hee unobserv'd
> Home to his Mothers house privat returnd,

that "privat" announcing both a return to privacy and a willful privation, a refusal of heroic status. *Samson Agonistes* likewise reaches its term in quietude, "calm of mind all passion spent."

With the Romantics, this habit of retrenchment becomes a positive—or perhaps I should say negative—creative scruple, a textual suicide. Friedrich Schlegel remarked in 1799 that the English wits, by whom he meant the early Shandyean romantics, "live wittily," and have a talent for madness. "They die for their principles." They make their poems die along with them, since they feel the very act of creating to be destructive. Poetry records an experience that is forfeited as soon as it is written down, so every poem is its own paradise lost. Wordsworth conceded this by saying that poetry is emotion recollected in tranquility: emotion, that is, subjected to the sedation Milton refers to in the last line of *Samson;* emotion known only at second or third hand, after it has been tranquilized and subdued by recollection. And because poetry can never translate into words the experience it is aroused by, it tactfully chooses words that paraphrase and circumlocute, nervously mediating their relation with what they purport to be describing—Wordsworth's unintelligible words for the "unintelligible world" in "Tintern Abbey," those equivocally indefinite articles and unspecific nouns manacled together by riskily overstated adjectives,

> *a* sense sublime
> Of *something* far more deeply interfused, . . .
> A motion and *a* spirit, that impels
> *All* thinking things, *all* objects of *all* thought,
> And rolls through *all things*.

In the preface to the *Lyrical Ballads*, Wordsworth calls the poet a translator. But if so, he presides over the devaluation of his own language, for poetry is that which is *lost* in translation. Wordsworth equivocates; Coleridge, more demoralized, sabotages his poems. The texts are deliberately confused or fragmented in the hope that, if the letter is cabbalistically deformed or doubled (as in the gloss to the "Ancient Mariner" or the prose preface to "Kubla Khan"), then the spirit may remain inviolate. A poem is for Coleridge an agonizing withdrawal symptom—a stage in his deranging ejection from the experience the poem is trying *not* to be about. Thus the "Ancient Mariner" and "Kubla Khan" belie themselves, pretending to be Gothic narratives rather than intimate, incriminatory revelations.

Poetically, the great tradition of English literature seems a history of lost causes, a succession of failed or unrealized epics. Beyond Wordsworth's *Prelude* to an epic he never wrote lie Tennyson's tragic postludes (the "Morte d'Arthur," even perhaps the "Charge of the Light Brigade") to an epic he too never wrote; beyond both, the edited, attentuated epic of *The Waste Land*. But it would be wrong to see this history as an accumulation of failures. In its idiosyncratic way, it represents a victory, for the most English quality of English literature is its renunciation of the classical curriculum of literary form, which places epic at the apex of the genres, and sees the composition of epic as an endeavor of national self-definition, a feat of arms performed with words, as it is for Virgil, Tasso, Camões, and even, mockingly, for Washington Irving, whose Diedrich Knickerbocker fabricates an epic genealogy for the Dutch burghers to justify their appropriation of Manhattan. The English have attempted this kind of hubristic project only so as, conspicuously and on purpose, to fail at it. The uniqueness of this literature is its reversal of the traditional relation between epic and pastoral.

In the classical graduation, the retirement and reclusion of pastoral must yield at last to the activism of the public life, which epic celebrates. This is the destiny of Marvell's Cromwell, sequestered only for the time being in the garden of his ignominy, in training there—while he plants pears—for a career of epic force and compulsion. The classical poet, like Cromwell, is apprenticed to pastoral while limbering up for epic. Marvell's character is dangerous precisely because he persists in the classical progress, defying the English retreat, exemplified in Marvell's own pastoral poems, from public embattlement to dreaming privacy. Whereas classical literatures are ambitious for the martial aggrandizements of epic, the aspiration of English literature is toward the condition of pastoral—toward its reticence, its quietism, its mystic fatigue. The belligerent epic heroism of Spenser's Red Crosse Knight mutates into the different, pastoral forbearance of Britomart, who underneath her travestying armor is a frightened girl, or into the lassitude of the drowsy Calidore. At its midpoint, *Paradise Lost* drastically declares a victory of pastoral over mettlesome epic, which is now the literary mode aptest for the devil. Satan has inherited the angry lust for self-immortalization of the epic protagonist. To his heroic wrath, Christ opposes the mental fortitude and sacrificial meekness that are the beatitudes of Christian pastoral; and when on the third day of the war in heaven he routs the rebellious devils, it is not as an aggressive general but as a shepherd chiding a refractory "Herd / Of Goats or timorous flock together throngd."

That reversal of genres, which pastoralizes the would-be epics of Spenser and Milton, becomes in Marvell a solacing regression: from public strife to private horticultural shelter, and what "restless Cromwell' disdains as "the inglorious Arts of Peace"; even, in "The Garden," from the "uncessant Labours" of politics and the contentions of sexual pursuit to the innocence and inanity of a vegetative life. With it, there occurs a miniaturization of poetic ambition, which is inimitably English. Spenser had hoped in his "Epithalamion" to arrest time or overcome it, and make "to short time an endless monument." Marvell in "To His Coy Mistress" takes over the same subject—the deathly haste of time, the self-immortalizing urgency of sex—but makes instead, in this abbreviated lyric, what we might call to endless time a *short* monument. His "On Milton's *Paradise Lost*" guilefully slights Milton's grand scheme while professing to revere it. He fears in prospect, he says, the reckless infinitude of Milton's plan, but in reading, he became reconciled to it by his awe. He ends, though, with the sliest of compliments. He is discussing Milton's banishment of rhyme, and he praises blank verse in his own adroit rhyming couplets:

> Thy verse created like thy *Theme* sublime,
> In Number, Weight, and Measure, needs not *Rhime*.

Not for Marvell the infinite spaces that Milton braves. He recoils into the insulation of the closed couplet, which for him, as for Pope, is a place of circular, enwombing safety. Within its bounds you can make whatever you wish to prove true sound true by an accord of vowel sounds. The couplet's symmetry offers to Pope a relief from faction and argument, a salving otium, and this, as much as Marvell's gardens, is pastoral in spirit:

> For Forms of Government let fools contest;
> Whate'er is best administered is best.

The couplet functions as a garden for Marvell, a grotto for Pope: a symbol, in both cases, of a pastoral beneficence. When Keats describes his ambition to desert a sensuous and blissfully indolent pastoral for the strife of epic, he still calls the long poem he wants to write a place to wander in—a pastoral enclosure, not an epic field of war; a bower of quietude such as is guarded, in *"Endymion,"* by the sacrosanct "thing of beauty."

The pastoral condition is, for the poets, a contemplative devotion. Christ in *Paradise Regained* replies temperately to the virtuoso enticements of Satan. The pastoral, as expressed in the patient passivity of Milton's Christ, begrudges speech, motion, dialectic—all the treacherous aptitudes of the active life that it resists. Hence, the Lady's minimal responses to the temptations of Comus, and her proud claim, "Thou canst not touch the freedom of my mind." When rigorously practiced, this meditative state becomes a mystic one. The mind, freed, withdraws to a distance to watch the antics of the body in which it was formerly housed: as Marvell does in "The Garden," or Wordsworth in the poems of tranquilizing recollection; as Coleridge nightmarishly does in his poems of psychic arrest and detention, where the meditative stasis is a purgatory; as Byron or Shelley suicidally do, consigning their imprisoning bodies to an elemental death. The romantic pastoral offers to the poets a desired extinction. Self-loss, annihilation in nature—in contrast with the heroic self-definition made by Whitman the initial act of the American bard—is the English poet's dream.

From poetry, pastoral extends into the English novel, where its continence and sequestered reserve become a quality of English manners. The novel invents a mental and social pastoral. In *Emma,* Jane Austen calls this "the true English style." Her characters have, she says, buried, "under a calmness that seems all but indifference"—she might be describing the Lady in *Comus* or Christ in *Paradise Re-*

gained—"the real attachment" they feel. They have trained themselves in a regime of pastoral self-suppression. Very often in the English novel this issues in the quietest and most discreet of despairs—the muffled scream of Marianne in *Sense and Sensibility;* the frustration and misery of those who, as Arnold said of the pastoralist Gray, cannot speak out, and who must write rather than speak, like Richardson's Clarissa. More sadly, yet more pastorally too, there are characters in English novels who do not even have the restitution, granted to Clarissa, of writing a novel. Their only hope, as in the case of Fanny Price at Mansfield Park, is to read the novels written by others on their behalf. When exiled to Portsmouth, Fanny cloisters herself upstairs, away from "the disturbances of the house," and by reading, studiously sedates the "daily terrors" that assail her.

The English novel has always had a special relation with such fugitive existences—social versions of the pastoral hermit. It has sought therefore, as Terence in Virginia Woolf's *The Voyage Out* hopes to do in his novel, to transcribe their silence, writing down "the things people don't say." Diderot, in his *Eloge de Richardson*, in 1762 argued that *Clarissa* would bore only the distracted social gadabout; it was addressed to the solitary in his shaded retreat—a pastoral cell existing now, with walls of paper, only inside the novel—and its longueurs were a discipline of negation, training us to renounce the active life and its itch for things to happen. Mme. de Staël considered the English the foremost practitioners of the novel because their society had perfected the protection, even the consecration, of privacy. More than other cultures, she says in 1800, England has turned away from public broils and exertions. It values above all else a domestic peace. "I sing the sofa," writes Cowper in *The Task,* bringing indoors the epic poet's vaunt about arms and the man, snugly furnishing his own pastoral den.

In place of the hermit's cave or grotto, which are the sanctums of pastoral, the novelist has that modicum of inviolable space that Woolf called "a room of one's own"; and a symbol of the English novel is a closed door. Richardson's heroines spend much of their mental effort in securing the privacy in which to write. Woolf made it a constitutional prerogative that one should have a door one could close. Henry James in 1906-7, by this time irreversibly anglicized, commissioned from A.L. Coburn a number of photographs of retentive, debarring portals for the uniform edition of his works: images of a novelistic probity—consciousness in architectural confinement, templed intelligence turning the key on its secrets. Another Europeanized American, Edith Wharton, in her treatise *The Decoration of Houses,* counted it as a special horror that American architects had made doors retract into walls or replaced them with portières, building "doorways *without doors.*" Such unsheltering rooms could never be houses for fiction. Among the exclusive rooms of one's own in the English novel are Fanny's library at Mansfield, or the inadvertent retreat of the Schlegel sisters in *Howards End:* "Their house was in Wickham Place, and fairly quiet, for a lofty promontory of buildings separated it from the main thoroughfare." Forster likens this enclave to "an estuary, whose waters flowed in from the invisible sea, and ebbed into a profound silence." That silence is the mood—the beatitude—of the English novel. It enables *Little Dorrit* to end pastorally, even in the midst of the metropolitan hubbub that Forster's Wickham Place shuts out. As Dorrit and Clennam leave the church—going down, as Dickens curiously says (it is as if they were "de-levitating," angelically quitting heaven to enter the novel's middle march of existence)—they "went down into a modest life of usefulness and happiness." But their twinned souls have no power over the melee of existences around them: "They went quietly down into the roaring streets, inseparable and blessed; and as they passed along in sunshine and shade, the noisy and the eager, the arrogant and the froward and the vain, fretted and chafed, and made their usual uproar."

This is moving because of its inefficacy. The two characters carry with them and within themselves a pastoral peace that the world ignores or denies, yet cannot harm. The endings of many English novels are footnotes to *Paradise Lost,* with the promise of a future paradise within, conclusions—like Johnson's in *Rasselas*—in which nothing can be concluded because the world lies ahead with all its travails, and pastoral trusts not in the completed actions and achievements of epic but in the steadying, cyclical toil of routine. English narrative subsides, therefore, into conciliatory anticlimax, as at the end of Wordsworth's "Ruined Cottage" or in the final lines of Shakespearean tragedies: after the expiry, the business of living must be resumed. Dickens in ending *Little Dorrit* has also annotated Milton. He has written an epilogue to *Paradise Regained,* a commentary on the lines I quoted about Christ's meek absenting of himself from the fete in his honor. The paradise gained by Dorrit and Clennam is their secret, an internal surety symbolized by the closed door or the enclosed garden. How often English novels end in that garden, which by now is a cemetery where the devout and meditative characters who remain can ponder the last things, like Lockwood, in *Wuthering Heights*, speculating on the disturbed slumbers of Catherine and Heathcliff "under that benign sky, . . . in that quiet earth"; or Nicholas Nickelby and his family visiting the grave of Smike and leaving there "garlands of fresh flowers, wreathed by infant hands"; or the obscurer "unvisited tombs" in which Dorothea and her kind—who have "lived faithfully a hidden life," subsisting in the pastoral quiescence of Dorrit and Clennam—will rest at the end of *Middlemarch*. Even after that paradise has been irretrievably lost, English literature dreams of regaining access to it. Hence the fantasies of H.G. Wells's "Door in the Wall," or Carroll's wonderland. But though Wells's door opens and in Carroll you can travel through the looking glass, perhaps the abiding image of the English novel is the closed door, declaring the jealous vigilance with which each person defends his dream. Returning to their garden, Adam and Eve voluntarily lock its gates behind them; or, in Marvell, Adam longs for the extra solitude of inhabiting it alone, without Eve.

Emerson, who visited England in 1847-48, commented that "every one of the islanders is an island himself, safe, tranquil, incommunicable." Odd that Donne's attestation to the contrary should be such a catchphase, for in English literature, every man *is* an island. Perhaps Donne claimed the opposite because his own ravening imagination coveted continents, not mere islands. "My America! my new-found-land," he calls the body of a mistress, which he intends to plunder. Emerson's perception was a very acute one. We are dealing with a literature of psychological insularity. The pastoral is a landscape of insulation. The shepherds complain of this in their double sestina in Sidney's *Arcadia*. They are immured within their poetic form as within their valley, since the sestina limits them to using the same reshuffled line-end words in each of their stanzas, and the words they are given to operate with are the perimeters of their circumscribed pastoral—mountains, valleys, forests, morning, evening, music. As the poem proceeds, the music they make with these words becomes increasingly disgruntled. They curse the mountains and valleys for penning them in, and the evening and morning for the tedious inevitability of their recurrence. The pastoral for them is a *huis clos*, a hell that is the *un*availability of other people. This is from the *Old Arcadia*, 1593; in 1933 Auden virtually wrote over again the same poem in his sestina "Paysage Moralisé." It is an urban pastoral, about the failure of revolution. One of its line-end words is actually "islands." In cities, Auden's people yearn for a freedom elsewhere:

"Each in his little bed conceived of islands." They set sail, are ship-wrecked, and must finally content themselves with envisioning those perfect islands in the distance, like Chaucer not arriving at Canter-bury or Spenser not attaining the court of Gloriana. If change could be made to occur, Auden avows, then we would "rebuild our cities, not dream of islands." The end of pastoral would be its overthrow: the raising of a city on a hill, the building of Jerusalem on English soil. Since they will never come to pass, we must spend the interim on one island, vainly imagining another.

The English novel is perpetually concerned with such islanded be-ings; the English drama controverts itself to accommodate them. Drama is the medium of extroverted character—character in action and reaction. Already in Shakespeare it has been monopolized by dogmatically antidramatic people, who spurn communication with others and turn in on themselves, like Hamlet, or like Macbeth at the banquet. By the nineteenth century, all that remains of the drama is the monologues of such characters, who now—in Tennyson, Brown-ing, and eventually Eliot—have no dramatic action to fit into. Defoe makes the desert island the hallowed location of the English novel, and that island can be reconstituted even in the populous center of London, as it is by the solipsist who keeps the *Journal of the Plague Year*. The plague enforces the shutting up of houses. Defoe's narrator recalls "several Dutch merchants . . . who kept their houses like little garrisons besieged." This fortification of the dwelling—a sanitary cordon placed around privacy—anticipates the islanding of charac-ters in the later novel: Clarissa kept prisoner in her own home; Fanny in Portsmouth retiring upstairs with a book; Wemmick in *Great Ex-pectations* castellating his villa and raising the drawbridge to dissoci-ate it from the city. These characters have all eccentrically recoiled into that nutshell that Hamlet—the patron saint of reclusive English monologuists—speaks of, and which he calls a kingdom of infinite space, because he occupies it alone.

Though Daniel Deronda wishes to restore "a political existence to my people," just as Chaucer or Langland or Spenser or Milton had, for a while, epically exerted themselves to contrive social union and national glorification, the tendency of English literature is to retire from such historical toil into privacy, which is where Gwendolen remains after Deronda takes off from the middling mediocre earth of the novel: "The world seemed getting larger round poor Gwendolen, and she more solitary and helpless in the midst." Deronda seeks to found a nation, to foregather in one place the diaspora of continents;

Gwendolen's fate is a diminished insularity. Often fictional conclusions protest, as Deronda does, against this fragmentation and cellulation of space, this psychic little Englandism, but the effort to connect—as in Forster's motto—is always frustrated. Birkin at the end of *Women in Love* wants company on his island solitude, "eternal union with a man" as well as the love of Ursula. She calls his insistence an obstinacy and a perversity, yet he persists in believing it might be possible. There the novel abruptly abandons him, unable to bring that conciliation to pass; and *A Passage to India* ends as the landscape vetoes the epic confraternity for which Fielding and Aziz long—"No, not yet" and "No, not there." That denial, though attributed to the obstructive Indian terrain, is the still, small voice of timorous Englishness, the voice that prefers to be overheard and not to assert itself by speaking out. Woolf's valedictory novel *Between the Acts* breaks off with Isa and Giles alone and exposed to the encroaching dark. "Then the curtain rose," Woolf adds. "They spoke." But they do not speak: the novel has hurriedly brought down the curtain before they can do so.

All these fictional conclusions execute dying falls into pastoral—Ursula and Birkin in exile from society at the Mill; Aziz and Fielding, who had desired an epic blood-brotherhood, domiciled apart in the landscape; Isa and Giles inundated by the shadows that seep in from the garden. It is a blighted pastoral though, incomplete and unsustaining. It recalls those criticisms of godforsaken England with which I began. Like Crusoe on his island, or Auden's fond fantasists on theirs, these people are condemned to a parody of the paradise they had hoped for. In this regard, it is peculiarly interesting that Lionel Trilling should have called *Emma* an idyll, representing a condition of bucolic innocence. He identifies the novel's genre rightly, but gets its mood wrong, perhaps because he had such a personal investment in what he refers to as the "legend and myth" of "Jane Austen's England." It was the imaginary, gravely peaceful region in which he—a refugee from the strife-torn Europe and America of literary modernism, extolled by his critical contemporaries—had elected to reside. He therefore cannot admit that Highbury, like the other English literary landscapes I've been describing, is a spoiled idyll, menaced by gypsies and robbers of poultry-yards from without, and mined by social malcontents from within. The nuptial celebration with which *Emma* ends is a reduced and sober affair, deficient in white satin and lace veils, and signifying the erection of another stockade, as the "small band" of like-minded castaways unite to defend their communal island against its enemies. English literary Edens are always imperfect. The courtiers in *As You Like It* imagine that the banished Duke disports himself in the forest as if in the Golden Age; but Arden is situated in those middle counties of England gloomily invoked by Henry Tilney, and contains, therefore, bitter winds, indigence, and human ingratitude.

The same qualification of Eden or Arcady occurs in the landscape paintings of the English Romantics. Their elevation of landscape to generic parity with history painting is itself a symptom of the change I have been describing—a reversion from epic (the noble attitudinizing and civic heroism of history painting) to pastoral. These painters now confide their historical fears or hopes to landscape rather than to epic tableaux, like David's *Horatii*. Turner's elemental vortices are the motors of revolutionary change, Constable's louring clouds, the warnings of social disturbance, steadfastly resisted by the spire of Salisbury Cathedral. In Constable and Turner alike, the unsullied pastoral is removed from reach within the picture, isolated far beyond the muddy impasto of the foreground by Constable as an aureole on the distant cathedral, and rendered inaccessible in Turner as well by the mess people make in the foreground, which is the painting's historical present: Turner's Malvern Abbey in his volume *Picturesque Views* is a mirage, trembling above the chaos of rough tumbledown shacks outside its gate. The ideal—in this pictorial structure—can be envisioned, but never arrived at. The grammatical equivalent of this postponement of paradise comes in Blake's poem of homage to Milton, where the building of Jerusalem is both nostalgic and millennial, belonging to the past ("We have built," Blake says, as if the heavenly city had since then been demolished) and to the future ("I will not cease . . ."), but never to the present. What is left is pastoral deconsecrated, or a pastoral that has degenerated into the merely agricultural. Instead of a place fit for "the holy Lamb of God," there are only the "pleasant pastures" or "green & pleasant Land" of England, as bereft of divine meaning as the landscape rid of fairies over which the Wife of Bath grieves, the wilderness cursed by the departing gods in Spenser, or the dryadless Hyde Park of Peacock. And a worse deconsecration is to ensue: the demise of the agricultural into the industrial, which builds Satanic mills instead of heavenly cities, and has its own sardonic definition of pastoral. For the industrial age punishes those who cannot or will not find work, by detaining them in a pseudopastoral existence—an eternity of unscheduled tedium, of hanging about on street corners or drifting aimlessly about the countryside—which Orwell describes in the up-to-date pastoral, *Down and Out in Paris and London.*

Blake does, in the prefatory poem to Milton, call for the weapons—bows, arrows, and spear—of the epic poet, who in singing of arms and the man is himself performing a deed of warlike valor. But he intends to employ this armory only to engage in "Mental Flight," and that—in the passive resistance of the Lady in *Comus* or Christ in *Paradise Regained* to their tempters, of Wordsworth in *The Prelude* to the French Revolution, or of Calidore in *The Faerie Queene*, unbuckling his armor and lying down to sleep—is the choice of the pastoral hero. Since America has an unmisgivingly epic literature, there is no such surrender of weapons in its history. On the contrary, the Western film, America's homemade mode of epic, regularly names itself after the particular firearm it is lauding, in films like *Winchester 73* or *Colt 45;* and when the Western urbanizes itself, Clint Eastwood stalks San Francisco brandishing what he affectionately apotheosizes, in *Dirty Harry,* as "a 44-Magnum—the most powerful handgun in the world." This small contrast of pastoral disarmament against the technological force saluted by American epic catches a larger dissimilarity between the two literatures, with which I shall end.

The characteristic gesture of English literature seems to be renunciation or wearied defeat. It complains of a land from which the gods have abdicated, and of a consequent imaginative impoverishment. So its recurrent mode is pastoral; its recurrent mood, elegiac. American literature, however, has always seen its destiny as epic. Its initial task is the epic and heroic one of conquering terrain—achieved in New York, in jest, by Irving's Knickerbocker, who forges deeds and lineages to legitimize the Dutch claim to the island; then in earnest by Whitman, who exponentiates the city from his own prolific, polymorphous ego, and populates it with comradely look-alikes; achieved continentally by the novels of Dreiser, Dos Passos, or Upton Sinclair, who, when running in 1934 for governor of California, acronymically called his party EPIC (after the slogan "End Poverty in California"). Because American literature assumes as its obligation the integration of a vast, uncharted national territory, its epics covet the status of grand industrial projects, bridging space and abbreviating time, engineering things into semblance or unison: hence the technological heroism imaged in Whitman's self-propagating printing presses, in Melville's try-works on the *Pequod,* or in Hart Crane's steely, tensile Brooklyn Bridge. But while American literature is constituting—or, given the alliance in it between imagination and industry, manufacturing—a new world, English literature is interring an old one. It is a literature strangely inured to failure and regret, modulating everything into pastoral elegy. Its sadness cannot be blamed on recent historical reverses, since it exists already in the earliest writing I have mentioned. England's antique ribald merriment is a dim memory even to the Wife of Bath (and to Falstaff). Centuries later, in *The Entertainer,* John Osborne makes a declaration similar to the Wife's: the closing of the music halls means—like the extinction of the fairies—the decease of old England.

The best that Shakespeare's John of Gaunt can say of his country is that it is a "demi-paradise." And he too is incorrigibly English in worrying, like Wemmick in his moated villa, about the immurement of his "other Eden," in contrast with the territorial expansiveness of the American imagination. "This fortress built by Nature for herself"—even Nature is in quest of a retreat, a retirement home—is served by the sea "in the office of a wall, / Or as a moat defensive to a house." Gaunt joins the other characters I have quoted in prophesying the depletion of pastoral, its lapse into mere agriculture:

> This land . . .
> Is now leas'd out—I die pronouncing it—
> Like to a tenement or pelting farm.

Later, in *Richard II,* this infested garden is seen being pruned and trimmed into discipline by horticultural politicians. This is English literature's notion of its allotted ground: the walled garden or the moated house, corresponding to the islanded self, private or privated, sundered from the unifying continent, as in the traumatic insulation Arnold describes in "To Marguerite":

> Yes! in the sea of life enisled,
> With echoing straits between us thrown,
> Dotting the shoreless watery wild,
> We mortal millions live *alone.*

Each literary generation describes, with its own differences, the same place. In Auden, it is the vicarage garden, the natural milieu of the detective story. But this pocket-sized Great Good Place contains, of course, a corpse. "Who is ever quite without his landscape?" Auden asks in his poem about those detective stories that he sees as fables of our guilt and our common perdition. More sadly scrupulous, Eliot in "Burnt Norton" declines even to enter that garden:

Footfalls echo in the memory
Down the passage which we did not take
Towards the door we never opened
Into the rose-garden.

How can this sense of loss be rationalized? Not by history; only by myth, which exists to explain to us our expulsion from heaven or from paradise. The English imagination mournfully cherishes the recollection of a defunct Golden Age, which, as Orson Welles says, "only the oak trees and the flowering chestnuts remember truly"; alternatively—in Arnold's poem, in Donne's indignant denial that we should be islanded alone, and in the landlocked seas of Wordsworth's "Intimations of Immortality"—it dreams of once belonging to a larger landmass from which it has been dissevered. Whatever its source, this dirge is the refrain of English literature, and defines, I think, its quietly aggrieved Englishness.

ENDNOTE

This essay was originally delivered as a talk at the annual meeting of the North American Conference on British Studies, held at Endicott House, Massachusetts Institute of Technology, October 30, 1982.

Stanley Fish

Short People Got No Reason to Live: Reading Irony

N OT TOO MANY YEARS AGO, Randy Newman wrote and recorded a popular song that quickly became notorious. It was called "Short People" and began by declaring that "short people got no reason, short people got no reason, short people got no reason to live." The song went on to rehearse in detail the shortcomings of short people, which included small voices, beady little eyes, and the inconvenience of having to pick them up in order to say "hello." It wasn't long before groups of short people were organizing to lobby against the song; it was banned in Boston, and there was a bill to the same effect introduced into the Maryland legislature. In the midst of the hullabaloo occasioned by the song, its author rose (metaphorically, of course) to say that he had been misunderstood: it was not part of his intention to ridicule short people; rather, he explained, it was his hope that by choosing an object of prejudice so absurd, he might expose the absurdity of all prejudice, whether its objects were Jews or women or blacks or Catholics, or whatever. He was, in short, or so he claimed, being ironic.

Not surprisingly, Newman's statement did not settle the matter. His critics, it seems, were unimpressed by what he said, and they had various ways of discounting it. Some simply declared that he had lied. Others invoked the familiar distinction between intention and utterance: he may have intended no slur on short people, but his words say otherwise. Still others turned to psychology and explained that while Newman perhaps *thought* that he was free of prejudice, his song displayed his true feelings, feelings he had hidden even from himself. In short (a phrase that should, I suppose, be used sparingly in this paper), rather than providing a point of clarity and stability,

Newman's explanations (not heard as explanations at all, but as rationalizations or lies) merely extended the area of interpretive dispute.

I find this incident fraught with implications for the practice of literary studies, and especially for the practice and perception of irony, for what Newman perhaps has learned (I say perhaps because I am in no better position than anyone else to rule absolutely) is what Defoe and others had already learned to their respective costs: irony is a risky business because one cannot at all be certain that readers will be directed to the ironic meanings one intends. According to our most recent theorist of irony, such problems are special or marginal rather than general, for in general, that is for the most part, ironies are stable. I am referring of course to Wayne Booth, who roundly declares, "I can without blushing say: I *know* that Jane Austen intended Mr. Bennet's statement as meaning something radically different from what he *seems* to say."[1] Indeed, Professor Booth knows a great deal more than that about a great many stably ironic works, and the principles underlying his knowledge are the subject of his book, *A Rhetoric of Irony*, a book that instructs us both in the ways of detecting irony and in the ways of processing it. Stable ironies, Booth explains, have four identifying marks:

1. They are intended, . . . deliberately created by human beings to be heard or read or understood with some precision by other human beings. . . .
2. They are all *covert*, intended to be reconstructed with meanings different from those on the surface. . . .
3. They are all nevertheless *stable* or fixed, in the sense that once a reconstruction of meaning has been made, the reader is not then invited to undermine it with further demolitions and reconstructions. . . .
4. They are all *finite* in application; . . . the reconstructed meanings are in some sense local, limited. . . . We can say with great security certain things that are violated by the overt words of the discourse.[2]

These "marks" are aggressively noted, and it is obvious that they represent an attempt by Booth to set limits on the operation of irony, so that its undermining of overt or literal meanings will have a fixed and specifiable shape, but unfortunately, they will not do as marks that *signal* the presence of irony (stable or otherwise), because it is precisely *their* presence that is in dispute when there is a debate as to whether or not a particular work is ironic. That is, one cannot argue for an ironic interpretation by pointing to these marks, because one will be able to point to them only as a consequence of an interpretation that has already been hazarded. Thus, for example, no one of the parties to the "Short People" dispute believes that the meanings he perceives were not intended; it is just that whatever intention is specified, it will be as much a product of interpretation as the reading it directs. Nor is it any help to say that an ironic meaning is always "covert," because the question of whether or not there *is* a covert meaning is precisely what is at issue, and therefore the covertness of a proposed meaning is not an argument of it; it is an argument. Things are no better with the third of Booth's marks, stability or fixity; the meanings proposed for "Short People" are *all* stable in that they do not involve further demolitions or reconstructions, but they are stable in different directions; that is, in as many directions as there are determinations of Newman's intention; and moreover, in their various stabilities, these same meanings are all finite and limited, offered, as Booth stipulates, with "great security" and certainty; it is just that not everyone is certain in the same way.

The certainty Booth desires is of quite a different order, for it would have to rest on something that was not itself a matter of opinion, and therefore subject to challenge; but what the Randy Newman example shows is that whatever one rests on in the course of identifying an irony will have exactly the same status as the reading that follows (with certainty) from it; that is, it will be the product of an interpretation. This holds equally for the steps, also four in number, by which an ironic meaning is supposedly processed or reconstructed. Step one, Booth tells us, is that "the reader is required to reject the literal meaning," because he will be "unable to escape recognizing either some incongruity among the words or between the words and something else that he knows." As an example, Booth cites this fragment from Voltaire's Candide, "When all was over and the rival kings were celebrating their victory with Te Deums in their respective camps," and declares that "the statement simply cannot be accepted at face value" (B–10). (The fact that I am always forced to explain the incongruity to an audience or a class in itself renders the declaration suspect.) But the incongruity will be inescapable only if it is assumed that the victory being celebrated by the two kings is the same one; if it has been established that the two kings entered the battle with different, but mutually compatible, objectives, then it would involve no contradiction at all to say that each had an occasion to celebrate a victory. The point is that incongruities do not announce themselves, as Booth assumes they do; rather they emerge in the context of interpretive assumptions, and therefore the registering of an incongruity cannot be the basis of an interpretation, since it is the product of one.

This means that Booth's second step—the trying out of "alternative interpretations or explanations" (B–11), will be performed in relation to an incongruity that is itself an "alternative interpretation." And when the third step is taken, and the alternative readings are sorted out by referring them to "the author's knowledge or beliefs," still another interpretive construct will have been introduced, for the characterization of that knowledge and those beliefs will be, as Booth says, a "decision" (B–11), a decision based not on direct inspection, but on a conjectural reconstruction of what the author might have known or believed. It is on the basis of that decision, made with reference to alternatives that are only alternatives in relation to an incongruity that is itself interpretively produced, that we finally take step four and "choose a new meaning or cluster of meanings with which we can rest secure" (B–12). That security, however, is as precarious as any of the interpretive links with which it has been fashioned. So long as they are in place, everything seems stable and incontestable; but so soon as any one of them is put into question— by disputing the presence of an incongruity, by adding one more to our list of alternative readings, by revising our sense of an author's beliefs—the entire edifice trembles, and the debate over whether an utterance is ironic or over which of several ironic meanings is the right one will begin again.

This is precisely the conclusion that Booth wishes to avoid, because he believes that to reach it is to abandon all hope of ever resting confidently in a reading or of being able to say to another, "My reading is better than yours." The stakes in this enterprise are very high, for, as Booth explains "if irony is, as Kierkegaard and the German romantics taught the world, 'absolute infinite negativity,' and if, as many believe, the world or universe or creation provides at no point a hard and fast resistance to further ironic corrosion, then all meanings dissolve into one supreme meaning: No meaning" (B–93). What Booth sees (although not always as clearly as one might wish) is that the shoring up of stable irony is the shoring up of meaning itself: "If the universe is ultimately an absurd multiverse, then all propositions about or portraits of any part of it are ultimately absurd ... [and] there is no such things as a 'fundamental violation' of the text" (B–267). This is a dark vision indeed, and one can only agree with Booth's desire to resist it and with his assertion that it is counterintuitive, given the wide range of communicative certainties that characterize our daily experience. What is required, of course, is an explanation of those certainties, and my quarrel with Booth is not that he seeks it, but that he finds it in the wrong places.

He finds it first of all in the Hirschian distinction between meaning and significance, a distinction between what the words say and what any number of interpreters, proceeding from any number of viewpoints with any number of purposes, might be able to make of them. Debates about significance are inevitable, but they can also be principled and grounded, because "running constant throughout any such debate would be agreement about meaning" (B–21); or again, "the central meaning of the words is fixed and univocal regardless of how many peripheral and contradictory significances different readers may add" (B–91). It follows, then, that "we have grossly exaggerated the actual disagreement even about the hard cases," for "in thousands of undisputed matters" we "read precisely the same work, but have chosen . . . to debate about what is debatable" (B–133). From this argument, it is a short step (really no step at all) to the notion of the "work itself"—identified with meaning—as the point of resistance to "ironic corrosion." That is, the work is "a structure of meanings, an order which rules out some readings as entirely fallacious, shows other readings to be partially so, and confirms others as more or less adequate" (B–242). It is the availability of that structure *before* significances are added to it that authorizes Booth to reject a reading in which "Claudius is the moral center of *Hamlet*," in the full confidence that "nothing in the work requires" him to accept it (B–19).

If these arguments seem circular, it is because they all rest on a single point, the perspicuity and independence of literal meaning. Indeed, each of Booth's key distinctions—between meaning and significance, between a "central meaning" and that which is debatable, between the "work itself" and what different readers and different circumstances might add to it—is no more than a distinction between a literal meaning, that which is indisputably and irreducibly "there," and interpretation, that which issues from some special perspective or set of interests. It is literal meaning, then, that grounds the interpretive process and provides a core of agreement, on the basis of which *principled* debate can then go on; for each of the readings generated in the course of debate will have to pass the minimal test of being compatible under the structure of meanings that remains fixed and univocal. In the case of "Short People," for example, any reading of Newman's intentions will at the very least have to take into account the fact that he uttered the words, "Short people got no reason to live," and meant them literally, even if it is then argued that he intends us to set aside that literal meaning for one that is ironic.

This argument will hold, however, only if the specification of literal meaning occurs independently of the interpretive activity of which it is to be the ground; that is, only if everyone who hears the utterance "short people got no reason to live," will hear it, at some basic level, in the same way. But, in fact, the dispute over the song is a dispute *about* its literal meaning, a dispute that arises because the words are heard, from the first, within different assumptions as to the circumstance of their production. If one assumes, as many of Newman's critics do, that the speaker, in saying that short people got no reason to live, is rendering a *judgment,* then the words will literally and immediately mean that short people do not deserve to live (and the way would then be open to arguing whether *that* literal meaning is offered seriously); but if one reconceives the speaker and imagines that he himself is a short person (as, in fact, Randy Newman is), then it is likely that the utterance will be heard as a *complaint,* and the words will literally mean that short people, because of the indignities and inconveniences they suffer, have nothing to live *for* (i.e., short people got no reason to live). In both cases there is a literal meaning and it is at once obvious and inescapable, but it is not the same one. The conclusion, a distressing one for Booth, is that literal meaning is no more stable (in the sense of being unchanging) than the interpretations it supposedly authorizes. Literal meaning, rather than being independent of perspective, is a product of perspective (it is the meaning that, given a perspective, will immediately emerge); it is itself an interpretation, and cannot therefore be the indisputable ground on which subsequent interpretations securely rest.

This is not an argument that Booth confronts because he never feels obliged to prove the case for literal meaning; he simply assumes it as something so necessary to his own position that any challenge to it would be unthinkable. There simply *must* be a level of fixed and unvarying meaning, for if there were not, rational inquiry would be impossible. To the extent that he provides evidence for his conviction, it is evidence drawn from the history of literary criticism, and more specifically, from events in that history that have *not* occurred. That is, whenever Booth feels himself in danger of giving interpretation more than its due, he pulls himself (and us) back into line by rehearsing a list of interpretations that have not been put forward:

We disagree about many "larger" issues: whether the Houyhnnms are to be seen as totally admirable, whether the Duke in *Measure for Measure* behaves badly, whether Mary Crawford in *Mansfield Park* is not unfairly treated by Jane Austen's moralizing voice. But nobody has suggested, even in this age of critical fecundity, that "A Modest Proposal" is a tragedy, or a paean to the British landlords or to Irish collaborators, or even a modest proposal for preventing the children of Ireland from being a burden to their parents or country. And nobody has suggested that "My Mistress' Eyes" or *Northanger Abbey* should be read either as non-ironic or as totally ironic, with no clear stop signs. Swift and Shakespeare and Jane Austen will not, after all, allow such freedoms; whether we like it or not, they determine, through the literary forms they created, both where we begin and where we stop (*B*–133-34).

The line of reasoning that follows from these examples is clear: in the long history of literary studies, there are certain interpretations that have never been offered seriously, interpretations that all of us would regard as obviously absurd. The explanation can only be that something is excluding these interpretations, while authorizing, at least as possibilities, a number of others; and that something could only be the intentions of the author as they are embodied in the verbal forms he has created, that is, in the literal meaning of the text.

This argument has a certain prima facie force, but it depends on an assumption that is never examined, the assumption that what *has* not happened is what *could* not happen. That is, for Booth, the fact that no one has ever suggested this or that reading is tantamount to a proof that no one ever will, or at the least, to a proof that if any one ever did, he would not be given a hearing. Unfortunately (or fortunately, depending on where you stand on these issues), Booth himself provides a counterexample to his argument when he turns, at one point, to Swift's "Verses on the Death of Dr. Swift," and specifically to the controversy over whether the lines spoken in praise of Swift by "one quite indifferent" are to be read ironically. Only in a footnote— it is almost as if Booth were trying to hide from himself the implications of what he is about to report—do we learn that the controversy is of recent date, and that, until 1963, "nobody had suggested irony in Swift's self-praise" (*B*–121). In that year, Barry Slepian published an article suggesting just that,[3] and, as Booth reports, "most of the discussions since 1963 have accepted his arguments." That is, the ironic reading did not exist until a single critic proposed it.

What is remarkable is that Booth, having taken note of this fact of literary history, does not see its relationship to his own position; in particular, he does not see that it undermines the case not only for stable irony, but for stability in general. It is crucial to Booth's argument that there be at least some works of which it can be said that they are indisputably either straightforward or ironic, and he takes great comfort from the existence of works that have always been read one way or the other. Here, however, is a work or a part of a work that until 1963 was considered ironic by nobody, and since 1963 has been considered ironic by nearly everybody; and if *A Rhetoric of Irony* had been published in 1962, the ironic reading of the last section of "Verses on the Death of Dr. Swift" might have been one of those of which Booth could have said, "No one has ever proposed it."

What are we to make of this? How can we take it into account without totally undermining our faith in rational inquiry and principled debate? The answer to this question will be found in a better understanding of how Slepian was able to do what he did. What is the explanation for his success? In Booth's model, the explanation could take one of only two forms: either Slepian is the first person in 230 years (with the exception of Swift) to have recognized the irony that was always there, or the lines are in fact not ironic, and for some reason, he has succeeded in exercising almost mesmeric powers over his fellow Swiftians; that is, he either saw the text clearly (where no one else had) or persuaded others to see a text that wasn't there. Of course he did neither; what he did was argue, and he argued in such a way as to persuade a significant number of his colleagues to see what he saw. He did not do this by simply *pointing* to the facts of the text (although that is the claim made by everyone who enters these waters); rather, he labored to *establish* the facts of the text, that is, to establish a perspective or a way of seeing from the vantage point of which the text would have for others the shape it had for him.

This is not to say that his was an act of unconstrained creation. The establishing of a perspective proceeds according to quite regular rules, rules that Slepian followed, even though he may have been unaware of them. The first rule is that one must remove the perspective that is already there, the perspective that is responsible for the text that everyone has hitherto seen. In this case, that perspective was established by two of the poem's first readers, Dr. William King, to whom Swift sent the manuscript for publication, and Alexander Pope, who apparently agreed with King's judgment that "the latter part of the poem might be thought by the public a little vain, if so much were said by himself of himself" (S–250). It was on the basis of this judgment that the two men, in consultation with others of Swift's friends, altered the poem and published a version that was immediately repudiated by the author. The text of the poem was therefore corrupt from its first appearance, and the "true" text was not available until 1937, when Harold Williams published his authoritative edition.

There is a lesson here for those who speak confidently of *the* text, but I will not belabor it, since I am more interested in the fact that the poem's textual history begins with the conviction that in lines 307-484, Swift is engaged in an indecorous act of self-praise. That conviction was not repudiated after 1937, but took a new and diagnostic form in the speculation by John Middleton Murry that at the time the poem was written, Swift's mind was already failing: "The sardonic objectivity gives place to an extravagance of self-laudation. So striking a lapse from decorum must be ascribed to a radical weakening of Swift's vigour of mind."[4] The Swift that Slepian inherits is the product of this interpretive tradition, and he makes his first and decisive move when he challenges that tradition in the name of the "real" Swift. "I think that a close look at 'Verses on the Death of Dr. Swift' will disclose that Jonathan Swift had a better understanding of the poem than Alexander Pope and John Middleton Murry" (S–251). This is a powerful move because it trades on the privileged status accorded to authorial intention in the Anglo-American literary institution; it is also something of a polemical sleight of hand, since Pope and Murry do not oppose their understandings to Swift's; they merely have a different view of Swift's understanding than Slepian does, or to put it more precisely, they see a different Swift in relation to whom the words they read have an obvious and immediate meaning. What Slepian must do is replace their Swift with another and when he does, the words of the poem will have the meaning that this new Swift *must* have intended. That is, while Slepian proposes simply to take a "close look" at the poem, what he really does is defer that look until he has positioned his readers in such a way that the look *they* take will produce the poem he wants them to see.

Slepian does this in workmanlike fashion, announcing that he will "first . . . dispose of Murry's biographical explanations" (S–251). By that he does not mean that he will challenge the relevance of biographical explanations in the manner of a doctrinaire New Critic; rather, he will propose an alternative set of explanations and thus dispose of Murry's Swift. In place of a Swift who is senile and wandering, Slepian puts the Swift of Thomas Sheridan, an early biographer, who declares that during this period, Swift's "faculties do not seem to have been at all impaired by the near approaches of old age and his poetical fountain . . . still flowed in as clear and pure a stream." Slepian then cites the evidence of "well sustained" poems that were written after this one, and concludes by asserting that "in 1732 Swift's mind was not 'weakening' " (S–253). (Of course, it could have weakened intermittently, but I am not so much interested in assessing Slepian's arguments as in analyzing the way in which he makes them.)

Slepian next disposes of the Swift of Pope and King, the man blind to his own vanity even in a poem whose very subject is vanity. He first argues from probability; it is much more likely "that Swift was up to his usual ironical tricks" (S–252). A second argument is stronger and more complicated: in the readings of Pope and Murry, the offending lines constitute an "incongruous addendum" (S–252); but Slepian promises to demonstrate that they are "the necessary completion of a complex pattern." That is, he promises to make the poem better. In the literary courtroom, there is no more powerful argument; for while critics, like other researchers, claim to be interested only in the truth, they are committed to finding a specifically *literary* truth, one that will validate the credentials of the work they have undertaken to examine. So that if Slepian can come up with a reading that improves the poem's reputation, the probability of its being accepted as a true reading will be very high.

Slepian begins by invoking another powerful institutional formula: the poem can be easily divided into three parts. An entire essay could be written on the effectiveness of declaring that a poem has three parts, an effectiveness that may have an explanation in the tendency of literary criticism, at least since Matthew Arnold, to appropriate the discourse of religion. At any rate, once you are told that a poem has three parts, and you know too that one of those parts has always been considered an excrescence, you know, with all the certainty that attends membership in the literary community, that the third part is about to be brought into a harmonious relationship with the other two and so contribute to the making of an "organic whole." Moreover, you know that that is what a critic is supposed to do, and when he does it, you are willing to give the reading that

results more than the benefit of the doubt. In this case it is done in
less than four pages and in two swift (no irony intended) stages. First,
Slepian points out that "no critic" in commenting on the first two
parts of the poem has mistaken Swift's ironies and exaggerations for
statements intended literally" (S–254). It follows then, from the un-
announced principle that the mode of a poem should be the same
throughout, that the third part is also ironic, and ironic in a way that
makes it compatible with parts one and two. That way is found
when Slepian declares that in this last section Swift makes himself the
object of his own irony; by characterizing himself as "humble, fear-
less, altruistic, diligent, innocent, and resolute, he is not presenting an
apologia, but making an assertion of his own vanity necessary to
complete his thesis that all mankind is egotistical, selfish and proud"
(S–256). The poem is thus given a perfect New Critical shape: "The
first part . . . says that people are vain; the second part that other
men are vain; the third part that Swift is vain" (S–256). *Quod erat
demonstrandum.*

Slepian, however, is unwilling to take credit for his accomplishment, and insists on yielding it to Swift, who, he says, "has left clues
. . . to show that he was not really taking himself seriously"; he himself has merely picked up on these clues, where others, for over 200
years, have missed them. Slepian's modesty is no doubt sincere, but it
is also (even if unself-consciously) strategic, since it displays his con-
formity with another unwritten, but powerful, rule, the rule that a
critic does not create, but only discovers meanings. Nevertheless, it is
obvious that the clues Slepian has persuaded so many other readers
to see become available only as a consequence of the change in perspective he brings about in this brief article. "Brings about" is perhaps too strong, because it suggests a wholly free act, whereas what
Slepian has wrought is a consequence of his having made arguments
that are recognized as telling by his peers, according to standards—of
truth, evidence, adequacy—that are inseparable from the institution's notions of what its members are supposed to do. These notions, or conventions, are enabling as well as constraining, and they
are in large part responsible for Slepian's success. In other words, he
succeeds neither because he alone is uniquely in touch with the work
itself nor because he has created the work out of whole cloth, but
because, in accordance with procedures authorized by the institution,
he has altered the conditions of seeing—the conditions under which
one might take a "close look"—in such a way as to cause many to

see a work other than the work they would have seen before he wrote.

Of course, the poem as it was previously seen was no less the product of some successful attempt (by a Pope or a Murry) to establish the conditions of seeing. To put it another way, while Slepian argues, as Booth insists that we must, from givens, he argues from givens that are only in place as a result of the kind of act he is himself performing. One of the givens that is in place when Slepian begins to write is the obvious irony of the poem's first two sections; and it is then open to him to presume on that irony when he moves to extend it to the third section, in a version of the "no one has suggested" argument ("no critic has mistaken Swift's ironies . . . for statements intended literally"); but it would be equally possible for someone to argue from the opposite direction, that is, from the fact that no one (before Slepian) had read irony into section three, to the demonstration that sections one and two are not really ironic either. And that is just what has happened since 1963. Writing in response to Slepian, Marshall Waingrow rejects the ironic reading of the encomium, but agrees that it does display Swift's vanity.[5] However, Waingrow contends, because the vanity is acknowledged, it can serve as a proper foundation for virtuous action (W–513). In effect, Waingrow is urging a change in the genre of the poem; in his reading it is less a satiric performance than a moral or homiletic one in which Swift offers himself as a model, necessarily flawed, of "moral perception." Of course, once the third section of the poem has been read in this way, it is inevitable that the first and second sections will be brought into line. This step is taken by John Irwin Fischer who sees in couplets like "I can not read a Line / But with a Sigh, I wish it mine" a "serious confession of Swift's envy" and "an act of true magnanimity." In Fischer's reading, every line "points" a moral, and the distinction between straightforward and ironic passages loses its force as what was once a poem becomes something very much like a sermon. (Swift's sermons are an important source for his argument.)

Of course, the poem can be read as a sermon only if the speaker is identified not with a persona, but with Swift himself, and indeed, the critical history of the poem coincides with the rise and fall of the persona as a central tool of literary analysis. As a notion, the persona operates to further the New Critical goal of enforcing a distinction between literary or aesthetic facts and the facts of an author's life. One sees this clearly, for example, in Maynard Mack's famous essay, "The Muse of Satire," which is essentially a set of directions for turning "apparently very personal poems" into satiric fictions.[6] By the time Slepian writes, this is a standard strategy, and he is able to rely on it (even though he does not invoke it) when he argues that Swift is not speaking seriously—that is, in his own person. But when Waingrow and Fischer elaborate a reading that is unashamedly autobiographical, it is a sign that it is once again becoming permissible to regard a literary work as the expression of deeply held personal views. In 1973 Robert Uphaus explicitly dismisses the persona theory—"Swift . . . is not exploiting a literary convention which we may conveniently dub the *vir bonus*"—and declares that "the man, Jonathan Swift, is the poem's matter, and his mind, rather than poetic convention, is the poem's governing form."[7] As more and more of the poem is returned to Swift, less and less is reserved for irony. Uphaus is willing to admit to the presence of some irony in the poem—it does not drop "completely out of sight"—but, he concludes, "the *over-all* effect . . . is hardly ironic" (*U–*415). In ten years we have gone from Slepian's all-ironic poem (itself put in place of a poem that was only two-thirds ironic) to a poem that is only fitfully ironic, if it is ironic at all.

This does not mean, however, that Slepian's reading has simply been set aside and no longer exerts any influence. Indeed, its continuing influence is seen precisely in the readings that are opposed to it, for they are constrained even in their opposition by what Slepian has established. In particular, he has established as central the issue of Swift's artistry. Having made the poem better by rescuing it from the charges of Pope and Murry, he has brought about a situation in which it would be professionally unwise for anyone to make it worse. As a result, a critic who wants to argue with Slepian has to argue in such a way as to validate Swift's artistry even more strongly than he does. That is, while one can certainly argue for a different "Verses on the Death of Dr. Swift," one would have great difficulty in arguing for a bad, or even an imperfect, "Verses on the Death of Dr. Swift." (Neither Murry's mad and senile Swift nor Pope's embarrassingly vain Swift is any longer with us, although one could certainly imagine circumstances under which they could be revived.) Just as Slepian could not have been successful had he not pointed to the givens and "taken-for-granteds" that were in place when he wrote, so no one who writes today will be successful if he fails to take into account the givens Slepian established.

This account of the critical process at once confirms and problematizes Booth's argument in *A Rhetoric of Irony*. In Booth's view, rational debate rests on a set of independent facts to which all parties subscribe; but what the recent history of Swift's poem shows is that, while debate is certainly grounded on facts, they are facts that have themselves been established as the result of debate. Membership in the category of the indisputable is determined in the course of disputes; givens are not given but made, and once made, they can serve as the basis for unchallengeable observations, until they are themselves challenged in the name of givens that have been made by someone else. The constraints and certainties that Booth seeks in all the wrong places—in a system of literal meaning, in the distinction between meaning and significance, in the fact that there are readings that no one has ever suggested—are to be found in the very process he would have them control. The result is that two of Booth's worst fears are confirmed, but in a way that removes their sting. The first fear is that what is ironic will be for the reader to decide, for in the absence of independent criteria, he may see ironies or not as he pleases. This, however, is an empty fear, for the decision a reader makes will have been possible only in relation to decision procedures that have been authorized by the institution. Someone who decides for reasons the institution doesn't recognize, i.e., someone who decides that the poem is ironic because its author's name is Jonathan, will not succeed in persuading anyone else to his view (at least not now).

This is precisely Booth's second fear: that the question of whether or not a work is ironic will be settled by whoever happens to be the most persuasive: "The critic with the most persuasive style wins because there are after all no rules imposed by 'the work itself' and there is no referee" (B–133). This is a fear Booth can feel because he conceives of persuasion as something that operates without constraints—as a form of sheer brute power—unless there is an independent object such "as the work itself" to control it; but power, like anything else, is a context-specific entity, and what will be persuasive in a situation is not a matter of "style" (a word that is particularly empty), but a function of the understood goals and practices, notions of what counts as evidence, and of what will be heard as a relevant argument, that define the shape of an activity in a particular historical moment. So that while there are no rules imposed by the work itself (an entity that is produced by persuasion and does not precede it), there are always rules, or rules of thumb, that are constitutive both of the possibilities and of the limits of what can be said and what can be demonstrated. One persuades neither on the basis of independent entities nor on the basis of pure will (another chimera), but on the basis of grounds that have themselves been established by prior acts of persuasion; and what one persuades *to* are new grounds. The whole of Booth's theory rests on the possibility and the undoubted fact of agreement; but he seems to think that there are two kinds of agreement, a good kind, to which persons are compelled by facts that are unassailable; and a bad kind, to which persons are forced by the illegitimate power of a discourse that rests on nothing. But unassailable facts are unassailable only because an act of persuasion has been so successful that it is no longer regarded as one, and instead has the status of a simple assertion about the world. In short, there are no facts that are not the product of persuasion, and therefore no facts that stand to the side of its operations; all agreements are the result of the process for which Booth seeks an independent ground, and therefore no agreement, however securely based it may seem for the moment, is invulnerable to challenge.

Thus, when a community of readers agrees that a work, or a part of a work, is ironic, that agreement will have come about because the community has been persuaded to a set of assumptions, to a *way* of reading, that produces the ironic meanings that all of its members "see"; and when and if that community is persuaded to another way, those meanings will disappear and be replaced by others that will seem equally obvious and inescapable. Irony, then, is neither the property of works, nor the creation of an unfettered imagination, but a way of reading, an interpretive strategy that produces the object of its attention, an object that will be perspicuous to those who share or have been persuaded to share the same strategy. In general, that strategy has just the shape Booth says it does. One assumes for the speaker an intention other than the intention that would have produced the meaning the words seem immediately to have, the literal meaning; but the meaning the words seem immediately to have is itself the product of an assumed intention within imagined circumstances; and therefore, when that literal meaning has been set aside for an ironic one, what has happened is that one interpretive construct has been replaced by another. That is to say, *if irony is a way of reading, so is literalness;* neither way is prior to the other, in the sense of being a mode of calculation rather than interpretation; both are interpretive ways, which are set in motion by cues and considerations that are themselves in place as a consequence of an interpretive act.

The point is a difficult one, but it may be clearer if we turn, for the last time, to Swift's poem. I can decide, as some readers have, that "Verses on the Death of Dr. Swift" is ironic, because there is a contradiction between Swift's claim that he lashes vices and not names (1.460), and his performance in this very poem. Or I can decide, as others have, that this claim is made seriously, and that for any number of reasons, Swift was simply blind to the contradiction. But I can also decide that the line is perfectly serious, because Swift conceives of the men he has named as the very incarnations of the vices he would lash, and therefore not as persons at all. In so deciding, I would be reading the line in such a way as to remove the contradiction it supposedly entails. But the presence or absence of a contradiction is one of those literal facts that are supposedly specifiable apart from interpretation. If contradictions can be made to appear and disappear by varying the assumptions within which reading occurs, then the literal level of meaning is as much an interpretive construct—the product of a way of reading—as the level of meaning we call ironic.

It is Booth's strategy in *A Rhetoric of Irony* to stabilize irony by linking it firmly to literal meaning. In my argument, that link has been made even firmer (indeed, too firm for comfort) by undoing the distinction between them, at least insofar as it is a distinction between something that is interpreted and something that is not. That is, by making literal and ironic readings equally the products of interpretation, I may have seemed to undermine stability altogether, because if interpretation covers the field, there is nothing on which a particular interpretation can rest. But what I have been trying to show is that interpretations rest on other interpretations, or, more precisely, on assumptions—about what is possible, necessary, telling, essential, and so on—so deeply held that they are not thought of as assumptions at all; and because they are not thought of as assumptions, the activities they make possible and the facts they entail seem not to be matters of opinion or debate, but a part of the world. Of course, it is not inconceivable that these assumptions could themselves be put into question, but that could only happen because other assumptions will have acquired the force once theirs, and are, at least for the time being, unquestioned in their turn. Rational debate— about whether or not a work is ironic or about anything else—is always possible; not, however, because it is anchored in a reality outside it, but because it occurs in a history, a history in the course of which realities and anchors have been established, although it is always possible, and indeed inevitable, that they will have to be established again. For Booth, the great question is, How can you know without doubt whether or not a work is ironic? My answer is that you always know, but that what you know, because it rests on a structure of assumptions and beliefs (which produce both literal and ironic meanings), is subject to challenge or revision, as a result of which you will still always know, even though what you know will be different. For someone like Booth, such a state of affairs is distressing, because it seems to doom us to an infinite regress of unstable interpretations; but one can just as easily say that it graces us with an endless succession of interpretive certainties, a reassuring sequence in which one set of obvious and indisputable facts gives way to another.[8]

ENDNOTES

[1]*A Rhetoric of Irony* (Chicago and London: 1974), p. 3.
[2]Ibid., pp. 5-6. All following (B—oo) quotes refer to this work.
[3]Barry Slepian,"The Ironic Intention of Swift's Verses on His Own Death," *RES* 14 (1963). All following (S–oo) quotes refer to this article.
[4]John Middleton Murry, *Jonathan Swift: A Critical Biography* (London: 1954), p. 459.
[5]Marshall Waingrow, *On Swift's Poetry* (Gainesville, Florida: 1978), p. 164. The following (W—oo) quote is from this work.
[6]Maynard Mack, *Yale Review* 41 (1951): 83.
[7]Robert Uphaus, "Swift's 'Whole Character': The Delaney Poems and 'Verses on the Death of Dr. Swift,' " *MLQ* 34 (1973): 403, 406. The following (U—oo) quote is from this article.
[8]This also holds for stable and unstable irony, insofar as the terms mark a distinction between ironies that are decidable and ironies that are not. Both decidability and undecidability are, like irony and literalness, ways of reading. That is, neither exists in the pure form (one constraining interpretation, the other allowing interpretation free rein) that gives Booth's argument its apparent urgency. The distinction between stable and unstable ironies is a real one, but its reality is a function of the availability at a particular historical moment of certain modes of reading; it is thus a conventional distinction that corresponds to conventionally produced entities. As a distinction between essences, however, it cannot be maintained, because the conditions of pure rationality and total interpretive freedom for which its poles stand would never obtain. To put the matter in the form of what is only an apparent paradox: all ironies are stable, even those that point in multiple directions, in that the shape they have (or don't have) will follow from in-place interpretive assumptions; and all ironies are unstable, even those that are sharply pointed, in that they are the product of interpretive assumptions, of ways of reading, and not the property of texts.

Wayne C. Booth

A New Strategy for Establishing a Truly Democratic Criticism

I wanted to be able to claim generality.
　　　　　　　—Stanley Fish

WHEN I FIRST GOT WORD that Stanley Fish was delivering "Short People Ain't Got No Reason to Live" at university gatherings throughout the land, I must confess that I was apprehensive. People kept telling me that he did not seem to be in total agreement with my views, and the title itself obviously contained some ironic reference, perhaps to the undeniable fact that I am tall, just under 6′2″, more probably to my notion that some interpretations ought to be given short shrift. Since I knew from experience that everything Fish does is done brilliantly, I feared that my goose was cooked.

Of course I had no real fear that any of my carefully wrought arguments would have been in fact refuted. Like everyone else, I had my interpretive assumptions in place, my trenches dug deep, my artillery at the ready. But I was still somehow scared. It seemed far too likely that careless listeners to his oft-repeated lecture might take whatever he had to say as confirming my already troublesome reputation as a well-meaning, even amiable, but rather muddle-headed, traditionalist.

I was in for two major surprises. On the one hand, as readers of *Daedalus* will have recognized, his lecture proves to be largely a generous elaboration and commendation of my work. On the other, I discover that where he disagrees with my work, I am for the most part persuaded by arguments that are not only temperate but just, based on a careful reading that is more concerned with understanding than with making debater's points.

There would be no use, all this being true, in my repeating here every step in my change of mind as I read and reread the essay and then returned to do a careful reading of his most recent book, *Is There a Text in This Class?*[1] After all, the readers of *Daedalus* can follow those steps in Fish's own pages, in a form much more cogent than I would be likely to achieve as a new—and probably *still* quite muddled—convert. Changing interpretive communities as I have just done is a slightly wrenching experience, and I may still have some things wrong. But I would like just to list, in Fish's own words, a few of the conclusions he has added to my beliefs.

First a few new truths from the book, before turning to the article in hand.

1. "Since others who have written on the poem [Milton's *L'Allegro*] have to a man sought to interpret it, they are necessarily wrong" (p. 6).

2. "There are as many meanings as there are readers" (p. 305).

3. "Unintelligibility . . . is an impossibility" (p. 307).

4. "No interpretation can be said to be better or worse than any other, and in the classroom this means that we have no answer to the student who says my interpretation is as valid as yours" (p. 317).

And here is a selection from the many I have noted in reading the present essay.

5. "That no one has ever suggested this or that reading is tantamount to a proof that no one ever will, or at the least, to a proof that if any one ever did, he would not be given a hearing" (p. 181).

6. "What is ironic will be for the reader to decide . . . he may see ironies or not as he pleases" (p. 188).

7. "In general, that strategy has just the shape Booth says it does" (p. 189).

A proper conclusion to a gratifying account.

II

Now, then, suppose I had gone to my final reward just as I typed that last word, "account." Suppose further that I had written those opening paragraphs in a tragic world where all the works of Stanley Fish and all *other* statements by Wayne Booth had been destroyed by some kind of demonically selective holocaust. While we're at the business of imagining one of those unreal interpretive communities that

Fish enjoys creating, let us imagine that not a single reader in that world is skillful enough to suspect that the statement is ironic from start to finish. In that world, the question of whether all or part of my statement was intended ironically would presumably be precisely the same question as it is in our world here—though no one would think of asking it. Yet every reader of *Daedalus*, in that world, would tacitly "vote" for a nonironic reading: Booth liked Fish's piece, and for the reasons he gave. In short, a whole world would read me wrong, *if* there is any sense to the notion of wrong readings. According to the question about intended ironies that lies at the center of *A Rhetoric of Irony*,[2] all such readers have everything backwards. Yet according to Fish, unless I have radically misunderstood him, we must say both that they have achieved one valid reading among many and that, even though they have misread the author's intentions, there is no sense in any claim that their reading is inherently inferior to a reading that someone coming from our world might offer them.

Shall we disturb them in their unanimity? Does it matter, to them or to us, whether the author intrudes now to tell them that every paragraph, every sentence, every clause of those opening paragraphs "says" something quite different from what he "means"?

All of the words I have quoted were actually written by Fish. All of them *could* conceivably be taken at face value by *some* careless or uninformed reader *somewhere*, in one of his imaginary communities. In Fish's terms, though not quite in my own, they could all be read "literally."[3] The character of the speaker who reports those words with approval (ostensibly some really knuckleheaded "Wayne Booth") is surely no more obviously absurd than the character of Mr. Collins in *Pride and Prejudice*, boldly rehabilitated by one of Fish's reading communities in *Text* (pp. 347-48). And he's not much more ridiculous than the portrait Fish gives of me in his essay. We can be sure that many inexperienced or uninformed readers (in Fish's terms, many interpretive communities) would find in his decontextualized words and my wild comments about them almost as much sense as they can make of what appears in our critical journals. But the whole statement was intended (note the word) to make no sense at all, except as a totally unfair distortion of Fish's views achieved by quoting his words out of the context of *his* intentions, insofar as I can infer them.

The facts are (note again my terms—though to talk of facts settles nothing in this particular debate) that Fish *intended*, in the book from which the first quotation is wrenched, a flat repudiation of what my stupid persona says he intended; the words quoted describe what he considers an unfortunate consequence of his earlier, not his present, views. He *intended* the second quotation as showing one unfortunate consequence of accepting a critical framework that he himself rejects explicitly. The words in the third quotation come closer to something Fish would himself say, but he did not *intend* them to be taken without the qualification that I expunge. The fourth quotation, again, is *intended* by Fish as a summary of what his enemies say about him, not what is true about him.

Readers of *Daedalus* cannot know any of this unless they happened to have read *Text*, just as they cannot be expected to catch the (slightly) milder wrenchings-from-context that Fish commits unless they happen to have read *A Rhetoric of Irony*. But when we turn to my three quotations from Fish's essay, any reader can easily check the distortions, suspect irony, and then move—perhaps instantaneously, perhaps laboriously—through the stages of interpretation that my book describes.

The point is not to describe that process here or to decide whether a nonironic reading of what I said does radical injustice to Fish; he knows as well as I know that it does. The point is that readers of my little spoof do not come bunched into two simple groups, those whose interpretive assumptions force them to ignore the ironies and those who catch them. Readers will fall along a vast spectrum, ranging from those of little skill and energy, who take every word straight, to those who sense something wrong from the first moment (with my weird title and my misquotation of Fish's), and then perform elaborate inferences about my intentions and even more elaborate evaluations of my success. We readers are, in the real world, though not in Fish's conceptual scheme, educable in short and manifold stages. We educate each other daily, if we are lucky, in how to move along a scale from misunderstanding toward understanding, and from varying degrees of dubiety to varying degrees of security (not "certainty," a word and a notion that Fish foists onto my talk about rhetorically established security and stability). We are quite unsure about many borderline matters, such as whether Swift meant the lines Fish discusses to be taken ironically. We have no doubt whatever about many other matters, such as whether Voltaire was intending irony when he showed both armies celebrating their victory (that the concept of victory is itself ambiguous and debatable, as Fish says, is another matter entirely). Some of these readings that now seem sure may later become unsure. But if they do, the change will not result from some total transmigration from one grand inter-pretive community to another; it will be much like the process Fish describes in the section on Slepian and Swift. Slepian, Booth, Fish, and others who care about what Swift might have meant will not share raw data from some imaginary "text in itself" (Fish is quite right in his claim that we never encounter such a thing). Rather, we try out possible pictures of the author as harmonious or inharmoni-ous with various hypotheses we form about what a given text might be doing. Unless he wants to argue that there is some sort of distinct interpretive community determining every conceivable reading and misreading of Swift's ironies, or mine—and that would mean an al-most unlimited number of communities—he will be forced, in deal-ing with my vile words, to enter the ordinary world in which bad misreadings can be talked about and turned into less bad ones, and less bad ones can become good, and good ones can be made better.

Does it matter to anyone but Fish whether some readers misread my words? (I know, as strongly as I know that Jane Austen was joshing in the lines Fish alludes to on page 176 of "Short People," that my misquotations will matter to Fish; indeed, he spends a lot of energy correcting people who give reductive reports of his views.) Are the notions of misreading and of improvement in reading of any real use to us? Is there no sense in which a straight reading of my jape is inherently inferior to an ironic reading? Fish concludes the title essay of *Text* as follows: "My message to them [people like Abrams and Hirsch who fear that Fish's views will lead to solipsism and relativism] is finally not challenging, but consoling—not to worry." Should we not worry? Are there consequences of his views that might justify at least some of the doubts people have raised?

III

I turn to consequences immediately, rather than to an attempt to show that Fish is wrong, because I suspect that his present position is in one sense irrefutable. The tight circle of his concepts appears im-pregnable, once we agree to abandon routine tests of experience in the real world and simply play with abstract concepts. Like many intellectual systems past and present (and by no means only systems of literary criticism), Fish's sociocentrism can handle quite nicely any objection to it by showing that, according to its own principles, the objection is both predictable and explicable within the system. The actual range of varieties of literary experience is simply put to one side while we theorize about what that range ought to be, given what we decide that certain concepts must mean. For Fish, the defined concepts are:

1. Assumptions, about the nature of readers, about texts, and about authors, the chief assumption being the seemingly self-evident point that we never have any version of texts and authors that is not in fact made by the reader, and its coordinate, that the reader is himself a product of a web of the conventional assumptions of his interpretive community.

2. Strategies or practices of argument, either "demonstration," which is impossible, or "persuasion," which is all we have.[4]

3. Purposes, which are finally reducible in all cases to the desire to persuade.

4. Facts or data, which are in all cases a product of the first three assumptions.

Working with these concepts, Fish has constructed a position that can handle every objection easily; it would be a fool's game to try to show that the structure is false or incoherent. A colleague of mine, the philosopher Ted Cohen, says that I am wrong in this, that in fact Fish's position is intellectually incoherent and quite flatly refutable. He may be right, but it surely depends on what we mean by refutable. The system covers the world nicely; it covers in advance any effort to shake it, because every criticism will be a confirmation of how the speaker's conclusions have been formed by the conventional interpretive strategy that his community imposes. And any reasons given for rejecting the system will either be simply ignored or, if noticed at all, reduced to an expression of groundless fears.

The marvelously efficient ways in which such monistic structures can work have been described with great care by a variety of pluralists in this century, and I do not have space to illustrate the matter here.[5] What their accounts show, finally, is that in the hands of any clever manipulator, closed systems are quite literally closed. It is simply wasted energy to try to break in at any point, whether at the level of fact (you misquoted me, you reversed my meaning) or at the level of assumption (why do you start *there* rather than *here?*). In talking of how our conceptual frames work, Fish is quite right to say that they constitute not only what we say but what we see. Another way of saying this is that, given his own conceptual framework—what

Ronald S. Crane would have called his "chosen critical language"—what he has to say about *A Rhetoric of Irony* is predictable and irrefutable.[6]

But of course that does not mean that we must buy either the system or its particular consequences for a particular text. As Fish himself would say, the way you can get at the problem of dispute about consequences is to find some way to "persuade" people that the assumptions should be changed. But we need not be bound by his peculiarly polar notion of persuasion versus demonstration. We can reason together about our critical languages, not in the sense of demonstrating that some are flatly wrong and others plainly right or true, but in the sense of probing whether they are more or less adequate[7] to our shared experience and more or less supportive or destructive of projects in the world that we all prize.

It is never easy to distinguish, especially at the borderlines, the useful theoretical structures, and the readings they generate, from the useless or harmful. Standards of usefulness obviously vary from system to system. Fish is himself quite explicit about repudiating concern for consequences; for his enterprise, they are irrelevant. On the one hand, the harmful consequences that people have feared—"the absence of any standards by which one could determine error, the impossibility of preferring one interpretation to another, an inability to explain the mechanisms by which interpretations are accepted and rejected, or the source of the feeling we all have of progressing" (*Text*–369)—all these and others will not follow on adoption of his views. The fears are in fact treated as the only conceivable reasons that might be offered against his system, and his chief strategy of persuasion is to address each of these fears, "one by one, and to remove them by showing that dire consequences do not follow from the position I espouse and that in fact it is only within that position that one can account for the phenomena my opponents wish to preserve" (p. 369). What is more important to him is that there *are no consequences* for the practice of criticism. "It does not follow from what I have been saying that you should go out and do literary criticism in a certain way or refrain from doing it in other ways. The reason for this is that the position I have been presenting is not one that you (or anyone else) could live by" (p. 370).

These claims should not deceive us into thinking that Fish himself does not try to live by the system he preaches. (Or should one perhaps say that he has gradually evolved a system that finally frees him to his preferred practice?) Indeed, my chief point is that in his current essay he does live by his own theory, and that the consequences of doing so are bad.

We should remember that the consequences of a theory are not to be judged primarily by the theorist. Fish may tell us again and again that there are no practical consequences, and that, besides, what consequences there are for theory are all to the good: "not to worry." But since he himself has relieved us from having to live by his elaborate structure, we are at least freed to decide for ourselves whether the theory, airtight or leaky, is useful or harmful.

Some of the bad consequences are demonstrable, in any sense of the word that matters. More of them are at most probable or possible. Fish's theoretical world has no room for this middle rhetorical ground between demonstration and his version of persuasion, but it is the ground on which we all live: a ground where tentative conclusions are tested by sharing opinions together, and then found to be more or less probable, according to criteria laid on the line.[8] Fish's language, in contrast, is all about totalities and necessities. "The extent to which this is a *decisive* break from formalism is evident in my *unqualified* conclusion that formal units are *always* a function of the interpretive model . . ."; "I wanted to be able to claim *generality*"; "solipsism and relativism . . . are *not possible* modes of being"; "there are *no* moves that are not moves in the game, and this includes even the move by which one claims no longer to be a player" (*Text*– 13, 15, 321, 355; *italics added*). In contrast, we who choose to dwell in the daily world of hard decisions about what to believe, in varying degrees of confidence and doubt, are free to say "maybe," and we know that our beliefs range, in the strength of our grasp, from firm to flabby.

What are likely to be the consequences, on our climate of argument, of Fish's quite different assumptions? The best evidence we have for an answer is Fish's own practice. Perhaps those converted to his views can escape the effects that his theory has on him, though that seems unlikely.[9] Certainly, in his works one finds a game played by rules that many of us will reject, even as we recognize why they appeal to many others in our beleaguered profession today—and not just in literary criticism.

In the first place, his pursuit of the absolute, irrefutable truth about how meaning is made by readers, not found in texts, has led to an increase of a tendency in his work that has always been a threatening one: to pursue abstract theory about what *must* be true rather than trying to observe what is true in the world as lived. This is unfortunate, for him and for us, because Fish has in the past shown an opposite tendency; in work after work, he engaged in an elucidation, often as good as any we have, of the powers of literary works, great and not so great. But he has also always been tempted by the appeal of startling theories about reading. Theory now seems to absorb him completely, and we must lament the rapid decrease of serious encounters with texts worth the effort and the corresponding increase of clever, but inconsequential, encounters with merely illustrative texts like "Private Members Only," "Is there a text in this class?" and an evanescent song.

His perfunctory discussions of the texts mentioned in "Short People" are by now all too typical. All of them, even the longest (the discussion of Swift's lines), tell us little about how to enrich or improve our own reading by attending to his. All are marshalled for the same repeated argument: no matter what happens in the world as lived, no matter what the patterns and purposes of texts as written, no matter how many thousands of stable (and unstable) ironies are shared every day (sometimes with great confidence, as in the question of whether Jane Austen is joshing in her portrait of Collins or whether I was being ironic in my praise at the beginning of this essay), no matter how much evidence or experienced critical opinion, including Fish's own, might be on one side of a question, one must *always* either find in the world of actual readers or invent in an imaginary world some alternative reading and then claim that "in theory" it is as defensible as any other—or rather, it would seem to be if we happened to belong to that maimed community.

Fish knows as well as you and I that people do understand ironies and reap rich rewards from doing so. He knows that people do misunderstand them and get in trouble (and cause trouble for others) by doing so. But theory says that all ironies are unstable (in the sense of being challengeable from some other position) just as they are all stable (in the sense of seeming self-evident to a given interpreter). So we must simply ignore what we know from experience and follow theory.

What we know in experience is that Swift intends many ironies, even in a poem with as many borderline and puzzling lines as we find in "Verses on the Death of Dr. Swift." When Swift shows us a mourner talking like this—

O, may we all for Death prepare!
What has he left? And who's his Heir?—

the ironic contrast of interests and tones is considerably clearer and surer than most inferences I make about my life in the real world of 1982. If Fish wants to imagine someone who will miss the contrast, let him, though one need not go to imagination. As reading speeds go up and reading skills go down, we can find plenty of interpretive communities who would not only miss the contrast if the poem were read aloud by a lecturer with a thesis, but who could not work it out on their own. The plain truth is—though I can only assert it here, without providing evidence—that students who read Fish's current theories do indeed feel a freeing from concern about getting things right. Fish has said that to be concerned about students' mistaken interpretations is simply an expression of fear about lost authority. Nonsense. It is quite precisely a fear that students will close off whatever chance they may have of gaining the joys and other rewards of learning how to read. But more of this later.

Dwelling with and on his abstract and nonconsequential theory leads him to another kind of harm that I am naturally aware of at the moment: a striking carelessness with other people's texts. It is true that the tendency to find what his theory seeks has always been a temptation for Fish. But the kind of casual distortion of other people's meaning that he exhibits in "Short People" has been increasing in the last decade, and one can only suppose that it springs from some sense, obviously reinforced by his current monism, that *getting the report as near right as possible* cannot really matter very much. "Not to worry."[10]

It would be tedious to dwell on all of the misreadings Fish constructs in order to buttress his case. In describing two of the more important ones, I should perhaps underline the ease with which Fish will be able to show that my claims demonstrate his position. To the degree that he has really seen the facts of the case in ways different from my own, we together will illustrate for him just how thoroughly facts are made by systems, not given by the text. Still, I think that any third party who takes a look at any part of my text to which he refers will find it—not surprisingly, except from Fish's view—falling somewhat closer to my interpretation than to Fish's co-optations.

Consider the picture he gives of my overall project. What he attributes to me is a failed effort to construct a general theory of interpretation.

The whole of Booth's *theory* rests on the possibility and the undoubted fact of agreement; but he seems to think that there are two kinds of agreement, a good kind to which persons are compelled by facts that are unassailable; and a bad kind, to which persons are forced by the illegitimate power of a discourse that rests on nothing (p. 189, *italics added*).

Now it is true that my project depends in part on the possibility and the undoubted fact of agreement. But it also depends on precisely the kind of disagreement that Fish seems to think should trouble me. The whole project is not about whether, in theory, interpretations can be authoritative, but about how, in practice, authors and readers get together—and fail to get together—through unusually oblique texts. "This is mainly a book about how we manage to share ironies and why we often do not; it is only secondarily a book of critical theory."[11] In focusing on "stable ironies" (except for a final two chapters on deliberate instabilities), I was quite explicit about their being stable only within the community of an intending author and a reader seeking to enjoy intended effects. Without that focus, every ironic statement can in some sense be taken straight, and every straight statement can be read as ironic. "Thus I can be sure that almost every statement that I label non-ironic, Kenneth Burke could prove to be ironic in a dozen different senses; so could I, in another kind of inquiry, and without contradicting my original claim, since I would not be employing the same question about the same subject or pursuing that question with the same methods" (p. xii). "Private interests or associations can lead to 'ironic' reversals of any passage. . . . Any statement can easily be turned into its opposite and made more 'interesting.' . . . Once you get the hang of it, you can go on indefinitely improvising reversals . . ." (p. 18).

Fish thus simply ignores most of what I care about—the whole effort to figure out how it is that sometimes irony works for rhetorical and literary power and sometimes produces muddle or total misreading or hostility. To put his systematic distortion in his own terms: his strategy of interpretation, dictated by the effort to prove his theory that no reading is inherently superior to any other (though it will always seem superior to those within any given interpretive community), determines his perception of the facts.

But we are really not all that helpless under the whip of theory, if we don't want to be. It is quite possible for a critic to give a more or less adequate account of a position before attacking it—one that the original author might at least recognize.[12] Everyone whose work has ever been discussed knows, as Fish must surely know, the difference between being addressed and being mutilated in the way that my opening words here mutilate his works. And we all have ways, some of them surprisingly effective, of recognizing subtle degrees of distortion, accidental and deliberate, and further ways of testing hypotheses about what authors mean behind their obliquities. *Irony* tries to describe those ways and to illustrate how they work, through a wide range of doubts and securities (never certitudes, in Fish's sense of "demonstration"). All of that drive for particularity is simply lost in Fish's account, as he turns the book into a clumsy effort at his kind of theoretical universality.

This leads us to the second distortion. In order to pursue and study what I called stable irony, I had to let my readers know at the beginning what it was we were trying to study. And so I gave an operational definition of such creatures—a list of the marks by which, *if* we saw one of this kind, we could recognize it. Those preliminary marks, explicitly announced as what "will give us a practical preliminary notion of the irony that for now concerns us" (p. 5), take up all of two pages of my book. Only then do I turn to the real task of reconstructing the steps we take in reading irony and then to the problems of how we employ, in detecting and interpreting actual ironies, clues provided by (1) straightforward warnings in the author's own voice, like my open declaration above; (2) disparities between claims made by a speaker and what we know to be true (modulated by our conviction that the author himself shares our knowledge); (3) "conflicts of facts within the work" (again provided that we have confidence that the author knows better); (4) clashes of styles that cannot be accounted for by the author's own carelessness or ignorance; (5) conflicts between an expressed belief and what we can infer of the author's beliefs; (6) violations or fulfillments of expectations produced by our past experience with various genres; and (7)—to cut a longer list short—that most unreliable of all clues, the ability of a passage to yield greater literary satisfaction when read ironically.

In Fish's account, those preliminary two pages of clarification are turned into almost the whole show. He deals with the four marks as an attempt

to set limits on the operation of irony, so that its undermining of overt or literal meanings will have a fixed and specifiable shape, but unfortunately they will not do as marks that *signal* the presence of irony (stable or otherwise), because it is precisely *their* presence that is in dispute when there is a debate as to whether or not a particular work is ironic.

Precisely: that is why I wrote an entire book about what *does* signal the presence of the marked beast.

That is, one cannot argue for an ironic interpretation by pointing to these marks, because one will be able to point to them only as a consequence of an interpretation that has already been hazarded. (p. 176)

Of course. I was not quite so foolish as to deny any of that. But because Fish needed the target of someone who is on a quest for certainty through recognition of easy marks, he simply ignores most of the book. And I would argue that though his particular theory did not absolutely coerce him into that kind of distortion, it can hardly be considered blameless, since its effect, if taken seriously, must be to make pointless my whole effort to discern distinctions of degree in what we "know," guess at, and fumble toward in reading irony.

Fish later does mention briefly the four "steps of reconstruction" that I turn to after the definition (*Irony*–10-12), and later still he says that the way we read irony, perhaps referring to those steps and the elaboration that follows them through many pages, "has just the shape Booth says it does." He then gives a much simplified version of that way ("Short People"–189). But in his zeal to show that all ironies are unstable (as of course they are, in his definition, just as they are all in a sense stable), he simply ignores my effort to deal with the vast domain of ironies that are unstable in everyone's view (poems by Sylvia Plath and Robert Graves, some Beckett, and some Plato). Unless the reader happens to read his last footnote, there is little hint that two out of my nine chapters deal with instabilities that in Fish's theory mark all ironies. The Wayne Booth that Fish constructs would of course never write such chapters; he would instead, on theoretical grounds, declare unstable ironies out of court, because they do not fit the theories that Fish wrongly attributes to me or allow for the certainties that he thinks must always be my goal.

And so it goes, through the whole essay. Points that I make in my book are made by Fish as if in refutation—for example, about the riskiness both of using and of interpreting irony. I am hectored for ignoring theses that in fact underlie my whole enterprise—for example, *"if irony is a way of reading, so is literalness"* (p. 189). And evidence that I cite in great detail, evidence that would fatally undermine Fish's closed circle of "we always know, but we never know," is simply ignored.

Nobody but me can be expected to care very much about any of this in itself; certainly one could name worse hatchet artists on our scene. But it should matter to everyone when a brilliant critic shows us that such practices do not matter to *him*. After all, does he not continue to get away with them? Does not his reputation seem to increase with each new slaughtering? It does not surprise me to find, in reading *Text*, that whenever Fish discusses a critic I know at all well, he almost unfailingly commits the same distortions, usually without troubling to mention the reasons the critic offers. (Perhaps we victims should form a club.)

The subject of reputation leads to a further bad consequence, the reduction of critical judgment to voting. Fish's whole argument about the radical indeterminacy of disputes about irony depends from the beginning on his finding examples, either in the real world or in his imagination, of counterreadings:

—Listeners disputed about the song "Short People."

—He finds that when he reads aloud the passage from Voltaire about victory Te Deums, his audiences (presumably all of equal intelligence and alertness and freedom from his influence?) don't see the irony on the spot ("Short People"–177).

—He can *imagine* an interpretive community whose members would take Mr. Collins as a moral center to *Pride and Prejudice* (*Text*,–347-48).

The curious assumption running through these and other examples seems to be that criticism should operate on the principle of one man-one vote. No matter who the man or woman might be who performs a reading, no matter how little experience with a given genre a judgment may spring from, no matter what forms of inattention, prejudice, ignorance, inexperience, or emotional crippling have been at work.[13] If someone calls "Hold!" Fish will report a new proof for the nonexistence of stability. As soon as anyone disputes

the presence of an incongruity, by adding one more to our list of alternative readings, by revising our sense of an author's beliefs—the entire edifice trembles, and the debate over whether an utterance is ironic, or over which of several ironic meanings is the right one, will begin again. ("Short People"–178)

Here is a democratic criticism with a vengeance.

That the debate will begin again, at least when certain readers offer a reversal of previous readings, is a simple matter of daily experience (though Fish in his essay insists, for his own reasons, that this is a conclusion I would wish to avoid; see "Short People"–178). But the fact that disagreement will lead to debate about a presumed stability says little about how the debate will or should turn out. When one of my colleagues, a psychologist, revealed to me twenty years ago that he had read *Brave New World* "straight," as the portrait of a desirable society, he gave me one vote on that side of the case. For Fish, such a vote must seriously undermine our knowledge that Huxley was engaging in satire. "Only if everyone who hears the utterance 'short people got no reason to live,' will hear it, at some basic level, in the same way," he says (p. 180), could we really talk about stabilities as I try to do.

His citation of the difficulties with Swift's ironies is revealing here. Fish writes as if the obvious creation of new votes as time passes could be generalized to the claim that all ironies are equally subject to similar questionings. But as Fish well knows, he has chosen a new reading that is (unlike many that he imagines, e.g., that of the admirable Mr. Collins) clearly borderline; if it had not been so, Pope and King could not have altered the one part of the poem without destroying the rest.[14] (Try to imagine their reversing the thrust of *A Modest Proposal* to protect Swift from the charge that he agrees with his projector's cruel plan.)

As my book insists, much of the delight in reading ironies like Swift's comes from making our way on very thin ice, risking hunches, admiring the author for *his* risks, discovering our errors, trying again, finding that the ironist was after all ahead of us once again— or that for once we have come out ahead. Every extended ironic work of any quality will necessarily offer large numbers of debatable invitations at the borderlines, and some of the debates will be irresolvable. New readings of such ironies, like new readings of any kind, can indeed, as both Fish and I say, tell us something about the culture in which they arise. But they say nothing whatever about the fundamental questions raised by my book: How is it that we manage, sometimes, wonderful moments of communion between ironic authors and ourselves, as we work through texts that seem to say "something else"? And what makes the difference between such ironic texts, like the couplet by Swift that I quoted above, and the seemingly similar passage from Swift that has become difficult to read in a single way? And how do both of those differ from still others, like many of the ironies in Beckett and Plato, that are finally irresolvable though at least as rewarding? All such complex questions get reduced in Fish to the simple claim that in theory we can never hope to collect enough votes to know that a given reading is better than any other.

No doubt I have sometimes seemed to rely on such popular polling when I have pointed out that nobody has ever questioned a given reading. But there is a great difference between the affirmative argument for the possibility of a kind of knowledge, on the grounds that everyone present in a discussion agrees (an ancient and honorable way of debating rhetorically about issues in the domain of opinion), and the negative argument that whenever any person or group questions a belief it instantaneously joins a vast undifferentiated mass of beliefs equally dubious. If Fish could find whole cultures who took Mr. Collins as an admirable moral center, or who thought Swift uniformly solemn, his discoveries would not count as evidence in the deliberately narrowed question I was asking about such passages: Did the author *intend* here an irony for our savoring or not? Though the fact that Fish and I and all other experienced readers laugh at Collins and at Swift's victims (including his persona) may not *demonstrate* irony, it surely puts the burden of proof where it belongs.

To attempt to get out the vote and count all votes equally is a marvelous way of stifling argument about real texts in real interpretive communities. As Fish often says, his system simply wipes out many problems that formerly plagued us. Those problems can only be dealt with by complex and indecisive arguments that turn on possibilities and probabilities, and it may at first seem legitimate for a theorist to come along and say, "Surely it is *possible* that a community could arise in which X would appear as Y. Therefore . . ." But to say that it is *possible* to imagine someone offering an absurd reading is only to play games with the word "possible." To say that it is possible—nay, even probable, since it has already happened—that some readers will take *A Modest Proposal* as a serious recommendation that we eat children teaches us nothing new. And to elevate such readings to democratic equality does not, as Fish seems to think, solve or dissolve complex intellectual problems. Unless we choose to follow Fish—"not to worry"—such readings raise immense practical problems, for the shade of Swift, for you and me in the classroom, for our culture.

In a curious passage in *Text,* Fish tries for once to imagine an argument that would establish the superior "normality" of one reading over another. First he sets up two real communities who would give contrary interpretations of the same "text," a question put by a student: "Is there a text in this class?" There seems to be a kind of plausibility, he says, about claiming that the group whose members hear this as a question about whether a textbook will be used is more "normal" than the group whose members hear it as a question about whether the unknown teacher shares Fish's beliefs about the irreality of texts. The only argument he can think of for such a claim is based on superior numbers: "more people would 'hear' " his key question in sense one than in sense two, and this might seem to suggest the superior "normality" of sense one (p. 308). Not so.

To admit as much is not to weaken my argument by reinstating the category of the normal, because the category as it appears in that argument is not transcendental but institutional; and while no institution is so universally in force and so perdurable that the meanings it enables will be normal for ever, some institutions or forms of life are so widely lived in that for *a great many people* the meanings they enable seem "naturally" available and it takes a special effort to see that they are the products of circumstances (p. 309; *italics added*).

They are *not*, that is, the product of more or less careful and attentive rhetorical negotiation of readers with authors through a text!

A further side to Fish's poll-watching is revealed whenever he talks, as he frequently does, about the reward system of "the profession." "The greatest rewards of our profession are reserved for those who challenge the assumptions within which ordinary practices go on" (*Text*–366). Again and again he reveals that, for him, success in getting a hearing is not only a primary goal; it is a prime validation of what one says. The ultimate vote is thus a vote for the critic, revealed in his popularity. The topics he has discussed, he says, "are basic topics, and anyone who is able to advance the discussion of them will automatically be accorded a hearing and be a candidate for the profession's highest rewards" (p. 371). And as if that were not clear enough, he adds, "One incontestable piece of evidence in support of this assertion is the fact that I have been here speaking to you for an entire week, and that you have been listening." In short: You wise people out there have chosen to listen to me. What better validation could one ask for?

In reading such passages, I am reminded of an anecdote from George Orwell's childhood. When he was about eleven years old, some acquaintances found him in the family garden, standing on his head rather than greeting them properly. "Why are you standing on your head?" "You are noticed more," he replied, "if you stand on your head than if you are right way up."[15] It is not hard to guess what Fish will think about my noticing his theory with all these attentive pages.

But poll-watching is only one of many bad argumentative modes that Fish's model is likely to encourage. Even at its most serious, even if we excuse his delight in constructing straw men, the model is a bad one for literary argument, as it would be a bad one for argument in any profession. (Again I should distinguish between Fish the theorist and Fish the attentive reader of any work he loves. In *Text*, for example, when he dwells on a work like *Coriolanus* for many pages, one can only admire the clarity of his gaze—except when theory dictates.)

The mode of argument can be easily summarized—too easily. First, you must find a simple polarity of two obviously impossible extremes, stated as abstract concepts. In his present practice, the two are his former reader-centered theory, shown with surprising ease to have been contradictory, and the (caricatured) "formalism" to which that theory was "rhetorically opposed." But any two seeming opposites will do.

Second, you choose an equally simple polarity of "models" of argument, in his case "demonstration versus persuasion," and you then develop "strategies" for convincing people that one of them, demonstration, is obviously impossible, and that the other, persuasion, can show both of the first two polar opposites—lectocentrism and formalism—to be egregiously false. Fish's argumentative world has no room for middle grounds. That middle ground of maybes, between demonstration and persuasive bludgeoning and trickery, that middle ground where traditional rhetoricians taught us "topical" reasoning, simply is wiped out.

Having thus reduced argument to skillful polemic, having not only "preserved generality by rhetoricizing it" (*Text*–16), but reduced rhetoric to the explicit goal of winning, you can then turn your strategies to the problem—not of meeting opponents' arguments about your central claims (why bother, since your claims are self-proving?)—but of meeting their "fears" about the consequences of your triumphs. Your opponents *must* be motivated not by good reasons, but by fears (or other irrational motives like the desire for power), since the conclusions that they attack have by now become indubitable to you, confirmed by everything you look at. And you then show, one by one, why the fears are unjustified—because your theory expresses a truth that has no consequences. Not to worry.

What is bad about this is not that Fish will win converts—as he surely will—to whatever position he next announces as the one and only truth about interpretation. What is bad is that, while all this is going on, those of us who attend to him (as I am now doing) fail to educate ourselves in the critical modes that have grappled with Fish's problems in subtler and suppler ways. There are models of rhetorical inquiry, for example Kenneth Burke's, Chaïm Perelman's, and Michael Polanyi's, that would enable us, if we studied them, to conduct real and important controversy in the worlds of criticism, of the social sciences, and of politics. There are models of how to deal with conflicting critical systems and the conflicting interpretations that they generate—Stephen Pepper's, Ronald S. Crane's, Richard McKeon's, and again Burke's—that would not leave us asserting one simple supreme truth while at the same time pretending to accept all comers. There are impressive programs that can accommodate the truth in Fish's claim that we are constituted socially, our judgments depending on communal norms, without the sacrifices Fish's program entails (Mikhail Bakhtin, Fredric Jameson). And there are current challenges to our beliefs that really go to our roots (for example, Jacques Derrida's). Meanwhile we fuss with Fish's simpler and easier views.

Fish's dogmatic refusal to look critically at his own current assumptions is curious when viewed in the light of his new emphasis on the importance of relating all observations and conclusions back to assumptions. By changing his system occasionally and rejecting *past* assumptions, he gives the impression of open-mindedness. But at any one point he is an absolute monist. No other way can be tolerated, and no other way needs to be brought seriously into the dialogue, as an alternative hypothesis to be tested with questions like those I have raised here.

Meanwhile, certain truths that are important for contemporary criticism become reduced in his embrace to dogma. He has discovered, one is glad to note, that the self is somehow social, not private or individual. But he then ties that discovery to a version of intersubjectivism that the great American social psychologists, Dewey or George Herbert Mead, or the great European critics of the private self, would have scorned. He has discovered that facts are not given by the real world but are constituted by our "interpretive strategies," strategies made up of "assumptions, practices, and purposes." But he then offers a version of this truth, a truth known to ancient rhetoricians and modern pluralists, that would make Cicero, Peirce, or McKeon weep. He has discovered that "sentences emerge only in situations"—that, in a nice formula now circulating, *words* do not mean, only *people* mean. But then he develops a version of that truth that ignores the transactions between two parties in "meaning," leaving the receiver gloriously in charge but in danger of remaining frozen in private—which is to say, in the new version, public—certitude.

Finally, a different kind of harm entirely, one that threatens not the would-be critic but the beginning reader. Consider again the misreading that Fish imagines, in *Text,* of the passages in *Pride and Prejudice* about Mr. Collins. The invented reading—Collins as moral center of the novel, not a comic figure at all—is of course useful to Fish and to any of his readers who find it representative of any possible community of readers. But to his imagined readers who really would fail to savor the delights of Jane Austen's portrait—what will be its use to them? It will be harmful, though to say so may seem a very undemocratic thing to say. It will be harmful, first, because it will deprive them of one of the world's available harmless delights—and as Samuel Johnson liked to say, we don't have so many of those that we can afford to squander any. But it will be harmful also because anyone who rests satisfied with it will be cut off, in this one instance, from genuine converse with a powerful mind and large spirit—from Jane Austen, that great conversationalist potentially living on the page. Such readings are harmful to their performers, in the precise and simple sense of limiting their access to a world richer than any they are likely to invent for themselves. Fish writes very well and he invents new readings very well; but nothing he has invented about Milton or Swift or Austen and nothing I can hope to invent myself should be allowed to replace the exercises in the imagination that attending to great imaginative works provides. Those works can provide what George Santayana called "imaginative rehearsals for living," what Kenneth Burke calls "equipment for living"—but they can do so only if we make them at least equal partners in the dance.

But we need not ascend so high. To take my opening pages "straight" is to close down one's world, at least at the moment of reading, narrowing it to an inane exchange between a mutilated Fish and a hermetically sealed Booth. To see them as ironic is to open outward into a debate between two quite different—and I hope more interesting—people about issues that matter. It would be absurd to see nothing wrong in the first reading, even if only you and I had managed the second. Why, in short, should we impose on ourselves a theory that encourages us in our far too natural temptation to wear blinkers as we move through the world?

IV

But I can keep up this posing no longer. It is high time to confess to the real strategy of this, my doubly ironic essay. Everything that I have said since Part II began has been an outrageously ironic spoof, parodying the kind of self-protective, fearful, traditionalist responses that Fish's brilliant and irrefutable work too often evokes. I know that it is not entirely fair to readers to have kept them in the dark so long, especially after having already played one ironic trick at the beginning. But I thought that there was no way to dramatize so well the true power of this new democratic criticism that I have embraced. I also know that the more skillful readers who have come to understand Fish's interpretive strategies from the inside will have recognized throughout that I was being ironic. But they will also have figured out that, for good or ill, there just may be other interpretive communities in which everything I have said will be taken entirely straight. And others still in which . . .

Oh, well—not to worry. As we have been assured, no consequences for our practice will follow from our decision about which interpretive community to join.

Meanwhile, I feel personally easy. Now that I know that attention from our peers is the best proof we have of our validity, how could I *not* feel easy in the discovery that Stanley Fish has chosen to validate *me*.

ENDNOTES

[1]Stanley Fish, *Is There a Text in This Class?* (Cambridge: Harvard University Press, 1980), hereinafter referred to as *Text*.
[2]Wayne C. Booth, *A Rhetoric of Irony* (Chicago, University of Chicago Press, 1974), hereinafter referred to as *Irony*.
[3]On the ambiguities in our notions of what is literal, see my *Critical Understanding* (Chicago: University of Chicago Press, 1979), pp. 54-58.
[4]See the final chapter of *Text*, "Demonstration vs. Persuasion: Two Models of Critical Activity." A shorter version of this essay is reprinted in *What Is Criticism?* edited by Paul Hernadi (Bloomington: Indiana University Press, 1981), pp. 30-37.
[5]A fine account of this matter is given in Walter A. Davis's "*Wille Zu Macht* in Baltimore," to be published this year in *Critical Inquiry*. I am indebted throughout to Davis's much more detailed and comprehensive arguments. See also his *The Act of Interpretation: A Critique of Literary Reason* (Chicago: University of Chicago Press, 1978). I have also profited from reading an unpublished essay by James Phelan and, on the earlier Fish, Phelan's *Worlds from Words: A Theory of Language in Fiction* (Chicago: University of Chicago Press, 1981), especially chapter 2.

6There are superficial similarities between Fish's current enterprise and Crane's effort to move his debate with the New Critics from the level of argument about data and interpretations to the level of a critique of "critical languages." But there are important differences, both in the reasons for pushing inquiry behind data to various assumptions and methods and in the way of moving once different assumptions are found. See Crane's *The Languages of Criticism and the Structure of Poetry* (Toronto: University of Toronto Press, 1953).

7On the criterion of adequacy as a source of choice among equally coherent systems, see Elder Olson, "The Dialectical Foundations of Critical Pluralism," in *"On Value Judgments in the Arts" and Other Essays* (Chicago: University of Chicago Press, 1976), pp. 327-59. See also *Critical Understanding*, pp. 90 and 200-3, and the index entries for "Comprehensiveness."

8For a cogent account of what happened over the past few centuries as the status of such thinking declined, see Stephen Toulmin's effort to renovate "topical" thinking, as represented in "Logic and the Criticism of Arguments," a lecture delivered recently at Michigan State University. For a more extensive renovation of the topics, see Chaïm Perelman and L. Olbrechts-Tyteca, *The New Rhetoric: A Treatise on Argumentation,* translated by John Wilkinson and Purcell Weaver (Notre Dame, Ind.: University of Notre Dame Press, 1969).

9For a scary exercise in similar procedures, see Walter Benn Michaels and Steven Knapp, "Against Theory," *Critical Inquiry* 8(4) (Summer 1982): 723-42.

10I was tempted here to report other people's complaints about Fish's recent distorted reporting—Ronald Dworkin, James White, and others. But—not to worry: I have the evidence in my files.

11*Irony*, p. ix.

12That the task is not beyond human capacities is suggested by one's encounters, rare but real, with critics who produce recognizable accounts. For a fine example, see Susan Suleiman's review of *Irony*, "Interpreting Ironies," *Diacritics* (Summer, 1976). See also her exchange with me in *MMLA* (Spring 1978 and Spring 1979).

13I discuss these "five crippling handicaps" in *Irony*, pp. 222-27. David Hume gives a fuller and better account of them in "Of the Standard of Taste."

14Note also that Fish radically underplays the importance of changes in the printed text of Swift's poem, as these changes supported differing readings ("Short People," pp. 181-183). I can't help wondering where in the world Fish thinks he will find, even among those who are far more wedded to "the text itself" than I am, anyone for whom the discovery of one more altered text will provide "a lesson."

15Bernard Crick, *George Orwell: A Life* (Harmondsworth: Penguin, 1980), p. 89.

Eugene Goodheart

The Text and the Interpretive Community

F OR ROLAND BARTHES, the pleasure of the text is in the making of one's own text at the expense of another's. "Thus begins
at the heart of the critical work the dialogue of two histories
and two subjectivities, the author's and the critic's. But this dialogue
is egoistically shifted toward the present: criticism is not an homage
to the truth of the past or to the truth of 'others'—it is a construction
of the intelligibility of our own time."[1] In shamelessly confessing the
egoism of the critical act, Barthes casts doubt upon the objective
existence of "others." If he were consistent, he would have also enclosed the past in quotation marks. His motive is to make the "other" vulnerable and defenseless, so that he can appropriate the text to
his own purpose: Barthes speaks of the critical act as theft. Interpretation, in this transvalued sense, is not obliged to represent the text,
which is, rather, broken up so that it can fill the critic's subjectivity.
In declaring "the death of the author," Barthes eliminates interference from an author's intention. The critical reader's access to the
text is immediate, dominant, and impermanent. The critic's text is
always provisional, his relationship to the text of the other in constant change. The critic need be faithful only to his own changing,
desiring subjectivity.

Barthes' nemesis—what makes the reader submissive to its meanings, extinguishing the reader's mobility and desire, and therefore the
possibility of pleasure—is "Replete Literature," "the monster of totality." For Barthes, Replete Literature is constituted by bourgeois
stereotypes (Balzac's *Sarrasine*, the text studied by Barthes in *S/Z*, is
an example). "Life, then, in the classic text [the replete and totalized
text], becomes a nauseating mixture of common opinions, a smoth-
ering layer of received ideas."[2]

More than any writer on either side of the Atlantic, Roland Barthes has brought the reader into the foreground of critical discussion. It was he who first undermined and usurped the independent text. When we turn to American reader-oriented critics, Stanley Fish, for example, we encounter significant differences. Barthes' vocabulary, in the French manner, has a metaphysical resonance. Words like nature, history, totality, suggest that every reading is more than an engagement with a particular text: it is a sort of philosophical or political meditation for which the particular text is an occasion. Fish's sensibility, in the Anglo-American manner, is empirical. If Fish denies the independent integrity of the text (which the New Criticism asserted), unlike Barthes, he virtually never rises above the interpretive occasion it offers, though he is continually theroretical about the nature of texts. Barthes' *pleasure* in and of the text disappears into a veritable *industry* of reader-oriented criticism, a reflection of another obvious cultural difference—though there is more intellectual pleasure in Fish's interpretations than in most American criticism. Whereas for Barthes the text is broken up or emptied so that the imaginative writer-reader may construct his own estate (Barthes is a lord of *écriture*), for Fish and his fellow readers, the text is largely an opportunity for interpretations by an academic community bound together by shared assumptions. The difference is between a kind of individualism and a kind of collectivism: Barthes, the exponent of a mandarin subjectivity; Fish, the democratic advocate of plural interpretive communities, though, as we shall see, Fish's pluralism is somewhat illusory.

I want to focus critically on the work of Stanley Fish, because among American reader-oriented critics, he has been in the vanguard as an abolitionist of the independent text and a foremost advocate of the interpretive community as the source of authority. Fish did not decide against the independent text because of the "monster of totality." According to the introductory essay in *Is There a Text in This Class?* (his collection of theoretical essays), Fish's career is the momentum generated by his attempt to answer the question, "Is the reader or the text the source of meaning?"[3] Against the prevailing New Critical orthodoxy that the text is the source of meaning, Fish decided in favor of the reader. As he discovered in the course of reading and debate, however, the idea of a stable, meaningful text did not disappear with the privileging of the reader. Like Barthes, Fish in his thinking about texts has undergone continual change (an abiding value for both), and the change has been in the direction of emptying the text, denying it inherent structure, properties, and intention: it is the reader who comes to realize the text.

Fish's conception of the role of the reader has also undergone change. If the reader is still in a privileged position in relation to the text, he is no longer an isolated entity; he now suffers the constraints of an interpretive community. Properties, structure, and meaning inhere neither in the reader nor the text. They emerge, rather, from a transaction between the communal reader and the text. It is the community that provides the constraints formerly attributed to the text. The effect of communalizing the reader is to avoid "the rankest subjectivism"[4] (Fish apparently believes that a communal consciousness is not a subjective one). Having already eliminated objectivism, he believes that he has also eliminated subjectivism, not only by communalizing the reader, but by creating a dynamic transactive model in which it is impossible to divide subject from object.

Nonetheless, the effect of the transactive model is to deny the substantial otherness of the text and to absorb it into the consciousness of the communal reader. Fish objects to another model of reader response, which holds that "the work is a repository of properties and meanings (corresponding to the intention of the author) which then come into contact with a reader more or less conformable to them." Fish speaks of this as an "adversary model" in which the work opposes the reader, and attributes to it a static view of the encounter between reader and work.[5] On this view (according to Fish), the reader confronts a work of fixed meanings with his own, possibly divergent, fixed views. What Fish proposes is a view of the work in which whatever resistance the text may offer to the reader is overcome by the activity of the reader. Fish overcomes the dualism of subject and object by effectively affirming the activity of the subject and denying the reality of the object.

Of course, one can never completely escape objectivism: it is, among other things, a necessary condition of polemic. Fish believes that a true, or at least false, interpretation of the post-structuralist, or Derridean, view is possible when he characterizes one of his own essays in the following way: "This essay is an attempt to dissociate myself from a certain characterization (*actually* a *caricature*) of the post-structuralist or Derridean position"[6] *(italics added)*. Objectivism is entailed in distinguishing between Fish's position and that of Derrida, and between Derrida's position and caricatures of it. It is difficult to see how Fish's transactive model would contribute to the making of these distinctions. His dissociation from the post-structuralist position, however, is revealing.

In the caricature . . . [of the post-structuralist or Derridean view] the denial of objective texts and determinate meanings leads to a universe of absolute free play in which everything is indeterminate and undecidable. In the view I put forward, determinacy and decidability are always available, not, however, because of the constraints imposed by the language or the world—that is, by entities independent of context—but because of the constraints built into the context or contexts in which we find ourselves operating. Thus I pursue a double strategy in the manner indicated by my title ["Normal Circumstances, Literal Language, Direct Speech Acts, the Ordinary, the Everyday, the Obvious, What Goes With Saying, and Other Special Cases"]. I want to argue for, not against, the normal, the ordinary, the literal, the straightforward and so on, but I want to argue for them as the products of contextual or interpretive circumstance and not as the property of an acontextual language or an independent world.[7]

The abolition of the independent text is not intended to change the way we live or, more specifically, the way we read, but only to change our theoretical understanding of what happens when we read. The intended effect is so benign that nihilism, even skepticism, seem to be inappropriate terms to apply to Fish's view.

For Fish, the normal, the everyday, and the straightforward cannot be taken for granted. They are sustained by an act of interpretive will that is always subject to collapse. Thus Shakespeare's *Coriolanus,* in Fish's view, is an expression, both in its theme and its form, of the precariousness with which "the social bond" (in which the everyday and the normal occur) is constituted. On his reading, *Coriolanus* is a speech act about speech acts, which constitute the social bond.[8] The play shows the precariousness of that bond, from which Fish draws the conclusion that "in fact men break those bonds whenever they like."[9] Fish could have said that men *may* break the bonds. The difference between the two conclusions is the difference between a logical and a historical view of experience. If one examines the logical conditions of the speech act as Fish does (following John Searle and J.L. Austin), one can draw the conclusion that men are free to deconstitute the social bond when they like. In history, however, men do not "enjoy" such freedom. More often than not, they maintain the bonds, because the risk of social or political retribution makes them fearful, or because the bonds have been internalized and present a psychological barrier too great to overcome. One of the citizens in *Coriolanus* says as much: "We have power in ourselves to do it, but it is a power that we have no power to do" (II. iii). What Fish does not take into account in his concern with the *logic* of speech act theory are the *historical* circumstances that make the breaking of bonds possible or not. In moments of social crisis (created by economic difficulties or war, for example), the social bonds may be weakened or possibly strengthened, but even then, the phrase "whenever they like" would be insensible to the constraints that exist for most men in any society. It is an ahistorical view that makes possible Fish's statement: "Institutions are no more than the (temporary) effects of speech act agreement, and they are therefore as fragile as the decision [how fragile is this decision?], always capable of being revoked, to abide by them."[10] "Temporary" and "fragile" (unmodified by a sense of how durable these qualities may be)—how temporary and fragile, for instance, is the division between East and West Germany?—underestimates the difficulty of unmaking institutions and institutional agreements. The absence of a historical perspective (which, as we shall see, is characteristic in Fish's theoretical work) has radically skeptical, if not nihilist, implications, which Fish does not pursue by disposition and preference.

Fish thinks that he gains all the determinacy and even stability that he needs from "interpretive communities," though, significantly, he does not tell us how these communities arise and gain authority. All he can tell us is that they exist. Jonathan Culler, another exponent of reader-oriented criticism, finds Fish wanting precisely at the point where he invokes interpretive communities. "The task of literary theory or poetics," Culler writes, "is to make explicit the procedures and conventions of reading, to offer a comprehensive theory of the ways in which we go about making sense of various texts. But here Fish's theoretical enterprise abruptly vanishes."[11] Such a theory would have to be, in part at least, a historical theory, which itself becomes a text or a series of texts as volatile as another text. (Where the independence and stability of texts are concerned, Fish makes no distinction, indeed argues against distinctions, between kinds of text.) I suspect that Fish stops short of offering a comprehensive theory of interpretive community because he wishes to exempt it from the unstable and dependent status of texts. The interpretive community, in fact, is the one relatively stable idea in Fish's constantly changing universe of reading. As a tacitly felt experience, the interpretive community paradoxically achieves the authority of constraint that it might lose if it became the explicit object of interpretive reading. If it became the explicit object of interpretive reading, we might see that it is an assumption as vulnerable to skeptical investigation as the view that meaning inheres in the text.

The result is that interpretive community in Fish's argument, despite the central place it holds, is far from clear.

> But given the notion of interpretive communities, agreement more or less explained itself: members of the same community will necessarily agree because they will see (and by seeing, make) everything in relation to that community's assumed purposes and goals; and conversely, members of different communities will disagree because from each of their respective positions the other "simply" cannot see what is obviously and inescapably there: This, then, is the explanation for the stability of interpretation among different readers (they belong to the same community). It also explains why there are disagreements and why they can be debated in a principled way; not because of a stability in texts but because of a stability in the makeup of interpretive communities and therefore in the opposing positions they make possible.[12]

Does this mean that people within the same interpretive community never disagree, or that agreement is possible only within the same interpretive community? I can imagine disagreement between persons who share the same assumed purposes that would not be resolved by our appeal to those purposes, the purposes themselves being subject to different interpretations. Readers, after all, are distinguished from one another not simply by their purposes and assumptions, but by differences in intelligence and temperament as well. I can also imagine agreement across the boundaries of different communities. Fish's model of community, to the extent that one can construe it from the passage above, suggests a tedious, even dangerous homogeneity and stability, belied, I might add, by the liveliness of his disagreements with members of his own interpretive community. As an interpreter of enormous skill and ingenuity, Fish presents himself as very much his own man in a community of diverse views.

If the meaning of interpretive community is unclear, so is the basis of its legitimacy. Fish deduces the necessity of interpretive communities: they supply the stability of interpretation that was once thought to depend upon the independent text. But he does not say where its authority comes from. In order to do so, he would have to provide a historical perspective that would yield, if not a general theory of the origins of authority, examples of how particular communities become authoritative.

One consequence of the absence of a historical perspective is that the existence of an interpretive community, necessary as it is for shared reading, appears to be an arbitrary construction. Fish himself does not recognize the arbitrariness of the interpretive community when he writes: "Thus the act of recognizing literature is not constrained by something in the text, nor does it issue from an independent and arbitrary will; rather it proceeds from a collective decision as to what will count as literature, a decision that will be in force only so long as a community of readers or believers continue to abide by it."[13] Fish does not explain why a collective decision is less arbitrary than a decision made by an independent will, though it is true that a decision that has the force of a collective will may have a less arbitrary *appearance*. The arbitrary basis of Fish's conception of the interpretive community (it is more than a matter of appearance) can be seen in the possibility of an indeterminate number of communities in which the most outlandish readings are possible. If each interpretive community is law-abiding, the universe of interpretive communities is anarchic. Fish speaks of the possibility of a *Pride and Prejudice* in which Mr. Collins is not seen as the object of irony and of a legitimate Eskimo reading of "A Rose for Emily."[14] Such readings are improbable, if not impossible, in the community that Fish inhabits (hence the confidence with which he affirms the normal, the everyday, the obvious), but Fish's theory (in which the text has no inherent structure) makes the outlandish always possible. There are no objective standards for discriminating between various communities. A historical perspective does not in itself provide standards for discrimination, but it does enable an understanding of why certain views gain authority and others do not. It also provides a place for the author: his intention and his situation.

By "author," I do not necessarily mean an agency or function that transcends the text. I mean what has gotten into the text to form its structure and properties. Though Fish on occasion seems to admit the author into the interpretive community,[15] the implication of his argument is that the author has no real place in it. It is not simply that the reader can never be sure about the author's intention; it is that whatever the reader may believe that intention to be (as it manifests itself in the structure and properties he perceives) is dictated by the assumptions of the community. Of course, this does not mean that the text is not already a constituted interpretation of something. The distance between interpreter and what is being interpreted does not require the view that the text not have an intrinsic structure. (It should be pointed out that, in Fish's view, the text produced by an interpretation is as uncertain in its "objective" meaning—indeed, it has no objective meaning—as the original text is to the first reader.) Fish seems to have converted the pragmatic difficulty, perhaps impossibility, of ascertaining and evaluating the author's intention into an epistemological denial of its objective existence. Simply to assume the existence of authorial intention is to require the effort to discover it; to dissolve the assumption is to eliminate a valuable constraint within the interpretive community.

Thus the typological reading of *Samson Agonistes* (a reading that assumes that the Old Testament anticipates the New) is for Fish simply one possible reading of the poem. "For some present-day readers Christ is 'in the text' of *Samson Agonistes,* for others he is not, and before the typological interpretation of the poem was introduced and developed by Michael Krouse in 1949, he was not 'in the text' for anyone."[16] If the question becomes one of evidence, the answer is that there is no objective way of establishing the presence of typology in the text. Fish is right in saying that the absence of reference to Christ may be evidence of "Milton's intention to respect typological decorum."[17] But the ambiguous nature of the evidence does not justify Fish's conclusion that it is the interpreter or the interpretive community that establishes its presence or absence. The question of the presence of typology should be addressed not only to the text, but also to the context in which it was written. (Fish is interested in the *present* context of the reader.) Continual reference to the assumptions of present interpretive communities dissolves attention to the text of the other and to the truth of the past.

The idea of interpretive communities has been with us for a while. Michael Polanyi has characterized the tacit assumptions by which scientists circumscribe the ground on which scientific progress occurs.[18] In *The Structure of Scientific Revolutions,* Thomas Kuhn argued that the motives which establish a particular "paradigm" as authoritative within a field are not purely scientific.[19] An understanding of scientific progress depends in part on a sociology of sciences. In his recent work, Frank Kermode appeals to an institutional (i.e., academic) consensus in establishing the freedoms and constraints of interpretation as well as the "canon" to be interpreted.[20] Yet the standards and commitments of the academy have been deeply affected by a pervasive skepticism. Kermode's own appeal to institutional standards is hardly untouched by this skepticism. In a review of Kermode's *The Genesis of Secrecy,* Michael Fischer remarks that, "to the extent that institutional pressures invest interpretation with appearance of significance, they also encourage the suspicion that criticism is an end in itself and foster the free play that Kermode thinks they restrain."[21] I suspect that Kermode is trying to add a voice to the need for restraint at the same time that he finds the seductions of free *skeptical* play hard to resist. Yet Fischer's point is an important one, because it calls attention to the problematic character of the idea of an interpretive community in a time when everything is under suspicion. Do agreements occur because of the existence of interpretive communities or despite their absence? It is impossible to answer the question unless we know more than we do at present about the character of such communities.

Kermode suggests what a consensus of genuine conviction and commitment is like, when he notes the belief in Christianity that motivates the work of most biblical scholars, who defend the truth of the Gospels against all challenges: "Few would undertake the ardors of the training held necessary for serious work in Biblical criticism without some such prior commitment." Fischer says, surprisingly, that "literary criticism is not all that different." For Matthew Arnold, it was "not all that different," because criticism was in a sense a transposition of biblical scholarship to secular literature—or rather, criticism, inspired by a cultural or spiritual significance in biblical literature from the dogmatizing and literalizing theological mind. But no such purpose determines the contemporary institutional study of literature. It is touching, but puzzling, that Fish should speak of "the bedrock of belief" that underlies the interpretive community.[22] This is the language of conviction singularly lacking in most interpretive communities today.

The interpretive community that sustains biblical scholarship depends upon a belief in the *presence* of the biblical text. Whether the presence is that of a divine voice or of an inspired human one is less important than the view that the text inherently contains something of utmost importance. Such a view makes it possible for the text to provide constraints to the interpretive community in addition to those provided by the social history of the community. I would guess that there is a correlation between the confidence that the members of any interpretive community have in the validity and value of their interpretations and in the authority of the community, and the belief that what they read has an independent reality.

Of course, Fish can assimilate the belief in the presence of the text to his theory of interpretive communities. He would have to characterize the community of biblical scholars as naive in failing to recognize that its conviction rests on the false assumption that the text has presence. Yet what Fish's demystifying sophistication (assuming for the sake of argument that it is a true demystification) cannot account for is the consensus of genuine conviction and commitment of biblical scholars. Fish says that the truth of interpretation is ultimately a matter of its persuasiveness, which he equates with politics.[23] Why should we be *persuaded* by an interpretation (as distinguished from being impressed by its ingenuity) if we don't believe that it corresponds—or better, responds—to a presence in the text? Whether such a view is naive or not, that is what it means to be persuaded. One is not persuaded simply because one belongs to the same interpretive community. Moreover, why should the view that the text has an inherent structure be more problematic than the view that the communal reader determines meaning, if all views are ultimately the products of assumptions?

The belief that a text has inherent properties need not severely curtail the freedom of the critical reader. It does not preclude the indeterminacy of texts. In fact, there is a degree of indeterminacy in all texts that varies according to the suggestiveness of the text. Indeterminacy is a perpetual provocation to readers to interpret texts again and again. There are even moments when a reader may be torn between possible interpretations and unable to decide between them, which is not the same as saying that undecidability is a condition of all interpretive situations. Indeterminacy is not necessarily a function of the absence of intrinsic structure or the substantial otherness of the text. It is in part what spills over the boundaries of the text (the implications beyond what is explicit) and in part the inherent incapacity of one mind (that of the reader) to make a perfect adjustment to the mind of another (as represented by the text). It is a false logic to infer a reader whose mind is *tabula rasa,* as Jonathan Culler does in his approval of what he calls Fish's "theoretical reorientation," from the idea "that the poem is some kind of autonomous object which contains its meaning as an inherent property."[24] The reader need not suspend his subjective disposition in reading a poem that is filled with meaning. Culler's statement is equivalent to a view that, in a relationship between two people, one has to be dead for the other to be alive.

Wolfgang Iser puts the case well for an indeterminacy that proceeds from the substantial otherness of the text. In speaking of a novel by Ivy Compton Burnett, Iser asks us to "bear in mind the fact that the speakers are not aware of the welter of the implications they bring about and can themselves only reveal these implications to a limited extent."[25] Presumably, the narrative consciousness has a fuller understanding of the welter of implications than the characters themselves. But it is also true that the narrative consciousness in fiction does not fully know itself, hence the need for the critical reader. In turn, the critical reader may not be fully aware of the welter of implications of his own discourse, hence the need for the critics of critics. Though "the welter of implication" complicates, it does not dissolve the substantial otherness of a text.

The welter of implications may never be possessed by any particular reader, who appropriates a work according to his disposition and purposes. But he is not given license to distort at will so long as the text has its inherent structures and intentions. An empty text is indeterminate only in the sense that there is nothing to determine in an objective sense. It is the reader who forms and determines the interpretation, or rather, forms and determines the text itself. "Indeterminacy" should be reserved for the full or structured, not the empty, text. I can illustrate degrees or kinds of appropriation (on this side of distortion) by contrasting two readings of Abraham's intended sacrifice of Isaac, one by Erich Auerbach and the other by Søren Kierkegaard.

In the opening chapter of *Mimesis,* Auerbach distinguishes between the biblical and the Homeric methods of the representation of reality as a basis for subsequent interpretation of Western representations of reality. The methodological interest of Auerbach's reading (genuine as it is) serves what might be called a pious view of the biblical story.

A journey is made, because God has designated the place where the sacrifice is to be performed; but we are told nothing about the journey except that it took three days, and even that we are told in a mysterious way: Abraham and his followers rose "early in the morning" and "went unto" the place of which God had told him; on the third day he lifted up his eyes and saw the place from afar. That gesture is the only gesture, is indeed the only occurrence during the whole journey, of which we are told; and though its motivation lies in the fact that the place is elevated, its uniqueness still heightens the impression that the journey took place through a vacuum; it is as if, while he traveled on, Abraham had looked neither to the right nor to the left, had suppressed any sign of life in his followers and himself save only their footfalls.[26]

Auerbach insists on the necessity for the empty spaces between the spare facts of the story. To fill the spaces between with descriptions of landscape or with psychological motivation would divert the reader from the goal of Abraham's journey: the reencounter with God on Mount Moriah. Auerbach's piety, perhaps an expression of the link between his secular humanism and an older religious humanism, is to make the text speak through him. That is, he tries to make the intention of the tale as transparent as possible. His reading is—or purports to be—a mimetic, and therefore a pious, act. It is an objective account in the sense that it is faithful to the facts of the story. But it is not an exhaustive account, since it avoids pursuing possibilities that the spareness of the tale implies through its suppressions. For example, when Auerbach says that "we are told nothing about the journey except that it took three days, and even that we are told in a mysterious way," the invitation to speculate about what transpired during the journey is suppressed. One might say that the author of the tale is responsible for the suppression, but the very fact that it is perceived or felt as a suppression means that there is something there or something experienced as absent.

It is this suppressed area that is illuminated by Kierkegaard in *Fear and Trembling*, the effect of which is to appropriate and subjectivize the story in two senses. We enter into the minds of the characters as we do not in the original story, and there is a sense in which the original story is rewritten or filled in by Kierkegaard, who is telling the story of his own consciousness of God and the Problem of Evil.

Then Abraham lifted up the boy, he walked with him by his side, and his talk was full of comfort and exhortation. But Isaac would not understand him. He climbed Mount Moriah, but Isaac understood him not. Then for an instant he turned away from him, and when Isaac again saw Abraham's face it was changed, his glance was wild, his form was horror. He seized Isaac by the throat, threw him to the ground, and said, "Stupid boy, does thou then suppose this is God's bidding? No, it is my desire." Then Isaac trembled and cried out in his terror, "O God in heaven, have compassion upon me. I have no father upon earth, be Thou my father!" But Abraham in a low voice said to himself, "O Lord in heaven, I thank Thee. After all, it is better for him to believe that I am a monster, rather than that he should lose faith in Thee."[27]

The effect of Kierkegaard's retelling is to displace attention from the goal to the motive. Though Kierkegaard remains on this side of blasphemy, he cannot avoid provoking the blasphemous sentiment that the very enterprise of responding to the empty spaces entails. It is difficult to resist the speculation that if Isaac believes that his father is a monster, it is because of a manipulated displacement from the real monstrous object: God himself. Kierkegaard fills the spaces between the facts in order to satisfy a modern doubt about Abraham's motivation. In this process of justifying Abraham's faith, he leaves a shadow about the divine conditions of that faith, which the modern reader may or may not choose to ignore. Yet for Kierkegaard, the text remains sacred; no fact is violated. If the surface of the story is insufficient, it must be enhanced, not penetrated to a darker and contradictory underlying truth.

The examples of Auerbach and Kierkegaard are meant to suggest both the appropriative activity of the reader and the constraints that the text imposes on the reader. The difficulties, if not impossibility, of establishing the true interpretation would seem to justify skepticism. But the radical version of skepticism that has gained authority goes beyond the claim that a true interpretation is impossible; it challenges the idea of objective constraints in the making of interpretations, because the text is intrinsically empty.

How did the literary intelligence arrive at this state? "The monster of totality" is not a presence in the work of Anglo-American critics like Fish, so they are not possessed by the desire to destroy it. But consciously or unconsciously, every serious reader of literature participates in a process of secularization (of which the totalizing ambition of the nineteenth century is a version). The disappearance of the objective text is a consequence of secularization that has its origins in the Enlightenment. Before the Enlightenment, one may have doubted the authenticity of this or that biblical text, but the existence of an authentic biblical text was assumed, and authenticity meant derivation from divinity. God had spoken through the mediation of inspired human voices in the stories of the Bible. Much of the energy of intellectual life before the Enlightenment was devoted to the right understanding of the Word, the Text of texts. No existence was as substantial as that of the holy text.

The traditional conception of the indeterminacy of the text derives from the belief that the text is divinely inspired. Indeterminacy is a function of the infinite mind of God, to which the finite mind of every reader is inadequate. Behind our secular interpretations of secular works are centuries of biblical exegesis. Interpreters may differ about what or how much we may know of a text, but interpretation (again in the traditional sense) regards the text with the respect and care—if not exactly the reverence—one reserves for sacred objects.

Very few, if any, contemporary secular interpreters are prepared to accept the religious aura that Arnold conferred on poetry in the famous, oft-quoted passage that begins "The Study of Poetry" (1880), but something of Arnold's habit of mind has persisted in the way close readers have talked about poems and poetry.

The future of poetry is immense, because in poetry where it is worthy of its high destinies, our race, as time goes on, will find an ever surer and surer stay. There is not a creed which is not shaken, not an accredited dogma which is not shown to be questionable, not a received tradition which does not threaten to dissolve. Our religion has materialized itself in the fact, in the supposed fact; it has attached its emotion to the fact, and now the fact is failing it. But for poetry the idea is everything; the rest is a world of illusion, of divine illusion. Poetry attached its emotion to the idea, the idea is the fact. The strongest part of our religion today is its unconscious poetry.

Arnold shares the desire for totality that animated other poets, novelists, and philosophers of the nineteenth century. The aura of the literary work is the result of a saving secularization that tries to disengage spiritual (i.e., symbolic) meaning from the dogmatism of literal belief. The claim for the literary work becomes excessive in the wholesale transfer of spiritual significance from religion to literature. If the work or text is drained of its spiritual significance, a danger if the spiritual assertion loses its dogmatic authority, then there may be no need to value the text. Certainly, piety before the text (biblical or secular) becomes unnecessary. The next stop is to deny the existence of the text. Since, however, the habits of reading and interpretation persist, the text is displaced from a world or space external to consciousness to the consciousness of the reader. Reading makes or unmakes the text. What survives of the older religious tradition in reader-oriented criticism is the talmudic habit of paying an inordinate amount of attention to every mark on the page—not in deference to the sacredness of the text, but in the desire to exhibit one's interpretive skill.

The "logic" that I am describing is not ineluctable. If a work loses its dogmatic character, we need not cease to value it. We may read the life of Jesus for the luminous suffering of a great human being, if not for instruction in dogma. A philosophy like Hegel's that appropriates providential history to secular purposes is meant to give us a rational experience of human history rather than an inscrutably dogmatic one.

But the logic by which a text is emptied of its objective meaning and significance is a possible one. With the emptying of the text, the reader no longer has a text to experience. If he can be said to experience anything in the act of reading, it is the activity of his own mind. But it is only by stretching the meaning of experience that we can speak of reading, thus understood, as experience of something beyond itself. Reading becomes an exercise in theory or theorizing, a reflection upon the conditions of reading. The skeptic does not simply read; he tells us what happens when he reads, or when we read. He may even tell us that it is impossible to read. This last is the claim of deconstruction, the most radical of skepticisms about the text.

A subjectivity that presupposes the emptiness of the text (or the world) can never remain secure even in its subjectivity. As the subjectivity is objectivized and scrutinized, it too becomes the object of doubt. Are we to trust the experiencing I? Do we know what constitutes the I? Are we even sure it exists? The deconstructionists, who pride themselves on the superior rigor of their skepticism, devote themselves to destabilizing all the terms of *their* understanding, including their own rhetorical tropes. The relation between reader and text can be understood as a relation between the "I" and the world, if the text is conceived as embodying a meaning that refers to the world. And if the world and text conspire to be radically indeterminate or empty of meaning, then reading itself (the activity performed by the I) becomes the object of interpretation and uncertainty. What survives the skepticism is the play of the skeptical will. Even as the skeptic doubts his own experience, the will asserts itself either in the form of an ingenious or creative reader, inventing doubtful "interpretive structures," or in the form of a deconstructive reader, dissolving structures, including the structure of interpretive community. It may be an expression of "the intelligibility of our time" that even the idea of an interpretive community (ostensibly an antidote to subjectivism) can exclude "the truth of the past" and "the truth of 'others.'"

ENDNOTES

[1]Roland Barthes, "What is Criticism," in *Critical Essays*, translated by Richard Howard (Evanston: University of Illinois Press, 1972), p. 260.
[2]Roland Barthes, *S/Z* (New York: 1974), p. 206.
[3]Stanley Fish, *Is There a Text in This Class? The Authority of Interpretive Communities* (Cambridge, Mass: 1980), p. 1.
[4]Ibid., p. 11.
[5]Ibid., p. 375. Only a view that demands that the world conform to one's idea of it would regard the encounter between reader and work (the meanings of which do

not conform to views held by the reader) as necessarily adversarial. Moreover, adversarial books (i.e., books that assault one's cherished beliefs and provoke resistance, which may or may not be overcome by the work) are among the most rewarding experiences we have of literature. Fish attributes to this "adversary" model a static view of the encounter between reader and work. The reader confronts a work of fixed meanings with fixed views, but the "adversary model" need not be a static one. I don't mean to suggest at all that my account fits Fish as a reader, but it does fit the *persona* who opposes the adversary model.

⁶Ibid., p. 268.

⁷Ibid.

⁸Fish's interest in speech act theory reflects his commitment to the constitutive character of utterance. Statements do not merely mirror or reflect; they constitute the only reality there is. "According to Searle, the rules governing the making of a request (and of any other illocutionary act) are not regulative, but constitutive; that is, they do not regulate an antecedently existing behavior but define the contitions under which that behavior can be said to occur." Ibid., p. 201. But then Fish's conception of the speech act is embarrassed by its intentional character. According to John Searle, speech act theory assumes the intentional character of "a noise or a mark on a piece of paper to be an instance of linguistic communication. . . . one of the things I must assume is that the noise or mark was produced by a being or beings more or less like myself and produced with certain kinds of intentions." (*Speech Acts: An Essay in the Philosophy of Language* [London: 1969], p. 16.) Fish allows the making of such an assumption as part of his theory, but would stress that it is only an assumption, which cannot be verified by reference to the text itself. "Only an assumption" weakens the necessity of making the assumption. Perhaps the nature of the intention is inaccessible or not fully accessible to another mind, but the fact of intention as something independent of that other mind is not merely an assumption: it is an intrinsic condition of the speech act and therefore *must* be assumed. In his prefatory note to his essay "How To Do Things with Austin and Searle," Fish corrects the objectivism of his discussion of *Coriolanus* (his claim that the play *is* a speech act), a necessary correction only if one remains faithful to the dubious premise that intentions do not inhere in a text. *Is There a Text?* p. 200.

⁹Fish, *Is There a Text?* p. 203.

¹⁰Ibid.

¹¹Jonathan Culler, *The Pursuit of Signs: Semiotics, Literature, Deconstruction* (Ithaca: Cornell University Press, 1980), p. 125.

¹²Fish, *Is There A Text?* p. 15.

¹³Ibid., p. 11.

¹⁴Ibid., pp. 342, 346-48.

¹⁵One circumstance in which an Eskimo reading of "A Rose for Emily" is possible "would be the discovery of a letter in which Faulkner confides that he has always believed himself to be an Eskimo changeling" (Ibid., p. 346). A frivolous instance that shows, I think, that Fish does not take authorial intentions seriously. Moreover, a letter after or beside the fact of a story is the least persuasive example of authorial intention. As I have already remarked, what counts is what has gotten into the text.

¹⁶Ibid., p. 216.

¹⁷Ibid., p. 273.

¹⁸See, in particular, Michael Polanyi, *Personal Knowledge* (Chicago: University of Chicago Press, 1960).

¹⁹Thomas Kuhn, *The Structure of Scientific Revolutions* (Chicago: University of Chicago Press, 1964).

20Frank Kermode, "The Institutional Control of Interpretation," *Salmagundi* 43 (Winter 1979): 72-86, and *The Genesis of Secrecy: On The Interpretation of Narrative* (Cambridge, Mass.: Harvard University Press, 1979).

21*Salmagundi* (Fall 1980-Winter 1981): 250-51.

22Fish, *Is There A Text?* p. 136.

23Ibid., p. 16.

24Culler, *The Pursuit of Signs*, p. 21.

25Wolfgang Iser, *The Implied Reader: Patterns of Communication in Prose Literature from Bunyan to Beckett*, (Baltimore: Johns Hopkins University Press, 1974), p. 248.

26Erich Auerbach, *Mimesis: The Representation of Reality in Western Literature* (Princeton: Princeton University Press, 1968), pp. 9-10.

27Translated by Walter Lowie (Princeton: Princeton University Press, 1968), p. 27.

Stanley Fish

A Reply to Eugene Goodheart

ALTHOUGH EUGENE GOODHEART makes several good points in his essay, I remain unrepentant, since it seems to me that he misunderstands the nature of interpretive communities, at least as I have tried to characterize them. Specifically, he seems to think that I think that an interpretive community is the result of an agreement entered into by individuals who choose its constraints; thus he describes the reader in my recent work as an agent who "now suffers the constraints of an interpretive community." "Suffers" is the key word here, because it suggests a reader who at some level exists independently of constraints and who, when he is not a member of an interpretive community, returns to a state of unbridled will. To put it another way, Goodheart imagines that I imagine a self *in need* of constraints, whereas in my account, the self is a *structure* of constraints, in that its very possibilities—of action, interpretation, and perception—are defined by the ways of thinking that have been furnished it by a culture. When I say in *"Is There a Text in This Class?* that "the 'you' who does the interpretive work that puts poems . . . into the world is a communal you and not an isolated individual" (p. 331), I do not mean to posit a stage *before* communalization when the "you" is still isolated and independent; communalization has always and already occurred, and therefore it is wrong to assert, as Goodheart does, that I affirm "the activity of the subject" by "denying the reality of the object." What is denied is the independence of either the reader or the text (and insofar as subject and object are the names of that independence, the words should perhaps be abandoned), and what I affirm repeatedly is the reality (itself a dynamic and changing one) of the interpretive assumptions or conventions or modes of being or forms of life (all names for "interpretive community") that inform and give a shape to the activities of readers as they in turn give shape to the texts they have been enabled to see. So that while it is in some sense true to say that the reader "comes to realize the text," it is true only if one remembers that the reader is himself realized, and does not have the independent status that would be necessary for it to be said of him that he "absorbs" or "overcomes" the reality of a "substantial otherness." Goodheart's mistake is to proceed as if I were doing what he is doing throughout his essay, leaving the reader and the text intact as competing sources of interpretive authority whose claims must be ajudicated and whose interaction must be explained. That is why he thinks my "model" is "transactive" (as in the negotiations between sovereign states): the better word would be "constitutive," so long as it is understood that the "constitutive" powers of the reader are themselves constitutively enabled by the community or communities of which he is an extension.

Once the notion of an independent and willfully constituting self is abandoned, some of Goodheart's other concerns lose their urgency. He is worried, for example, that there are "no objective standards for discriminating between various communities"; but again, to so worry is to assume that standards are something the self must seek, when it is my thesis that, as a structure of constraints, standards are something the self can never be without. Of course these standards will not be "objective" in the sense that they stand outside the self, but that is just the point; they are the content of the self, the very motor of its apprehending; which is not to say that they originate in the self, but that the self originates in them, and because the self originates in them, discrimination has always and already occurred.

Goodheart would no doubt object that discrimination as I describe it will still be occurring *within* rather than *between* interpretive communities and therefore will not provide what he requires, an *objective* basis for judgment; but in terms of the argument I have been making here and elsewhere, that requirement would be incoherent, for it would itself require a self not yet constrained by any interpretive assumptions, not yet situated and constituted by any community, or alternatively, a self capable of standing to the side of assumptions and communities and therefore capable of deciding between them. But what would a self abstracted from all conventional ways of knowing be like? And *with* what would such a self (if it could be imagined) decide? There is, I contend, no answer to these questions, and moreover, there is no *need* to answer them, for in my account (and of course it is not only or even chiefly mine), the self is always situated, and therefore always in the position of being able to decide. That is why Goodheart's charge of "anarchy" cannot be sustained, at least if what one means by anarchy is the state of being paralyzed by indecision or of being in possession of no standards with which to make decisions. Of course he may have in mind a state in which everyone's mechanism of decision is not the same, but it is surely somewhat melodramatic to call that anarchy, since there is no one for whom it is debilitating or even in the slightest way disabling. I have already put it as well as I can in *Is There a Text in This Class?*, although obviously it wasn't put well enough:

The fear that in a world of indifferently authorized norms . . . the individual is without a basis for action is groundless because no one is indifferent to the norms and values that enable his consciousness. It is in the name of per-sonally held (in fact they are doing the holding) norms and values that the individual acts and argues, and he does so with the full confidence that attends belief. (p. 319)

Goodheart is puzzled to find me using the word "belief," because he thinks that the ingredient of belief "is singularly lacking in most interpretive communities today," and attributes this sorry situation to arguments that deny the independent text and thereby "weaken the possibility of reasonable consensus." But "consensus" is precisely the wrong word to use, because it implies that an interpretive com-munity is made up of individuals who meet to decide what they be-lieve or whether or not they believe anything at all. This is once again to make the mistake of positing an ungrounded self who is looking around for a ground, when it is my argument that the self is always grounded by the assumptions that constitute it, assumptions that form a system of belief in relationship to which certain facts will be inescapable. Those who share this system or, more properly, are shared by it, will "naturally" agree about many things, including the features of a text; not, however, because the text has compelled them to agreement or because they have gotten together and resolved to agree, but because agreement will be an unsought consequence of minds similarly constituted. This does not mean that disagreements between members of interpretive communities cannot occur, but that the shape of possible disagreement would itself be a function of com-munity assumptions. Two critics might, for example, disagree over the correct characterization of the affective structure of *Paradise*

Lost, but their disagreement could only occur if they both assumed that there was such a thing as affective structure and that it was the proper object of literary analysis. Someone who held or was held by neither of those assumptions could not even agree to disagree. Both agreement and disagreement are activities rather than states of mind, and they are activities that can only be performed in the ways made possible by the community, by the taken-for-granteds and goes-with-out-sayings that must be in place before samenesses and differences can even emerge. Similarly, someone who was uncertain about an interpretation could only be uncertain about alternatives already marked out in advance by the set of practices in which he was embedded. Radical uncertainty—the uncertainty of an independent mind confronting an abyss or an *aporia*—is, on this analysis, neither a danger nor a possibility. To be uncertain, in short, is to have already decided (again, it is an activity, not a state of mind), so that rather than "saying that undecidability is a condition of all interpretive situations," I am saying that it is a condition of none.

I am aware that to have characterized interpretive communities as sets of assumption or beliefs that inform minds rather than as aggregations or collections of minds that meet to determine what they believe is only to have raised in a more urgent form some of the questions Goodheart poses. What is the origin of these beliefs? How do they become authoritative? How do they change? These are questions of history, and at several points Goodheart complains that my account of interpretive communities lacks a historical perspective. To this I would reply, in part, by citing the final chapter of *Is There a Text in This Class?*, "Demonstration vs. Persuasion: Two Models of Critical Activity," in which persuasion is defined as the "attempt on the part of one party to alter the beliefs of another so that the evidence cited by the first will be seen *as* evidence by the second" (p. 365), an attempt that is, I assert, "the whole of critical activity." This of course means that the configurations and boundaries of interpretive communities—and therefore the configuration of the activities of mind they make possible—are not fixed but continually changing. It means, in short, that an interpretive community is a historical entity. I am still left, however, with the task of explaining how changes in interpretive communities occur, what provokes them, and how they take hold. I make some small gestures toward such an explanation in my discussion of the rise of Reader Response criticism, and in my rehearsal of the interpretive career of Blake's "The Tyger," but these gestures fall far short of the full scale analysis for which Goodheart quite properly calls. Something more substantial is attempted in my essay in this issue of *Daedalus*, but for now, the best that I can do is offer the reader a promissory note. For some time I have been preparing an account of the critical history of Books XI and XII of *Paradise Lost*, from 1942 to the present. That history addresses itself to two questions: How is it that in 1942 C.S. Lewis was able to dismiss Books XI and XII as an "untransmuted lump of futurity," whereas by 1982 those same books (apparently no longer the same) had come to be regarded as the poem's very center? How is it that a negative judgment that had been in force at least since 1712, when it was delivered by Addison, was overturned in the space of only five years (1958-63)? In the course of answering these questions, I consider such matters as the prevailing definitions of poetry, the kinds of arguments that were recognized as literary, the shape of current critical orthodoxies, the investment of literary history in Milton's reputation, the rise and development of modernist forms of thought, the effect on Milton scholarship of his appropriation as a source of propaganda for the Allied cause in World War II, and so on. The result of this inquiry is an essay entitled "Transmuting The Lump," which traces out, at least in the context of this one example, the emergence, development, and decline of interpretive communities, and of the texts and activities they make available. One thing, however, that this essay will not do is provide "a comprehensive theory of interpretive community," because such a theory would require a theorist who could move away from his own assumptions and beliefs to a place where a "comprehensive" view became possible. Everything in my argument militates against that possibility, which means that the historical account I offer in "Transmuting The Lump" or in any other essay will be just one more interpretation. This, however, would be a debilitating admission only if interpretation were an activity opposed to something more stable or "objective," whereas in fact stability and objectivity are what interpretations establish when they have been so persuasively urged that the assumptions underlying them have acquired the status of general truths, of truths so deeply held that, for a time at least, they seem unchallengeable. Of course this will not satisfy someone like Goodheart who demands truths and objectivities that are unchallengeable *forever;* but that is to demand that I provide a perspective behind or beyond interpretive communities, a perspective beyond culture, and it is my entire thesis that no such perspective (which would be the absence of perspective) is or ever could be available.

Alvin C. Kibel

The Canonical Text

WHAT FOLLOWS is an attempt to say something about a particular kind of relation between texts and interpretation. The relation I have in mind is one in which interpretation aims to make available what a text is saying while refusing to substitute any paraphrase for the original. The matter cannot rest there, however, since paraphrases of a given text always differ from it (and each other) to some degree, so that contexts can sometimes be found where substitution is impermissible. The point is that, in the case of particular texts, this difference is held to be *never* trivial. There are texts that we read as if they can be formulated in other words; what they have to offer by way of meaning can be put into general circulation without scrupling about minute details of the form in which they were first articulated. With other texts we insist upon the return of interpretation to those details, which are preserved in artifactual form as something more than a record of the way in which a paraphrasable message was first expressed. I suggest that this is a matter of cultural practice: we believe, or rather, we behave as if we believe, that it is not strictly necessary to read, say, the Decretals of Pope Alexander II or the English Act of Reform or Newton's *Opticks* to know what is in them, but anyone proposing to discuss the works of Plato, St. Mark, Rousseau, or Freud had better know them by direct acquaintance, not by hearsay. The particular examples shift about—what goes in the first category today may fall into the second tomorrow, and vice versa—but the distinction itself survives these alterations. We preserve texts in the first category for the sake of a record, thereby acknowledging that a change in context or the turning up of new information may lead us to reinterpret them occasionally. But reinterpretation here amounts to discrediting existing paraphrases and putting a new stock into circulation. With the second sort of text, the case is otherwise. Exegesis is continual rather than intermittent; it does not try to circulate the meaning of a text by replacing an original form with a number of versions more adequate to the context of our needs or understandings. It treats the original not as a textual deposit (a hedge against discovering that we haven't understood it) but as a continual source of meaning.

I offer the foregoing, despite obvious faults, as the beginnings of a description of something intensely familiar to members of learned institutions—namely, the ideal of a canon, a body of privileged texts with a reserve of meanings accessible only through special disciplines of interpretation. The canonical ideal is surprisingly difficult to talk about, even among those committed to it, and not only, as Frank Kermode remarks in an intelligent essay on the subject, "because its familiarity may have come to conceal from us its mode of operation."[1] A canonical text is one whose importance we recognize, although in some radical sense we are not able to understand it. Accordingly, we do not simply interpret the text, making its message available; we also insist that its given form is the only means through which its message can be reliably transmitted. This frequently produces oddities: Origen, for instance, corrected scribal errors and mistranslations in the Septuagint, but also kept them in, side-by-side with his emendations, in order to argue their wrongness with the rabbis; once this text acquired canonical status, no one could excise them, and the text circulated in a form that sometimes made no sense at all. Incoherence is no doubt easier to tolerate when one believes that messages issue from a divine author who might work through human error, but even modern editors dealing with the secular canon hesitate to correct misprints when these are of sufficiently long standing, and often put their revisions into footnotes instead. The essential conservatism of the learned institution on this point has a number of sources (not the least being that authors have been known to prefer copyists' errors to their own work), but all of them are supported by a characteristic hesitancy about letting our capacity for paraphrase settle doubts about meaning. The text must be treated as a kind of artifact. Of all possible versions of a message, one has a form that cannot be tampered with, even though, for various reasons, we can never be absolutely sure which version is the one in question.

Gerald Bruns points the issue neatly in connection with the scriptures: "You cannot enter into an understanding of them until you know that you have actually got them in front of you, but it is diffi-

cult to say when you have actually got them."² Is the notion prepos-
terous? Interpretation is generally inspired by the perception of some
discrepancy within a text, some gap or hiatus resulting from the fact
that different portions of it match up with the general run of discourse in different ways. Now, in most cases, the aim of interpretation is to reconcile a text to current discourse, to what we know
about the world and how we express it; what we derive from a text
by way of paraphrase is referred, for its systematic intelligibility, to
our tacit understanding of discourse as a system. In this connection,
the ideal of a canon proposes that texts exist whose importance we
can recognize even though they escape our tacit dealings with the
system of current discourse. The notion is granted that the original is
not a version of some composite of meaning-types generated by current discourse; along with certain other texts, consonance of a
unique sort—what Augustine refers to as "the concord of canonical
writings"—is assigned to it. Accordingly, its original form is recognized as the only trustworthy expression of its meaning, and whatever can be derived from it by way of assertion about the world must
be referred to this form for its systematic intelligibility. The very idea
of *version* is discredited; that of *original* is put in its place. However
odd this seems abstractly, it follows directly from the distinction between canonical and noncanonical texts. With the latter, you preserve the meaning of a text by disseminating interpretations; with the
former, preservation and interpretation are distinct.

Perhaps this can be clarified by the instance of oral narrative. In
the case of a joke, one doesn't think of a text as existing in any
particular version of it; the process of dissemination is at the same
time a process of interpretation. You don't keep a good story in circulation by memorizing it word-for-word and then repeating it but
by remembering its essential details, tacitly ascribing a hierarchical
order to them, and then using your grasp of their overall point to
reinvent it, adding one detail or deleting another to accommodate its
meaning to the circumstance of narration. Studies by Milman Parry
and Albert Lord,³ among others, suggest that in so-called preliterate
or subliterate cultures, extensive oral narratives are preserved
through similar feats of remembrance and improvisation; the text is
divided imaginarily into large paratactic units, each of which is composited of episodes; these in turn are composited of narrative and
descriptive units and subunits, whose order relates to a hierarchical
arrangement of materials derived from various schematisms useful
throughout cultural life, which everyone, therefore, may be expected

to carry in their heads. It is reported that artists in oral cultures, recounting the same tale in different ways, deny ever changing a line; for them, the story is "the same" despite minor accommodations to the varying conditions of performance. The artifactual presence of a privileged version does not exist: the text here leads an immaterial life as an ideal type informing every one of its utterances, none of which is privileged as its absolute representative.

It was this ideal, immaterial aspect of spoken discourse that led Plato in the *Phaedrus* to discredit writing in favor of speech as a medium for the communication of knowledge. Writing, he has Socrates maintain, promotes *lethe*, forgetfulness, rather than *aleth-eia*, truth, despite its utility as a record; it frees those involved in conversation from the need to remember what they have heard and understood—that is, from the need to sort and arrange units of discourse according to schematisms of types and then reinvent the whole of which these are parts in ways adapted to different occasions and turns of argument.

You know, Phaedrus, that's the strange thing about writing, which makes it truly analogous to painting. The painter's products stand before us as though they were alive, but if you question them, they maintain a most majestic silence. It is the same with written words; they seem to talk to you as though they were intelligent, but if you ask them anything about what they say, from a desire to be instructed, they go on telling you just the same thing forever.[4]

Plato lived well before a time when the development of collective views through a written exchange of exposition, argument, and summary became possible on a massive scale. The medium of scientific publication, in particular, offers precisely the sort of accommodation of original messages through reformulation and redaction in written form that Plato thought was exclusively in the power of speech. From the standpoint of canonical practice, the exchange of scientific messages is an antitype. Here, interpretation and perpetuation are so closely intertwined as to be virtually inseparable; the individual text is thought to have no value save as it is consonant with the general run of current discourse, and what it has to say is immediately absorbed in the form of summary, paraphrase, and selective duplication. The scientist assumes that he shares a system of discourse with the texts that he exposits, and reinterprets them constantly in view of changing experience; the authority of what he has to say derives from the intelligibility of his own discourse as the light of experience is refracted through it, and a return to his sources when these are more than a few years old seems to him a pointless antiquarianism. "Whitehead," writes Thomas Kuhn,

caught the unhistorical spirit of the scientific community when he wrote, "A science that hesitates to forget its founders is lost." Yet he was not quite right, for the sciences, like other professional enterprises, do need their heroes and do preserve their names. Fortunately, instead of forgetting these heroes, scientists have been able to forget or revise their works.[5]

Where Plato thought that only slavish duplication was possible, the modern historian of science is led to surmise that the wholesale transformation of viewpoint through the medium of the written message renders the documentary past irrecoverable save by acts of interpretative distortion.

I began by speaking of a relation between texts and a particular kind of interpretation. In his magisterial study *European Literature and the Latin Middle Ages,* Ernst Robert Curtius talks about the gradual formation of a secular canon as an outgrowth of the habit of thinking of a distinct textual corpus in connection with various ecclesiastical practices, so that there was first a liturgical canon of Fathers, then a juristic canon of Doctors; from this point of view, there is no reason why every institutional activity requiring textual material should not generate its own canon. What is wrong with this conception is that it ignores an essential feature of the canonical text—namely, that it is established as such only in relation to a secondary kind of writing, which demands the continued presence of an original in the course of transmitting its meaning. The canonical is determined against the noncanonical, but there is one sort of noncanonical text especially required by the canonical and without which it cannot be said, properly, to have an existence. I refer, of course, to commentaries—the sort of interpretative writings that, unlike those produced in scientific discourse, do not depend upon an assumed participation in the system of discourse exhibited by the text under exposition.

Among the ancient Hebrews, a body of writings considered holy and subject to exegesis was clearly extant before the historical recognition of the canon, as many canonical texts themselves bear witness. Until the advent of canonization, however, interpretations important enough to be written down and repeatedly transcribed could be embedded at various points in the original text, which might then be recast to smooth out transitions—a process analogous to the composition of a modern text by a single author, whose secondary and tertiary revisions include new materials meant to elucidate the old. The practice of interpreting scripture, or midrash, is not a postbiblical phenomenon, but until the formation of an explicit canon, no essential distinction was observed between "primary" and "secondary" materials; indeed, recognition of the canon is coterminous with the historical advent of the secondary text, a new sort of writing, which seeks neither to substitute for the primary text nor to add itself to the textual deposit wherein the primary is recorded.

Post-biblical midrash is to be distinguished from the biblical only by an external factor, canonization. By common though mysterious consent, and using criteria which largely elude us, the Palestinian religious authorities decided, probably at about the end of the third century B.C., to arrest the growth of sacred writings and to establish a canon. With one exception, Daniel, their policy was carried through, and from then on the nation's religious and moral guidance was entrusted not to writers but to interpreters.[6]

In the last sentence of this passage (from the *Cambridge History of the Bible*), the distinction between writers and interpreters is hardened into an opposition in a way that overrides the connection of each with the production of documentary materials. By means of "an external factor, canonization," the procedures for making continually accessible to a community certain messages deemed essential to its life are kept rigidly distinct from all attempts to accommodate the form of those messages to the changeful assumptions of that life. Access to the meaning of a text is tied to the availability of a particular artifactual form—or, rather, interpretation ensures the preservation of a textual deposit by making direct acquaintance with the text a precondition of its own intelligibility. A new kind of writing appears, animated by what one modern bibliographer, the late Fredson Bowers, called "concern for the exactness of representation given to the physical form of the work to be handled."[7] The division between writers and interpreters becomes one between primary and secondary discourse, or text and commentary—the former an election of the latter, which sets off to reconcile a text with current discourse, then aborts its own project and declares what it has to say incomplete without direct reference to a set of primary documents. (Here, by the way, is a clear distinction between earlier and modern ideas of the canonical; when the Christian canon was in process of formation, lists of accepted texts could include the text proferring the list. In the modern ideal, the canonical is recognized by a mode of discourse that eschews self-nomination.)

Situated between two systems of discourse, the commentator recognizes their incommensurability as an important factor in the articulation of meaning. In a recent book, Richard Rorty has identified the struggle against the assumption that all contributions to a given discourse are commensurable as the effort of hermeneutics:

By "commensurable" I mean able to be brought under a set of rules which will tell us how rational agreement can be reached on what would settle the issue on every point where statements seem to conflict. These rules tell us how to construct an ideal situation, in which all residual disagreements will be seen to be "noncognitive" or merely verbal, or else merely temporary—capable of being resolved by doing something further. What matters is that there should be agreement about what would have to be done if a resolution *were* to be achieved. In the meantime, the interlocutors can agree to differ—being satisfied of each other's rationality the while.[8]

The interlocutors in Rorty's "commensurable" discourse can rest content with discord because they agree on what would count, were it accessible, as a decision in either's favor. The hermeneutical attitude resists the very possibility of such agreement; in Rorty's description, it is expressed chiefly by mutual respect among interlocutors for what each cannot understand. The commentator, however, is animated by a one-sided version of this passion. A prototype is found in the example of Philo of Alexandria, who found himself situated between the discourse of Hellenic culture and the authoritative canon of Hebraic scriptures, which he could neither accept nor deny. In her study of the interpretation of the Bible in the Middle Ages, Beryl Smalley remarks on the inappropriateness of various attempts to systematize Philo's opinions:

Scripture enabled Philo to make his conceptions more precise and intelligible. Further, it allowed him to develop a train of thought and yet dispensed him from the need to build up a system. . . . The free and flexible exegesis of revelation suited his mental attitude of compromise between creative thought on the one hand and acceptance of authority on the other. Those of his readers today who prefer to do their thinking in the margin of a literary or historical text will sympathize with him.[9]

Philo is an ancestor of the interpreter who believes that certain important features of reality can be addressed only through the medium of commentary upon a body of particular texts. Appearances to the contrary, interpreters write by means of, not about, canonical texts—in their margins, as it were. The literary or critical exposition that takes the form of an essay may have left the margins of the page, but its reference to the text is still essential and specific. One might think of criticism as *discussion conducted in the presence of specific artifacts;* what it has to say about the world will not make sense unless access is possible to particular embodiments of meaning rather than to alternative versions of what they appear to be saying.

The seemingly unstructured nature of this enterprise issues from an unwillingness to abandon certain texts to the general flow of messages in culture, or if you will, from a refusal to reduce them (in the manner of the oral bard, the Platonic interlocutor, the practitioner of Kuhnian "normal" science) to a composite of types according to received schematisms. This puts those who believe in canons at odds with the system through which messages are generally exchanged; it makes them look worshipful of the sheer presence of words on a page, blind sticklers for the letter rather than the spirit of communications—a vice to which, it must be admitted, many of them are liable. The vice is ecclesiastically castigated as bibliocentrism; in reaction to it, at times, the inutility of scripture has been seriously proposed, and there are secular parallels—Derrida and the present "deconstructive" phase in literary criticism, for instance. Since the meaning of a canonical text is problematical, every variation may prove of consequence; we cannot trust our grasp of its point to secure a chain of transmission. Those who view textual discourse as the linguist views language—namely, as a composite of thoroughly abstract entities, accessible, to be sure, through the materiality of speech or writing but identical with none of their instances—will always regard the canon with suspicion. The various texts whose elements lead the kind of ideal life appropriate to the linguist's view, however important to a culture, are not canonical in my sense, which is bound up with material embodiments privileged in kind and, therefore, with the idea of rote or mechanical transmission.

An oddity connected with this subject is the currency of the notion that the invention of movable type or other means of mechanically reproducing works of art should discredit, of itself, the valuation put upon artifactual presence. The very existence of a canon absolutely depends upon the availability of means for identifying a text as "the same" through a discrimination of artifactual properties rather than through a grasp of its meaning. Just this is also the presupposition of

mechanical duplication. Where mechanical duplication of such properties is, for various reasons, not possible, as is generally the case with
pictorial art, the artifactual presence has to be identified by its prove-
nance and career, that is, with much of what Walter Benjamin, in a
famous essay, has termed its "aura." The paradoxes of this situation
are familiar: since interpretation cannot be trusted, identification of
the artifact begins with descriptions clearly relevant to an attributed
meaning but depends finally upon contingent factors, such as the
chemical makeup of paint or the nature of the wood-frame stretching
the canvas, or a history of origin, sale, exhibition, and storage. The
situation doubtless changes in many aspects when a text is originally
produced by means of transcriptive or reproductive techniques, as in
the writing of a manuscript or in the construction of representational
images by feeding digital instructions to a computer, which then
transmits them to an analogical plotter. Yet even here, a duplicable
artifact is nonetheless an artifact. The invention of movable type and
possible techniques of photography alter the system of arrangements
through which artifactual presence is made accessible, but they do
not eliminate the need to respect it.

For that matter, neither does alphabetic writing, the first reliable
method of reducing messages to composites of meaning-types suitable for mechanical duplication. The mistake of thinking otherwise
rests upon the assumption that knowing what properties of an utterance bear upon the meaning of a text is equivalent to knowing how
to relate them in interpretation. Benjamin's celebrated essay on
"aura" rests upon a hidden assumption of this kind. He argues that
our respect for the artifactual presence of works of visual art is an
obfuscating mysticism, no more than a veneration of the significance
fortuitously acquired by particular objects during their history, not a
regard for meaning. Accordingly, he suggests that photographic reproduction of painting and the production of works directly created
through techniques of mechanical duplication will soon rid the
artwork of the last vestige of its mystical, specific presence, much as
the invention of printing earlier destroyed the "aura" of the auto-
graph manuscript.

An analysis of art in the age of mechanical reproduction must do justice to
these relationships, for they lead us to an all-important insight: for the first
time in world history, mechanical reproduction emancipates the work of art
from its parasitical dependence on ritual. To an ever greater degree the work
of art reproduced becomes the work of art designed for reproducibility.

From a photographic negative, for example, one can make any number of prints; to ask for the "authentic" print makes no sense.[10]

For Benjamin, the work of art here rejoins the visual or auditory image of the word—the physical token of an immaterial type, which may be represented indifferently by any member of a class of such tokens. But the ability to duplicate the relevant properties of a text simply does not guarantee knowing what relationships obtain between those elements in every context where they carry meaning. Imagine a courier in wartime entrusted with accurate repetition of a coded message whose cipher he does not possess; his feat is not an isolated oddity but one that reflects a basic reality of articulated communications. Every articulated message is potentially multileveled in relating its constitutive units. Linguistic messages, most famously, have secondary and tertiary levels of articulation—that is, they are constituted of units, the units of subunits, and so on. The point of this is that while units of an uppermost tier (composed, let's say, of sentences and phrases) convey portions of the meaning of the whole, units of a lower tier (say, words and letters or phonemes) do not: the initial *I* or the segment *It* in *It is raining,* although a distinctive unit of the message, does not correlate with any distinctive part of its meaning. This holds for photographs as well; part of the photograph of a dog may stand for part of a dog, but the tiny dots of hue and value that constitute the units of contour and mass on the image do not stand for anything in what the picture represents. They are pre-semantics. Now, the genius of any system of transcription, like writing or photography, is to short-circuit the uppermost levels of articulation— ignoring phrases and sentences or contour and mass—in order to deal straightaway with units of a lower level out of which uppermost units are composed. This is why accurate transcription can be mechanical: you don't have to pay attention to meanings to do it properly. For the same reason, the fact that we can duplicate the elements of a particular text in their given arrangement, as in writing down words or printing off books and photographs, shows only that we can treat lower, pre-semantic elements as representing known types. It implies nothing about our understanding of the ways in which such elements combine into units of a higher level—units that may or may not represent known types—to generate meaning.

Why would anyone suppose the contrary? In Benjamin's case, at least, the motives are clear. The multileveled nature of linguistic articulation is often taken as defining our uniquely human capacity for speech. From this standpoint, the possibility of repeating an utterance by rote and only subsequently discovering its meaning is a feature of human communications as such: one can say, paradoxically, that a distinction between the spirit and the letter was a reality before the advent of alphabetic script, which only realized what repetition had already presupposed in principle—namely, the reduction of utterance to assemblages of units determined at levels below those at which speech takes on meaning. Benjamin's essay hails the invention of mechanical means of reproduction in the visual arts on the grounds that they, too, realize the essentially transcriptive nature of pictorial statements, which only our fetishism about pictures prevents us from acknowledging. Such a view inevitably supposes a distinction between a hard core of meaning, freely transcribable, and a vague "significance," projected upon the material embodiment of that meaning by reason of its contextual associations. This distinction, it seems to me, must be sustained by a belief that those lower-level, pre-semantic units constituting the repertoire of types in any transcriptive system can be determinately linked (at higher levels) only to the realization of meanings that are context-free. What photographs, let us say, can transcribe through their arrangements of dots will suffice to communicate the meaning of any pictorial statement; in contrast, what cannot be put on film and then printed off or flashed on a screen is mere "aura," the effect of a particular material embodiment in its contextual associations. *Et tout le reste est littérature.* Notoriously, the material embodiments of meaning (that which can be seen or that which can be read or heard) are always in particular contexts, which transcription ignores: Benjamin regards this ignorance as a liberation. The mechanically duplicated work of art can be transported and encountered in virtually any context, much as a given sentence can be repeated almost anywhere. Freed from its material envelope, every pictorial statement is also largely freed from the determinate conditions of its exhibition, from its specific location in the place of worship, the museum, the gallery, the various sacred repositories of "art." Transcription overcomes, for Benjamin, the systems of physical access through which society attempts to regulate our approach to works of art. It delivers simply the meaning of pictorial statement; what we choose to project upon it by way of "significance" (derived from its chance associations with details of our private lives) becomes henceforth our own business.

The notion that transcriptive units exist in determinate *liaison* with meanings only on a context-free basis is also a commonplace of literary studies and is similarly invoked, although seldom this pointedly, in connection with the distinction between meaning and "significance" (most notably by E.D. Hirsch). As it happens, there is some support for this in linguistics, both of the Saussurean and Chomskian varieties, where natural language is conceived as a context-free abstraction for the purposes of scientific study. Currently, however, linguistics appears to be busy changing its mind about the value of this conception to its own enterprise. In this connection, it is useful to draw a distinction between *discourse,* the linguistic act in its communicational setting, and the context-free abstraction designated as *language* by many theorists. As John Lyons, among others, has pointed out, linguists establish the character of their subject matter by a process of "idealization," in which the linguistic phenomenon is reduced to standard paradigms of combinatory units by the presumed elimination of all context-dependent features.[11] Considered in this fashion, the elements of language become ideational posits, disembodied presences represented by material tokens only to the extent that the latter are disposed according to a uniform system of context-free rules. Accessible either through utterance or inscription, the linguistic unit is not the material token but the type lurking behind it: this Platonic conclusion follows upon a process of idealization that every linguistics pledged to the study of timeless universals is bound to honor. From the standpoint of actual discourse, however, all this must be reconsidered, for discourse is constituted of linguistic units employed in particular contexts, as a result of which the stability posited by the linguist is provisionally disturbed and regularities of usage are altered, however slightly, even at the bottommost tier of phonemic units. My point here is that the distinction between language and discourse is a necessary assumption of the historical study of language, and that in proportion as discursive context does qualify or alter meanings, the words composing it lose their disembodied, spiritual character and resume a measure of artifactual life. As material forms of words, they remain duplicable, but the relational properties disambiguating them as transcriptive counters are no longer identical with the relational properties that carry discursive meaning. This holds for speech as well as writing, each existing as an independent system of discourse in dialectical interplay with the other through the relatively stable base of the transcriptive system. The mutual dependency and distinction of the two systems of discourse is what makes any piece of writing, at least potentially, something other than the record of speech—a fact usually ignored in most dealings with texts but made much of by those who recognize a canon.

You might think that literary theorists, given their stake in the issue, would be alert to the inadequacies of positions like Benjamin's, but in fact this seems not to be so. A famous chapter in Rene Wellek's *Theory of Literature,* long a standard work on the subject, argues Benjamin's case:

the lines in black ink are merely a method of recording a poem which must be conceived as existing elsewhere. If we destroy the writing or even all copies of a printed book we still may not destroy the poem, as it might be preserved ... in the memory of a man like Macaulay, who boasted of knowing *Paradise Lost* and *Pilgrim's Progress* by heart. On the other hand, if we destroy a painting or a piece of sculpture or a building, we destroy it completely, though we might even try to reconstruct what has been lost. But we shall always create a different work of art (however similar), while the mere destruction of the copy of a book or even of all its copies may not touch the work of art at all.[12]

Bringing in Macaulay cheats a little, for if Macaulay really has the work down word for word, the way to destroy all copies would include destroying Macaulay. The main point of Wellek's argument is, however, clear: since the elements constituting a literary work exist independently of their embodiment in any given bit of physical material, like a particular set of lines in black ink on a particular white page (but where, then, do they exist?), it is wrong to hold that "a poem is an 'artifact,' an object of the same nature as a piece of sculpture or a painting." But this is to regard poems as language, not as discourse. Most of what Wellek has to say about the literary work of art—that it leads an ideal existence as a system of "intersubjective norms" hovering behind every one of its material embodiments— applies to jokes, laundry lists, exclamations of surprise, letters of resignation, telephone books, to anything, in short, conceived primarily as concatenations of elements of language.

Since the meaning of a message varies relative to the circumstances of its transmission in ways uncovenanted by the linguist's abstract system, the alignment between token and meaning is perpetually disturbed. In some cases, this will not matter, but where it does, artifactuality comes flooding back in: the need arises to preserve as much as possible of discursive context, simultaneously recognizing the individual words while suspending the interpretation of meaning that enables this recognition. I would suggest that something of this sort—call it "rote recognition"—takes place to an important degree every time that we read a book. The sheer size of the book as an artifact is important here, as is the introduction of the codex as opposed to the scroll as the preferred form for extensive written presentations; not merely the word but whole passages are preliminarily grasped and subsequently reinterpreted as we turn back and forth the pages. Despite Hegel, literature need not be more spiritual than painting. A composite of intellectual parts, writing can be nonetheless earthbound, dense, refractory—the poet's flawed words and stubborn sounds.

The difference in this connection between works of literature (or computer-produced drawings) and induplicable works of art is not that the former are transparent to meaning while the latter bear mystical significances, but that literature makes use of a system of transcription through which regularly established differences between writing and speech may be exploited.

While the artist of the other arts begins by conquering the resistances of raw materials, the poet struggles with a new type of resistance, the word, which not only gives forth spiritual products, but also constitutes the very material with which he works. Words, in contrast with stone, or coloring matter, or moving air, are themselves significations of the human element to which the poet must give new meaning.[13]

I am quoting from a modern Spanish poet, Antonio Machado, because his remarks on the materiality of words are accompanied by a sense of the difference between duplicable and induplicable systems. The idea behind them is, of course, in no way exceptional. It is not true, however, as Machado implies, that the medium of pictorial statement entirely lacks its own reduction of messages to composites of schematic types, as a number of studies have shown. Just as the poet gives "new meaning" to everyday discursive significations, so the artist makes use of the pictorial lingua franca, the commonplace discourse of illustration in his day. What is the case is that no regular system of transcription between pictorial and nonpictorial messages has been developed akin to the system bridging spoken and written discourse. In this sense, the devices of mechanical reproduction celebrated by Benjamin may yet have an effect, although not the one that he intended.

The amount of time and economic resource that manuscript culture had to devote to the perpetuation of its textual inheritance made it unlikely that anyone would scorn the idea of the written text as an artifactual presence. In an age of printed texts, thoughtless veneration of artifactual qualities is harder to come by. We have come a long way since Erasmus could exult on finding a random scrap of printed paper. When the text left the silence of the copy-desk, the chained lectern, the monastic library, it lost much of what Benjamin calls its "aura." Still, the idea of the canon survived the advent of the printed book, and the notion of the text as artifact can still be justified in an age of mechanical reproduction. Whether it can survive an age of modular communications is less likely. Benjamin cites Paul Valéry: "Just as water, gas, and electricity are brought into our houses from far off to satisfy our needs in response to a minimal effort, so we shall be supplied with visual or auditory images, which will appear and disappear at a simple movement of the hand, hardly more than a sign."[14] Ours has been for a time the general culture of the printed book; it is fast becoming a culture of the visual narrative, the broadcast speech, the illuminated printout recovered from a databank and flashed upon a computer screen. As a result of current developments, one can now envisage a culture of high literacy whose members cannot arrest the flow of message-bearing units, actually lay hands on a text, and peruse it at will, glancing repeatedly back and forth among its parts as a matter of first reading. Certain linguists have recently challenged the classical notion that written language is simply a faithful transcription of speech; it is ironic that the independence of writing as a separate linguistic function should be affirmed just when the transmission of messages commonly tends to equate visual with auditory presentations, as things that do not absolutely require placing a text with a recipient in palpable form. We know as yet very little about the psychological configurations of reading or the structures of attention and revision through which it takes place. One can only surmise that when the experience characteristic of advanced literacy is of an unimpeded linear flow, the idea of special meanings that emerge only slowly, through successive revisions of the weight given even to minute detail, will seem an aberration, rather than an extension of normal practice.

ENDNOTES

A shorter version of this paper was delivered as the keynote address at the conference "Conventions, Canons, and Criticism," sponsored by the Department of Architecture at Massachusetts Institute of Technology, April 1982.

[1]Frank Kermode, "Institutional Control of Interpretation," *Salmagundi*, no. 43, Winter 1979.

[2]Gerald L. Bruns, *Inventions: Writing, Textuality, and Understanding in Literary History* (New Haven: Yale University Press, 1982), p. 34.

[3]See especially Lord's *Singer of Tales* (Cambridge: Harvard University Press, 1960).

[4]Plato, *Phaedrus and the Seventh and Eighth Letters*, translated, with introductions, by Walter Hamilton (Harmondsworth, England: Penguin, 1973), p. 97.

[5]Thomas S. Kuhn, *The Structure of Scientific Revolutions* (Chicago: University of Chicago Press, Phoenix edition, 1964), pp. 137-38.

[6]The Cambridge History of the Bible, vol. 1 (Cambridge, England: Cambridge University Press), p. 199.

[7]Fredson Bowers, *Textual and Literary Criticism: The Sanders Lectures in Bibliography 1957-58* (Cambridge, England: Cambridge University Press, 1966), p. 1.

[8]Richard Rorty, *Philosophy and the Mirror of Nature* (Princeton: Princeton University Press, 1979), p. 316.

[9]Beryl Smalley, *The Study of the Bible in the Middle Ages* (Notre Dame, Indiana: University of Notre Dame Press, 1964), p. 4.

[10]Walter Benjamin, "The Work of Art in an Age of Mechanical Reproduction," in *Illuminations* (New York: Schocken Books, 1969), p. 224.

[11]John Lyons, *Semantics*, vol. 2 (Cambridge, England: Cambridge University Press, 1977), p. 588.

[12]Reńe Welle and Austin Warren, *Theory of Literature* (New York: Harcourt Brace, Harvest Book edition, 1956), p. 130.

[13]Quoted and translated by Fernando Lázaro Carreter in "The Literal Message," *Critical Inquiry* 3(2) (Winter 1976): 316.

[14]Benjamin, "The Work of Art," p. 219.

Herbert S. Bailey, Jr.

Reading, Writing, and Publishing in Academia

IN GENERAL PUBLISHING there are authors, then publishers, and then readers "out there," but in scholarly publishing the authors *are* the readers. The writers write to be read and the readers read to write. Knowledge builds upon itself. The university publisher, as part of this circle, is a facilitator and a validator. My perspective is that of one who has been a university press publisher since World War II. What follows is some observations on various aspects of the cycle.

Changing Times

It is not news that the prospects of higher education for the 1980s and 1990s are far different from those of the expansive 1950s and 1960s. The 1970s, largely because of the psychological, intellectual, and economic effects of the Vietnam War, were a decade of transition. The momentum of expansion continued through this period, but difficulties began to appear, and although the extension of knowledge can always be justified on philosophical grounds, its material base was eroded. We are now in a period of adjustment, reassessment, and consolidation in almost every area of higher education. This has had its effect on careers, on research, and on the communication of scholarship.

In 1973 a few directors of university presses saw trouble ahead and persuaded the American Council of Learned Societies (ACLS) to sponsor the National Enquiry into Scholarly Communication. Funds were raised, a study was undertaken, and the report appeared at last in 1979.[1] The principal recommendations of that report—a national bibliographic system, a national periodicals center, a national library agency, restraint in the founding of new journals, a broader role for foundations, an office of scholarly communication, and the increased use of technology—are still mostly valid. If, as is hoped, the Office of Scholarly Communication and Technology can be established under ACLS, the chance of achieving many of the goals of the National Enquiry will be enhanced. In particular, the National Enquiry was weak in the area of technology—the microcomputers were not yet ubiquitous—and new evaluations must be made. An image of what we need technologically should be projected on the basis of the requirements of scholarship, and we should then work to achieve that constellation. It will not be achieved by just letting things happen.

Let us look at the dimensions of recent change. In the United States there were 3,290 Ph.D.'s awarded in 1940, 9,829 in 1960, and 32,615 in 1980. The number of scientific journals increased by 50 percent between 1960 and 1975; in the same period, the number of humanities journals more than doubled. University presses, which are the principal publishers of advanced scholarship (except in the natural sciences, which are more attractive commercially), grew in number from 35 in 1940 to 57 in 1960, and 116 in 1980. The college-age population (already countable) is expected to level off and decline in the next two decades. Universities and university presses are adjusting their programs, seeking ways to adapt to new conditions. Some will not survive. The number of academic jobs available for younger scholars is decreasing, and since scholars are expected to do research and to publish, competition in universities and for publication by university presses has become fierce.

Scholar-Authors

There is a romantic image of the unworldly and somewhat impractical scholar: devoted to his obscure subject, reading mountains of books, thinking and writing for years, and eventually producing a monument of scholarship. Before World War II there may have been some truth in that image, but today's competitive world does not permit that style of scholarly life. Scholars need jobs, have families to feed, and are required to publish to attain academic appointments and advancement. In a famous book that is still relevant, Jacques Barzun addressed the problem of "the Ph.D. octopus."[2] The octopus has become a hydra-headed sea monster, a creature from Jules Verne. The intrepid scholar can escape only into tenure; until that safety is reached he can only swim desperately against the current. Even when success is achieved, the joy of scholarship may be replaced by exhaustion.

The Role of University Presses

Since publishing is required for academic advancement, and since in many fields university presses are almost the only publishers, the presses serve to some degree as validators of scholarship. Their review processes, attempting to measure scholarly value, set critical standards. Moreover, presses have reputations based on the quality of past publications, and there is an unwritten ranking (which may vary from field to field), just as there is for journals. Editors are uncomfortable in the role of validators—they just want to publish good books—because it puts them under heavy pressure from authors and occasionally from deans. A year may pass between a decision to publish and the appearance of the book, and another year before reviews in scholarly journals begin to appear. That is a long time in the life of a young scholar, covering a period in which a tenure decision may be made. Often a scholar is forced to try to publish before his work is thoroughly thought out and ready.

Let us look again at the individual scholar who wants to study, write, and publish in his or her field. He or she must have access to a good research library. Twenty years ago research scholarship was concentrated in a few large centers, well served by libraries, but the difficulty in getting academic jobs has led to a much wider dispersal of active scholars to small institutions. These institutions previously did not support or expect faculty to do research, and they do not have research libraries. Computerization of bibliographies in library networks, along with interlibrary loans, has eased this situation somewhat, and new technologies may alleviate it further. Let us suppose that the scholar has written a research monograph that, though not attractive to a commercial publisher, may be publishable by a university press as a contribution to knowledge. After consulting with colleagues and observing which university presses publish in his or her field, the author writes to several presses, sending a description of the work and its table of contents. Three respond expressing interest. What next?

The author has a choice of submitting to one press or to two or three, the only condition being that the publisher must be told if it is a multiple submission. Most university presses now ask, and the answer will affect their consideration of the project. Reviewing scholarly manuscripts is time-consuming and expensive. Resources for publishing scholarship are in short supply, and an editor will reject a multiple-submission manuscript more quickly than otherwise—or, if he or she is enthusiastic, will accelerate the review process to beat the competition. The author, especially if he or she is beginning an academic career, will be under pressure for a publishing contract and may take the risk of multiple submission. My own belief (perhaps prejudiced) is that this is usually undesirable. It wastes publishing resources, and the author, especially a beginning author, is usually better off to submit to one publisher at a time, seeking a sympathetic editor.

Nonetheless, multiple submission is more and more frequent. It is an anomaly that this should be so when publishing resources are squeezed, but it is an understandable response to pressure both on authors and on presses. The authors want and need to publish; the presses are under pressure to find excellent scholarly books that can sustain themselves in the market. The result is that for such manuscripts the competition among university presses is ferocious, a situation experienced relatively rarely before 1980.[3] For works by established scholars in fields that are commercially attractive, high royalties and large advances are offered. Leading authors are wined and dined—or the scholarly equivalent. As a publisher I do not object to competition, but the effects of all this on young scholars are, I think, unfortunate. Editors have less time and less incentive to guide an author through the revision of his dissertation, since the outcome is uncertain. It is more efficient to seek manuscripts from scholars of proven ability in fields where sales are better. Fortunately the National Endowment for the Humanities has a modest program to aid publication, and the A.W. Mellon Foundation has recently made a series of grants to university presses for publication in the humanities.

Ph.D. Dissertations

For the reasons given above, many university presses will not look at dissertations. Yet sometimes the best book a scholar will ever write is an outgrowth of his dissertation; his days as a graduate student are the one time in his life when he can devote himself wholly to his subject, undistracted by teaching or administrative chores. The publication problems of younger scholars are, I think, unnecessarily aggravated by the traditional requirements of the Ph.D. dissertation, necessitating extensive rethinking, reorganization, and rewriting after the dissertation is completed. Universities expect faculty members to write and to be published, but they train young scholars to present their first important and intensive research in unpublishable form.

The obvious mark of a dissertation, unwanted in a book, is an opening chapter in which the author proves that he or she has read all the right literature, discussing it in superfluous detail. Another objectionable feature is excessive footnoting; the writer is not allowed to assume any previous knowledge on the part of his reader. Standard sources and every statement of fact, even those well known to likely readers, are referenced. Sources are quoted, in text and in footnotes, at excessive length. Many dissertations are written not for readers but for an individual professor. Finally, the dissertation is usually written in a dry, impersonal, academic style, without passion and with the most hesitant expression of personality and opinion. If young scholars in academic careers are expected to produce publishable books, they could be helped along more effectively by their professors—without lowering academic standards.

I suggest that a Ph.D. candidate should be required to write an extensive critical bibliographical essay on his subject, separate from the text itself, not as an introduction to it. If it is good enough it might become an appendix to the published work, perhaps in condensed form. Such an essay would have to be written along with the thesis itself and be submitted with it, but would not be part of it. It could serve to show the examining committee that the student had mastered the sources.

Next, the student should be encouraged to regard the dissertation as the first draft of a possible book, or as part of the first draft of such a book. I do not mean that professors should require dissertations to be, in effect, finished books, but they could go some distance down that line, far enough to satisfy themselves that their students are able and promising original thinkers and writers.

The student should also be encouraged to write for a readership of his peers—other graduate students, for example, not just the examining professor. He or she should be expected to relate the topic to the field generally, at the same time assuming that the readers are themselves scholars or advanced students. It is to be hoped that his style would be charged with his own interest in the subject, the interest that inspires him to make the field his life's work. For this he will need some scholarly latitude, not a lessening of rigor but room for the clearly identified expression of opinion or conjecture, of a sense of excitement and pleasure and quest. This is not unreasonable; the best senior scholars do it. Their books show that they care.

Finally, and this is not trivial, graduate students should be required to turn in their dissertations in the form expected by publishers and required by printers. This should be a part of their training as scholars and authors. Everything should be doubled-spaced, including notes, extracts, quotations, bibliography—everything! Notes should be gathered at the end of the manuscript, numbered within each chapter. There are many useful style manuals. If dissertations are to be sent to editors, they are much more likely to be read if presented in proper form, and the editor is more likely to be willing to work with the author to achieve a publishable book if it is already partly along the way. It is unnecessarily discouraging to young scholars to have to undo and redo so much of their dissertations in order to ready them for publication. It is also unnecessarily discouraging for editors.

In this regard, a very promising development is the increasing use of word processors for writing. A manuscript from a word processor is much easier to revise, and virtually all dissertations must be revised for publication. Also, if the output of the word processor is compatible with computer-based phototypesetting equipment (not to be assumed), there can be a large reduction in typesetting costs and in the cost of proofreading. This technological change is especially helpful for scholarly publication where, because the print runs are small, typesetting is a very large part (often half) of manufacturing cost.

The Growth and Fragmentation of Knowledge

Sir Francis Bacon's tree of knowledge, perhaps a sapling in his day, is now a giant redwood. This growth is traced in Fritz Machlup's classic *The Production and Distribution of Knowledge*[4] and in his *Knowledge: Its Creation, Distribution, and Economic Significance*, three volumes of which he completed before his recent death.[5] The ten volumes he planned would have given us an extraordinarily comprehensive and original insight into the ramifications of knowledge in our world.

Machlup was interested in the classification of knowledge, which is a continuum, and which is arbitrarily divided by universities into departments and by libraries into a bewildering structure of categories and subcategories. The evolution of library cataloging techniques in this country is a story in itself; the rules are rigid and the discipline is a mystique, sometimes producing surprising results. Publishers often observe strange classifications of books in the Library of Congress's Cataloging-in-Publication (CIP) program. With the explosion of knowledge in modern times, this is a serious problem for librarians and scholars, especially since the card catalog is being displaced by the computer. When scholars must rely on computer searches instead of browsing, cataloging becomes vital. In our preoccupation with new technologies (optical laser disks, micromachines, etc.) we must not overlook this essential intellectual problem. The solution will require the cooperation of scholars, librarians, and publishers. Present systems are not sufficiently discriminating; more abstracting and evaluation will be necessary.

Readers

I have already pointed out that in the scholarly world the writers and the readers are the same people; there is a circularity in which university presses play a role. They evaluate, select, and disseminate. At present they disseminate through books and journals, in the future perhaps by electronic means, though I believe the physical book (however produced) will be with us for a long time. In order to disseminate effectively, university presses must identify the potential readers of a work and inform them of its existence; this is a significant function in scholarly communication, as evidenced by the sale (usually) of more than half of the first printing of each new book before reviews appear in scholarly journals. Press editors must be aware of the directions scholarship is taking, of schools of thought, of intellectual fashions (even fads), of new interdisciplinary trends. Sometimes they can foster or reinforce or occasionally invent areas of publication, having in mind the readers who will benefit.

Scholarly readers are informed of new works by mail and by advertising, but mostly they borrow these books from libraries. Clothbound books have become too expensive for most individuals. A promising development in the past decade is the scholarly paperback, printed in small quantities and sold at perhaps half the price of the clothbound edition. A $15 paperback of a $30 clothbound book may be within range for a graduate student or professor. American libraries tend not to buy the paperbacks because of the expense of processing and binding them individually (about $15), because the process of rebinding keeps the book off the shelves for several months, and because the paper used for paperbacks usually does not have the permanence and durability of the clothbound edition. This is significant because the sale of the clothbound book pays the fixed cost that makes the paperback possible. Unfortunately there is an increasing tendency for European libraries to buy paperbacks; if this practice spreads, publishers will have to cut back or discontinue scholarly paperbacks, which are such a boon to individual scholars.

The Problems of "Big Books"

In this essay I have focused on the publication of specialized scholarship because that is the main concern of most scholars and of most university publishers. This is as true of senior professors as it is of the younger scholars who have yet to make their reputations. The primary role of university presses is to disseminate scholarship, and most scholarly writing is too specialized for even the well-informed general reader. The results of scholarship are usually interpreted, condensed, synthesized, and explained for the general reader in textbooks and in trade books written specifically for that purpose, although a few original scholarly works also have wide appeal. Such books are appropriately published by university presses, though most are issued by trade publishers.

Although it is appropriate and even desirable for university presses to publish such books, there is a danger in it too. The prospect of big sellers can lure university editors and publishers away from their main task, and in hard times this is a strong temptation. Citing several recent university press books that had made headlines in the popular reviews, a friend recently wrote to me, "The age of the monograph is not over; the age of the big book is here, and the university presses are not disinclined to publish such."

In contrast, the director of a press that is known for its big books remarked to me not long ago, "It just isn't possible to do big books any more. They are few and far between, and the market is bad."

For university presses a big book can be a will-o'-the-wisp. Such books are hard to find, risky, and they require heavy investment (because of the competition that always surrounds them), price-shaving, large discounts, heavy advertising, and expensive bookstore promotions. It is easy to show large losses on a book that sells 25,000 copies or more and is considered a huge success. Especially for smaller presses such losses, or even such a large effort and investment, may seriously impair their ability to publish scholarly monographs.

In another sense it can be truthfully said that the age of the big book is here—it has been here all along. There have always been a modest number of scholarly books, or books written by scholars, that are important enough or controversial enough and well written enough to appeal to a broad public. University presses over the years have published a fair number of these, and often, because a big book for a university press may be a "not so big book" for a commercial publisher, the university press will make a greater effort to sell more copies than a trade publisher would. But no press can build a program on such books.

The academic superstars who write the relatively few scholarly books that sell in large quantities for the most part made their reputations by publishing monographs with university presses. But usually their loyalty is diminished when they are offered much gold and heady fame by trade publishers for their long-awaited big book. Each university press must decide for itself how it will deal with each situation. I think it is reasonable to compete—up to a point, and university presses have benefits to offer that trade publishers do not—but I also think it is reasonable to be glad that one has played a part in developing a leading author, and go back to the main job of publishing books that advance knowledge, by scholars for other scholars. Such books can be as exciting and satisfying as big books.

The age of the scholarly monograph is indeed not over. The best way for a university press to prosper is to publish many truly excellent scholarly monographs on which it can break even at 1,200 or 1,500 copies. Some of these books will be reprinted and sell in thousands, or even tens of thousands, of copies, in hardback or paperback, in years to come. The most successful frontlist for a university publisher is one that will become a strong backlist in years ahead. This approach is not only most successful financially; it is doing what university presses were invented to do.

The Future

As I emphasized earlier, we are going through troubled times, and the sources of the present troubles are likely to be with us for a decade or more. Nevertheless, I am optimistic about the future of scholarship and of scholarly publishing.

I am optimistic first because the world needs the results of scholarship, and I do not believe that our society will allow scholarship, which depends on scholarly communication, to be seriously diminished. Crises will be met by universities, by university presses, by foundations, by government, by corporations, and by the ingenious use of new technology. The shape of their activities, including their institutional arrangements, may change, but the substance will remain.

Universities (and university presses), like the church, are slow to change but in the long run are very adaptable. Oxford University Press is over five hundred years old. The oldest American university press is past one hundred. Institutions with such stability and adaptability are needed for long-term progress.

We are in the age of the computer, and most publishers have been using the new technology for business functions for more than a decade. Computers are rapidly being adopted for editorial, marketing, and various management functions. Not long ago I spoke to a group of publishers about the importance of printing books on paper that will last; the speaker following me had as his topic "the paperless book"! I do not see the paperless book as imminent, but publishers are now marketing computer data bases by wire or satellite, and computer programs are being sold in bookstores. These developments in the general market will be adapted and adopted for scholarly communication. There will be new alliances between university computer centers and university presses, with the presses marketing the products of the computer centers, particularly those specialized products needed by scholars—just as the university presses have found their special role in the book market.

Still, computers and the paperless book will not replace the book in codex form in the near future. Books may be produced and distributed differently, but the selective editorial function of the publisher will continue to be important. Tools may change, but the basic process of reading and thinking and writing will not change greatly. Computers are a long way from becoming a substitute for mind; and as a means of presenting serious thought, nothing has yet come even close to the printed book.

ENDNOTES

1*Scholarly Communication, The Report of the National Enquiry* (Baltimore: Johns Hopkins University Press, 1979).
2Jacques Barzun, *The Teacher in America* (Boston: Little Brown, 1945).
3Sanford G. Thatcher, "Competitive Practises in Acquiring Manuscripts," *Scholarly Publishing* 11(2) (January 1980): 112-132.
4Fritz Machlup, *The Production and Distribution of Knowledge* (Princeton, N.J.: Princeton University Press, 1962).
5Fritz Machlup, *Knowledge: Its Creation, Distribution, and Economic Significance*, vol. I, *Knowledge and Knowledge Production*, 1980; vol. II, *The Branches of Learning*, 1982; vol. III, *The Economics of Information and Human Capital*, forthcoming. (Princeton, N.J.: Princeton University Press, 1980-).

Notes on Contributors

Daniel Aaron, born in 1912 in Chicago, is Victor S. Thomas Professor in the Department of English and American Language and Literature, Harvard University. He is the author of *Men of Good Hope: A Story of American Progressives* (1950), *Writers on the Left: Episodes in American Literary Communism* (1961; 1977), and *The Unwritten War: American Writers and the Civil War* (1973). Professor Aaron is president of the Library of America.

Herbert S. Bailey, Jr., born in 1921 in New York City, is Director, Princeton University Press. He is the author of *The Art and Science of Book Publishing* (1971), *The Traditional Book in the Electronic Age* (Bowker Lecture on Book Publishing, 1976), and various articles on publishing. Mr. Bailey is a past president of the Association of American University Presses.

Wayne C. Booth, born in 1921 in American Fork, Utah, is Distinguished Service Professor of English and Ideas and Methods at the University of Chicago. His works include *The Rhetoric of Fiction* (1961; 1983), *Modern Dogma and the Rhetoric of Assent* (1974), *A Rhetoric of Irony* (1974), *Critical Understanding: The Powers and "Limits" of Pluralism* (1979), "The Company We Keep: Self-Making in Imaginative Art, Old and New" (*Dædalus*, Fall 1982), and "Bakhtin and the Ideology of Feminism" (*Critical Inquiry*, Summer 1982). Professor Booth is the current president of the Modern Language Association.

Benjamin M. Compaine, born in 1945 in Philadelphia, is executive director, Media and Allied Arena, Program on Information Resources Policy, Harvard University. He is the author of *Who Owns the Media? Concentration of Ownership in the Mass Communications Industry* (second edition, 1982), *The Book Industry in Transition: An Economic Study of Book Distribution and Marketing* (1978), *The Newspaper Industry in the 1980s: An Assessment of Economics and Technology* (1980), and many monographs and articles on technology and the media of information and communication. Mr. Compaine's current work involves investigating the forces and trends—political, social, economic, and technological—that may affect the decisions of policymakers in the rapidly changing area of information resources.

Peter Conrad, born in 1948 in Australia, is a Fellow at Christ Church, Oxford. He is the author of *The Victorian Treasure-House* (1973),

Romantic Opera and Literary Form (1977), *Shandyism* (1978), *Imagining America* (1980), and *Television: The Medium and Its Manners* (1982).

Stanley Fish, born in 1938 in Providence, is William R. Kenan, Jr., Professor of English at Johns Hopkins University. His works include *John Skelton's Poetry* (1965), *Surprised by Sin: The Reader in Paradise Lost* (1967), *Self-Consuming Artifacts: The Experience of Seventeenth Century Literature* (1972), *The Living Temple* (1977), and *Is There A Text in This Class?* (1980).

Eugene Goodheart, born in 1931 in New York, is professor of English at Boston University. He is the author of *The Utopian Vision of D.H. Lawrence* (1963), *The Cult of the Ego: The Self in Modern Literature* (1968), *Culture and the Radical Conscience* (1973), and *The Failure of Criticism* (1978).

William B. Goodman, born in 1923 in New York City, is editorial director at David R. Godine, Publisher, Inc., in Boston, and a lecturer at Harvard. Mr. Goodman writes occasional reviews for *American Quarterly, The New England Quarterly,* and *The Yale Review.* Before joining Godine, Mr. Goodman was college and trade editor at Harcourt Brace Jovanovich and general editor at Harvard University Press.

Elizabeth Hardwick, the novelist and critic, was born in 1916 in Lexington, Kentucky. She is a professor at the Graduate School of the Arts at Columbia University and advisory editor for *The New York Review of Books.* Her works include *Seduction and Betrayal* (a collection of essays, 1973) and *Sleepless Nights* (a novel, 1979). Her most recent work, *Bartleby in Manhattan and Other Essays,* will be published this year.

Frank Kermode, born in 1919 on the Isle of Man, is a professor at Columbia University. He is the author of *Romantic Image* (1957), *Wallace Stevens* (1960); *The Sense of an Ending* (1967); *The Classic* (1974), and *The Genesis of Secrecy* (1979).

Alvin C. Kibel, born in 1933 in New York City, is professor of literature and head of the literature faculty at Massachusetts Institute of Technology. He has written articles on literary theory in relation to the theory of history and the theory of fine arts for *Partisan Review, American Scholar,* and *History and Theory.*

Dan Lacy, born in 1914 in Newport News, Virginia, is senior vice-president of McGraw-Hill, Inc. He is the author of *Freedom and Communications* (1961), *Meaning of the American Revolution* (1964), *The White Use of Blacks in America* (1972), and *The Birth of America* (a text, 1975).

Walter W. Powell, born in 1951 in Raleigh, North Carolina, is assistant professor at the School of Organization and Management, Department of Sociology, Yale University. He is the author of *Getting into Print: The Decision-Making Process in Scholarly Publishing* (forthcoming) and co-author of *Books: The Culture and Commerce of Publishing* (1982). Professor Powell has also written numerous articles on the production and dissemination of culture. His major interests are in the area of organizational theory and public policy and the sociology of culture.

Al Silverman, born in 1926 in Lynn, Massachusetts, is president and chief operating officer of the Book-of-the-Month Club. Mr. Silverman is the author and co-author of many books, the most recent being *Foster and Laurie* (1972).

Lola L. Szladits, born in 1923 in Budapest, is curator of the Berg Collection of English and American Literature of the New York Public Library. Her works include *Pen and Brush: The Author as Artist* (1969), *Charles Dickens: An Anthology* (1970), *1922: A Vintage Year* (1972), *Independence: 1770-1850* (1975), and "The Art and Craft of Collecting Literary Manuscripts," in *Book Collecting: A Modern Guide* (1977). Dr. Szladits paid her first visit to the New York Public Library in 1946 while a student at Columbia, and joined the staff in 1955.

Paul Starr, born in 1949 in New York, is assistant professor of sociology at Harvard. He is the author of *The Discarded Army* (1974) and *The Social Transformation of American Medicine* (1982).

Samuel S. Vaughan, born in 1928 in Philadelphia, is editor-in-chief and vice-president of Doubleday. He is the author of several children's books and has written for the *New York Times Book Review,* the *Sunday Times of London, The Writer,* and other publications. Mr. Vaughan has lectured on publishing at various colleges and universities, and for the past five years has taught a course, "The Author and the Publisher," at Columbia.